Non-Invasive Data Governance Unleashed

EMPOWERING PEOPLE TO
GOVERN DATA AND AI

FIRST EDITION

Robert S. Seiner

Technics Publications
SEDONA, ARIZONA

115 Linda Vista
Sedona, AZ 86336 USA

https://www.TechnicsPub.com

Edited by Sadie Hoberman

Cover design by Lorena Molinari

First Printing 2025

Copyright © 2025 by Robert S. Seiner

ISBN, print ed.   9781634625937
ISBN, Kindle ed.   9781634626132
ISBN, PDF ed.   9781634626149

Library of Congress Control Number: 2024952299

Contents

Introduction

Non-Invasive Data Governance Unleashed: Empowering People to Govern Data and AI is a comprehensive guide designed to transform how organizations approach data governance in an era defined by the recognition of the role people play in governance, the rise of Artificial Intelligence (AI), data-driven decision-making, and the continuous flow of information. This book is not a step-by-step manual; it is a strategic roadmap that reframes how to embed data governance into the DNA of organizations by following a Non-Invasive Data Governance® (NIDG) approach, which is practical, adaptive, and minimally disruptive to existing operations. For organizations grappling with the complexities of data stewardship, AI governance, and cross-functional collaboration, this book offers the tools and insights necessary to create a data governance framework that is not only effective but also scalable and future-proof.

The Non-Invasive Data Governance (NIDG) approach introduced in this book builds on a simple yet powerful principle: the data will not govern itself.

This foundational truth is the driving force behind the methodology presented, which integrates governance into the fabric of organizational processes without imposing heavy-handed controls. NIDG recognizes that data governance is not solely about creating policies, assigning responsibilities, or setting technical standards—it is about people. Every individual within an organization who interacts with data, whether directly or indirectly, has a role in ensuring its quality, accuracy, security, and proper use. By formalizing and recognizing people's existing roles, NIDG democratizes data stewardship, making governance a shared responsibility that permeates all levels of the organization.

Throughout the book's ten chapters, readers are guided through the essential elements of implementing NIDG, starting from foundational concepts to more advanced applications in the age of AI and beyond.

We need to structure data governance in a way that aligns with business objectives while minimizing disruption.

At the heart of NIDG is the belief that governance should complement the natural workflows of employees, seamlessly integrating into the organization's day-to-day operations. This people-centric approach not only makes data governance less intimidating, but ensures that it becomes a sustainable, enduring practice that delivers value over time. The book provides real-world examples and strategies for building a governance framework that grows with the organization, adapts to its needs, and empowers individuals to contribute to its success.

One of the critical aspects that sets *Non-Invasive Data Governance Unleashed* apart from other governance manuals is its focus on proving the value of data governance through the focus on people and measurable outcomes. In today's business environment, leaders are increasingly asked to demonstrate the Return On Investment (ROI) of every initiative, including data governance. This book equips readers with the tools to measure the tangible and intangible benefits of implementing a robust governance framework. It provides a set of clear, actionable metrics that organizations can use to track improvements in data quality, operational efficiency, decision-making capabilities, and regulatory compliance. Readers will find practical guidance on presenting these metrics to stakeholders in a way that highlights the business value of governance efforts, thereby making a compelling case for continued investment in data governance.

In addition to providing strategies for measuring ROI, the book explores how to effectively communicate the importance of data governance to key decision-makers. The chapters offer convincing arguments demonstrating how a well-executed data governance framework enhances organizational performance, mitigates risk, and positions the business for long-term success. For organizations operating in highly regulated industries, where compliance and data privacy are paramount, NIDG offers an approach that aligns governance practices with regulatory requirements without creating unnecessary bureaucracy. Through a combination of strategic insight and practical advice, the book empowers data professionals to build governance programs that not only meet the needs of the present, but are also flexible enough to evolve with emerging data challenges and opportunities.

Another key theme in *Non-Invasive Data Governance Unleashed* is its exploration of leadership's role in fostering a culture of governance and stewardship. Effective data governance is not just a bottom-up process; it requires top-down commitment and alignment with the organization's strategic goals.

The book highlights the pivotal role that leaders play in shaping governance practices, from setting the vision and expectations to ensuring that data governance becomes a core element of the organizational culture. Leaders are tasked with building a governance framework that transcends silos, encourages collaboration across departments, and ensures that data is managed as a valuable asset. The book provides actionable advice for leaders on how to champion governance initiatives, allocate resources effectively, and build a lasting culture of data stewardship that supports innovation and growth.

The book also focuses on the evolving landscape of AI and its intersection with data governance. As AI becomes increasingly integrated into business operations, the need for governance frameworks that can manage both data and AI processes becomes critical. The book addresses this challenge head-on, offering insights into how the NIDG approach can be adapted to govern AI systems, ensuring transparency, accountability, and ethical decision-making. AI systems are only as good as the data they are trained on, and the book underscores the importance of governing that data to prevent bias, ensure fairness, and maintain trust. By integrating AI governance with traditional data governance practices, readers will learn how to build a holistic governance framework that safeguards against the risks associated with AI while unlocking its potential for business innovation.

Practicality is woven throughout the book, offering readers step-by-step guidance on implementing NIDG in diverse organizational contexts. Whether a company faces budget constraints, decentralized data management, or a large-scale digital transformation, *Non-Invasive Data Governance Unleashed* provides actionable strategies for overcoming these challenges. The book includes case studies and examples illustrating how organizations have successfully implemented NIDG, from smaller enterprises to global corporations. Readers will also find advice on how to make their data governance framework AI-ready, ensuring that their data is well-governed and fully prepared for use in AI applications, thus maximizing the value of both data and AI investments.

Finally, *Non-Invasive Data Governance Unleashed* emphasizes the importance of continuous improvement in data governance. It presents NIDG as a living, evolving framework that requires regular assessment, refinement, and adaptation to meet the changing needs of the organization. The book encourages readers to see data governance not as a one-time project, but as an ongoing journey that drives sustainable business value. With its combination of strategic insight, practical tools, and a clear focus on the human element, this book provides readers with everything they need to master the future of data governance and AI stewardship.

In essence, this book is more than just a guide to data governance—it is a call to action for organizations to rethink how they approach data management and stewardship in a rapidly evolving digital world. Whether you are a seasoned data professional or new to the concept of data governance, *Non-Invasive Data Governance Unleashed* offers the insights, strategies, and tools you need to build a governance framework that not only works today but will continue to drive value for years to come. This is your roadmap to mastering the future of AI and data stewardship, while ensuring that data governance remains a core, enabling force within your organization.

Foundations of Data Governance

In a world where data drives innovation, decision-making, and growth, the foundations of data governance are more critical than ever. Chapter 1, *Foundations of Data Governance*, lays the groundwork for empowering people to govern both AI and data effectively. This chapter takes a close look at the essential principles, approaches, and frameworks that make governance not just an operational necessity, but a strategic enabler for any organization.

The chapter begins with *The Data Will Not Govern Itself*, a powerful reminder that data governance is not a passive activity. This essay emphasizes that without active management, data can become a liability rather than an asset. Introducing the Non-Invasive Data Governance (NIDG) approach, the essay demonstrates how governance can seamlessly integrate into existing workflows, ensuring success without disruption.

From there, *What Data Governance ROI Looks Like* demystifies the value of governance by presenting clear, tangible ways to measure its return on investment. Too often seen as a cost center, governance is reframed as a value driver that delivers improved data quality, compliance, and operational efficiency—all of which are indispensable for organizations leveraging AI and advanced analytics.

In *There Are Only Three Approaches to Data Governance*, the chapter explores the core governance strategies: Command-and-Control, Traditional, and Non-Invasive. This essay simplifies a complex decision-making process by helping readers understand which approach aligns with their organizational culture and goals.

Next, *Is Data Governance Just Government for Data?* takes on a common misconception by comparing governance to government, questioning whether the analogy holds true. This thought-provoking piece sheds light on the unique aspects of governance, moving beyond bureaucratic comparisons to highlight its role in fostering collaboration and innovation.

Informal to Formal Data Governance transitions the discussion to the journey many organizations must undertake. By addressing how informal governance practices can evolve into formalized frameworks, this essay provides a practical roadmap for organizations looking to scale their governance efforts without overwhelming their teams.

The chapter also emphasizes the importance of aligning governance with technology functions in *Why IT Needs Data Governance*. Here, the connection between IT and data governance is explored, demonstrating how effective governance enables IT systems to deliver reliable, high-quality data that fuels AI and analytics initiatives.

Finally, *Why Information Governance Needs Data Governance* underscores the interconnected nature of structured and unstructured data. By illustrating how governance practices bridge the gap between these two realms, this essay highlights the critical role governance plays in supporting comprehensive data strategies.

Through these essays, Chapter 1 serves as the perfect starting point for understanding the critical importance of data governance in empowering people to manage AI and data effectively. It builds a compelling case for organizations to prioritize governance not just as a technical requirement, but as a catalyst for innovation and success.

The Data Will Not Govern Itself

In my years of working in the field of data governance and stewardship, I've encountered a recurring truth that remains as relevant today as it was when I first started: the data will not govern itself. This simple yet profound statement encapsulates the essence of Non-Invasive Data Governance (NIDG)—a philosophy and methodology I've championed and refined over the years.

NIDG is not just about managing data; it's about empowering every individual in an organization to take an active role in this process. Let's see how following the principles of NIDG activates and energizes your organization, and how transforming every individual into a data steward enables the implementation of effective data governance.

The Essence of Non-Invasive Data Governance

At its core, NIDG is about recognizing and formalizing the roles that individuals already play in data management.

It's a strategic approach that champions efficiency, collaboration, and adaptability. This approach contrasts with the more authoritarian models of data governance that impose rigid structures and stringent policies. Instead, NIDG recognizes that governance is already happening, albeit informally, leading to inefficiencies and ineffectiveness within organizations.

Democratizing Data Stewardship

The democratization of data stewardship is a fundamental aspect of NIDG. In this model, every individual interacting with data, whether defining, inputting, analyzing, or making decisions based on it, is a steward of that data. This inclusive approach lays the groundwork for a more collaborative and adaptive framework.

Cultural Transformation and Leadership Buy-In

Implementing NIDG requires a cultural shift within the organization. This shift starts with leadership buy-in and commitment. Leaders must champion the values of NIDG, emphasizing the importance of collaboration and recognizing the potential in every individual to contribute to the governance landscape. The transformation also involves targeted training sessions, workshops, and communication initiatives to embed these values into the organizational DNA.

Breaking Down Silos

Traditional governance models often result in limited adoption and organizational silos, where data is hoarded within departments, hindering its free flow and optimal utilization. NIDG, by design, seeks to break down these barriers, promoting collaboration across departments and encouraging the sharing of insights, data, and expertise.

Strategic Considerations and Assessment

Implementing NIDG requires a strategic roadmap that considers the unique needs, goals, and challenges of the organization. Key strategic considerations include a comprehensive assessment of the existing governance landscape, leadership alignment, training and skill development, technology integration, effective communication strategy, pilot programs, and continuous monitoring and improvement.

The Transformative Impact of NIDG

The adoption of NIDG within an organization leads to the democratization of data, enhancing data quality and reliability. It fosters a culture where data becomes a shared asset, and its accuracy becomes a collective responsibility. This approach also contributes to a more agile and responsive organization, where decisions are based on a comprehensive understanding of data, leveraging it for strategic advantage.

Realistic and Operational Implications

Accepting the notion that everyone is a data steward leads to a significant operational shift in how data is managed. It means that accountability for data-related actions is spread across the organization. This accountability extends beyond mere compliance; it encompasses the stewardship of data quality, its ethical use, and ensuring its alignment with business objectives.

Activation and Engagement of Data Stewards

Under NIDG, activating data stewards involves recognizing and leveraging their existing interactions with data. Training and skill development focus on enhancing their understanding of their role in data governance. This approach does not seek to impose new responsibilities but to formalize and acknowledge the existing contributions of each individual.

The Role of Technology in NIDG

In the NIDG approach, the strategic integration of technology is pivotal. This encompasses adopting data cataloging tools that facilitate the organization and retrieval of data, thereby streamlining governance processes. Collaboration platforms play a significant role, offering a centralized space for stakeholders to communicate and share insights, which is essential for fostering a culture of shared data responsibility.

Communication and Cultural Change

A well-defined communication strategy that includes the three Os of data governance communications (orientation, onboarding, ongoing), is principal in NIDG. Transparency and effective communication ensure that all stakeholders are informed about the changes, understand their role in the governance framework, and feel empowered to contribute.

Pilot Programs and Iterative Implementation

In the journey of implementing NIDG, initiating pilot programs is a strategic step. These pilot programs serve as testbeds, allowing organizations to apply NIDG principles on a smaller scale before rolling them out organization wide. This approach facilitates iterative implementation, where each phase of the pilot provides valuable insights and learning opportunities. Through these pilots, organizations can closely monitor the successes and challenges encountered, enabling them to make informed adjustments to their governance strategies.

Continuous Monitoring and Improvement

NIDG is a dynamic and evolving approach, mirroring the continuous growth and transformation of an organization. It thrives on regular monitoring and assessment, ensuring that the governance framework remains in harmony with the shifting goals and strategies of the organization. This ongoing evaluation process is crucial, as it allows for identifying areas needing improvement, adjusting practices to meet new challenges, and capitalizing on emerging opportunities.

Overcoming Challenges and Resistance

While the benefits of NIDG are substantial, organizations may encounter challenges during implementation, such as resistance to cultural change and potential disruptions to existing workflows. To address these challenges, the strategic plan includes change management initiatives, targeted communication campaigns, and phased implementation to help individuals and teams adapt gradually.

Conclusion

In the digital age, where data is a crucial asset, NIDG emerges as a signal of innovation and adaptability. Implementing this governance paradigm by design is a commitment to fostering a culture where data is a shared asset, decisions are informed by collective intelligence, and the organization thrives in the face of evolving challenges.

In conclusion, "The Data Will Not Govern Itself" is more than just a saying; it's a philosophy that underpins the success of NIDG. By embracing this approach, organizations can effectively activate and energize their workforce, turning every individual into a data steward. This transformation is essential for achieving a robust, agile, and responsive data governance framework, ensuring organizations not only survive but thrive in the data-driven future.

What Data Governance ROI Looks Like

When implementing an effective data governance program, calculating the return on investment (ROI) can often feel like an elusive goal. Unlike more straightforward investments where we measure ROI in clear financial terms, data governance benefits are frequently intangible, spread across various departments, and realized over time.

In the era of data analytics, AI, and AI governance, measuring the ROI of a Non-Invasive Data Governance (NIDG) program is more important than ever.

Not only does it justify the resources allocated to these initiatives, but it also provides a clear picture of their impact on the organization's overall success.

The most effective way to gauge ROI is by implementing specific metrics that capture the core benefits of data governance. These metrics should be easy to implement and directly tied to the goals of the organization, particularly as they relate to data quality, decision-making, compliance, and operational efficiency. In this short essay, I explore five of the easiest metrics to implement (the fifth metric will surprise you!) for measuring the ROI of a NIDG program and explain why these metrics are crucial in today's data-driven world.

Data Quality Improvement Metrics

Data quality is at the heart of any data governance program. Improving data quality ensures that the data used across the organization is accurate, complete, and consistent. The first and most straightforward metric to implement measures the improvement in data quality over time. This can be tracked by monitoring the number of data errors identified and corrected, the reduction in duplicate records, or the percentage of data that meets predefined quality standards.

Why is this important? In the context of data analytics and AI, data quality directly impacts the outcomes. Poor data quality can lead to inaccurate insights, faulty predictions, and ultimately, bad business decisions.

By tracking data quality improvements, organizations can directly link their data governance efforts to better business performance, providing a tangible ROI that resonates with stakeholders.

Data Quality Improvement Metrics include:

- Number of data errors identified and corrected.
- Reduction in duplicate records.
- Percentage of data that meets predefined quality standards.
- Time spent on data cleansing before and after governance implementation.
- Frequency of data audits and the outcomes.
- Improvement in data accuracy scores over time.

Compliance and Regulatory Adherence Metrics

Another critical area where data governance demonstrates its value is in compliance and regulatory adherence. This is particularly important in finance, healthcare, and other sectors with stringent data protection laws. A useful metric here is the reduction in compliance violations or the percentage of data that meets regulatory standards.

This metric is particularly relevant in the age of AI and AI governance. As organizations increasingly rely on AI for decision-making, ensuring that data used by these systems complies with regulations becomes paramount. Failure to do so can result in significant financial penalties, reputational damage, and loss of customer trust.

Measuring compliance adherence not only protects the organization but also showcases the ROI of data governance by preventing costly regulatory breaches.

Compliance and Regulatory Adherence Metrics include:

- Number of compliance violations before and after governance implementation.
- Percentage of data that meets regulatory standards.
- Cost savings from avoided regulatory penalties.
- Frequency and outcomes of internal compliance audits.
- Time taken to comply with new regulatory requirements.
- Improvement in data privacy and security measures.

Decision-Making Efficiency Metrics

One of the key benefits of a robust data governance program is the improvement in decision-making processes across the organization. A practical metric to assess this is the time taken to make critical business decisions before and after the implementation of a NIDG program. This can be further refined by measuring the speed at which data requests are fulfilled or the time saved by having accurate data readily available.

In the world of AI and data analytics, quick and informed decision-making is a competitive advantage.

Organizations that can harness accurate, well-governed data to make decisions faster are better positioned to capitalize on market opportunities, respond to threats, and innovate.

This metric directly ties the ROI of data governance to business agility and competitiveness, making it an essential consideration.

Decision-Making Efficiency Metrics include:

- Time taken to make critical business decisions before and after governance.
- Speed at which data requests are fulfilled.
- Reduction in decision-making bottlenecks due to poor data quality.

- Number of data-driven decisions made in a given period.
- Improvement in the quality of business insights and forecasts.
- Efficiency of data-driven meetings and discussions.

Operational Efficiency Metrics

Operational efficiency is a clear indicator of the ROI of a NIDG program. This can be measured by tracking the reduction in time spent on data-related tasks, such as data retrieval, cleansing, and management. Another approach is to measure the reduction in costs associated with these tasks, whether through automation, improved processes, or reduced errors.

Operational efficiency is particularly critical in the context of AI governance, where the ability to manage large volumes of data quickly and accurately is essential. By demonstrating how data governance improves efficiency, organizations can justify the investment in NIDG not just as a cost-saving measure, but as a strategic initiative that supports the broader goals of the organization.

Operational Efficiency Metrics include:

- Reduction in time spent on data retrieval and management tasks.
- Cost savings from automating data processes.
- Improvement in the speed of data-related operations.
- Reduction in errors and rework due to better data management.
- Improvement in resource allocation due to streamlined data processes.
- Efficiency gains in cross-departmental data collaboration.

Measuring Non-Invasiveness

And finally, and this metric may surprise you, measuring the non-invasiveness of a data governance program involves assessing how seamlessly governance principles are integrated into the daily operations of an organization without causing disruption. We can evaluate this metric through awareness, adoption, and application. Awareness looks at how well employees understand governance policies and their importance. Adoption measures the extent to which governance practices are embraced by various departments. Application evaluates how effectively governance principles are implemented in daily tasks.

These factors combined provide a clear picture of how naturally data governance fits into the organization's workflow, which is crucial for the overall success of the program.

Relating this to ROI, the non-invasiveness metric directly impacts the return on investment of a data governance program. A program that integrates smoothly with existing processes without creating resistance or requiring significant additional resources tends to have a higher ROI. This is because the organization can achieve its governance objectives—such as improved data quality and compliance—without incurring the costs and disruptions often associated with more invasive approaches. Therefore, a higher score on the non-invasiveness metric generally correlates with greater efficiency, quicker realization of benefits, and, ultimately, a stronger financial return.

Non-Invasiveness Metrics include:

- Employee awareness levels regarding governance policies.
- Rate of adoption of governance practices across departments.
- Smoothness of governance integration into existing workflows.
- Level of resistance or pushback from employees.
- Impact on employee productivity before and after governance implementation.
- Overall satisfaction with the governance program across the organization.

Conclusion

Measuring the ROI of a Non-Invasive Data Governance program is not only possible but essential in today's data-driven landscape. By focusing on metrics related to data quality improvement, compliance, decision-making efficiency, operational efficiency, and non-invasiveness, organizations can provide clear, quantifiable evidence of the value their data governance initiatives bring. In the age of AI, where data is the fuel that powers innovation, these metrics are not just useful—they are critical. Senior data leaders who understand and leverage these metrics can drive their organizations toward greater success, ensuring that their data governance efforts are recognized as a key driver of business value.

There Are Only Three Approaches to Data Governance

The other day, I overheard someone tell a large audience of data people that there are "hundreds of approaches to data governance." I beg to differ. There are only three approaches to data governance.

Organizations often struggle with choosing the Data Governance approach that aligns with their culture, resources, and objectives. Three universal approaches— Command-and-Control, Traditional, and Non-Invasive Data Governance—offer distinct perspectives on how to implement effective data governance programs. Let me boil them down for you.

Command-and-Control Approach: Mandating Governance Responsibilities

The Command-and-Control approach to data governance involves assigning individuals as data stewards and instructing them to take on governance responsibilities beyond what they recognize as their "regular duties." This approach relies on a structured hierarchy, where specific roles and responsibilities are appointed without necessarily considering individuals' existing relationships with the data. While this approach can bring swift organization to governance efforts, it often faces challenges in terms of employee engagement and the added burden on designated stewards.

This approach compels a thorough consideration of the impact on employees who are assigned governance responsibilities. Mandating additional duties can potentially lead to a sense of obligation rather than enthusiasm for the governance role. In some cases, individuals may perceive the imposition of these responsibilities as disruptive to their existing workflow.

To mitigate these challenges, effective communication becomes paramount. Clearly articulating the strategic importance of data governance, emphasizing the shared benefits for the organization and individuals, and providing necessary support and resources can foster a more positive reception. Incorporating feedback mechanisms and recognizing the contributions of data stewards within this structured framework can contribute to a more collaborative and motivated governance environment.

Traditional Approach: Identifying and Trusting Governance Inclinations

The Traditional approach to data governance appreciates the importance of individuals who naturally lean towards governing data but may encounter challenges in scaling this disposition across the organization. Depending solely on inherent leanings often results in an uneven distribution of the governance efforts, with certain subject areas or datasets receiving more attention than others. To address this, organizations should establish a clear framework that not only identifies individuals with inherent governance inclinations, but also actively encourages others to participate. This involves creating a culture that values formal data stewardship and provides opportunities for skill development and engagement.

Acknowledging and rewarding the contributions of stewards under this approach becomes crucial for sustaining motivation and ensuring a more widespread and equitable distribution of governance responsibilities. By combining the strengths of identified natural stewards with a structured engagement strategy, the Traditional approach can enhance its effectiveness and inclusivity.

Non-Invasive Data Governance Approach: Recognizing Existing Data Relationships

The Non-Invasive Data Governance (NIDG) approach recognizes individuals based on their inherent relationships with data. In other words, as the definers, producers, and users of data. Rather than imposing additional responsibilities, NIDG acknowledges existing data-related activities and formalizes these roles. This approach emphasizes engagement and collaboration, aligning governance with daily workflows. By organizing individuals based on their natural connections to data, NIDG promotes a culture of shared responsibility and leverages existing data expertise.

NIDG refrains, to the extent possible, from burdening individuals with additional governance tasks but instead formalizes and acknowledges their existing contributions. This approach fosters a sense of ownership and accountability, as individuals are engaged in governance activities that directly relate to their areas of expertise.

The NIDG approach thrives on collaboration and inclusivity, as it allows various departments and teams to contribute to governance efforts without disrupting established workflows. By aligning data stewardship with individuals' natural roles and responsibilities, NIDG builds a sustainable and integrated governance framework that capitalizes on the organization's existing data expertise.

NIDG builds a sustainable and integrated governance framework that capitalizes on the organization's existing data expertise.

Contrasting the Approaches

In comparing the three approaches to data governance, the aspect of imposition versus voluntarism stands out prominently. The Command-and-Control approach adopts a top-down strategy by designating individuals and mandating governance responsibilities, potentially facing resistance and challenges in engaging individuals who may perceive it as an added burden to their existing roles. On the other hand, the Traditional approach relies on voluntarism, expecting individuals to naturally gravitate toward governance due to their inherent interest or experience. This approach, while fostering enthusiasm among those naturally inclined, might lack a systematic and consistent engagement framework across the organization.

In the context of engagement, Command-and-Control might encounter difficulties in motivating individuals to actively participate, as the imposed responsibilities may not align with their daily workflows. The Traditional approach relies on the voluntary engagement of those with a predisposition for governance, potentially leading to uneven participation across different departments or teams. In contrast, the NIDG approach engages individuals by recognizing and formalizing their existing data-related roles, ensuring that governance activities seamlessly integrate with their regular responsibilities. This not only enhances engagement but also aligns governance efforts with the natural workflows of the organization.

Regarding formality, the Command-and-Control approach introduces formal roles and responsibilities, potentially creating a rigid structure that might not resonate with the organizational culture. The Traditional approach relies on informal inclinations toward governance, which, while flexible, might lack a structured framework. In contrast, NIDG combines formality by acknowledging and organizing based on existing relationships, providing a balance that leverages the strengths of both formal and informal structures. This hybrid approach ensures effective governance without disrupting established workflows, making it a practical and adaptable solution for organizations seeking a cohesive data governance strategy.

Conclusion

To summarize, while each approach has merits, the Non-Invasive Data Governance approach stands out by integrating recognition, engagement, and formalization, creating a harmonious and effective framework for governing data within the organizational landscape.

Is Data Governance Just Government for Data?

When people hear the term "Data Governance," it's natural to think of it as a sort of government for data—a structure of rules, regulations, and oversight aimed at managing data like a government manages its citizens. This comparison is apt in some ways, as governance involves setting policies, enforcing standards, and ensuring compliance. But is this all there is to it? Let's explore the comparison further, understand why it can be beneficial, and consider whether there might be a downside or even a better way to describe this essential practice.

Throughout this short essay, I will explain how Non-Invasive Data Governance (NIDG) provides a framework that goes beyond the simple comparison of governance to government. NIDG emphasizes the importance of embedding governance practices into existing processes and roles, rather than imposing them from the outside like a government might impose laws. This approach allows for a more natural integration of governance into the daily operations of the organization, reducing the perception of governance as an external or bureaucratic force and instead positioning it as a supportive structure that enhances the organization's ability to manage and utilize data effectively.

The Positive Side of Governance as Government

The analogy of data governance to government has its merits. Just like a government establishes laws to maintain order and protect citizens, data governance sets the rules for managing data to ensure its quality, consistency, and security. In a well-governed environment, data is treated as a valuable asset, with clear guidelines on how it should be handled, who is responsible for it, and how its accuracy and integrity can be maintained. This structure helps organizations ensure that data is reliable and available when needed, much like how a government ensures that public services are accessible and efficient. The order and discipline that come with governance provide a sense of stability and predictability, which is crucial for making informed business decisions based on trustworthy data.

Just as governments protect the rights and privacy of citizens, data governance plays a crucial role in safeguarding sensitive information. In today's data-driven world, where data breaches and privacy violations are real threats, a robust governance framework is akin to strong laws protecting against misuse and abuse. It helps organizations stay compliant with regulations, reduces risks, and fosters stakeholder trust. This protective role is undeniably a good thing, ensuring that data is not just managed but also respected as a critical resource.

NIDG enhances this positive aspect by ensuring that governance is non-invasive, meaning it doesn't disrupt existing processes but rather supports them. By integrating governance into the natural workflows of the organization, NIDG ensures that protective measures are in place without adding unnecessary complexity or burden. This approach makes it easier for organizations to adopt and maintain governance practices, ensuring that data is protected and managed effectively without being seen as a hindrance.

NIDG ensures that protective measures are in place without adding unnecessary complexity or burden.

The Potential Downsides of the Government Analogy

However, the comparison between data governance and government is not without its drawbacks. One of the key issues is that "government" often carries connotations of bureaucracy, red tape, and inefficiency. When employees hear "governance," they might immediately think of slow-moving processes, rigid rules, and an overall sense of constraint. This perception can lead to resistance, with individuals viewing data governance as something that stifles innovation or makes their jobs harder rather than a beneficial framework that aids their work.

Another downside is the fear of over-regulation. Just as citizens sometimes feel burdened by excessive laws and regulations, data professionals might worry that too much governance will limit their ability to work with data freely and creatively. In a fast-paced business environment, where agility and flexibility are key, the idea of being bound by stringent governance policies can be off-putting. This can result in a lack of buy-in from the very people whose cooperation is essential for governance to succeed.

NIDG addresses these potential downsides by promoting a governance approach that is both flexible and adaptable. It recognizes that one size does not fit all, and that governance should be tailored to fit the unique needs of each organization. By embedding governance into existing roles and responsibilities, NIDG ensures that it supports rather than stifles innovation. This approach helps mitigate the negative perceptions of governance as overly bureaucratic and presents it as a necessary and beneficial part of the organization's operations.

NIDG ensures that it supports rather than stifles innovation.

Explaining the Relationship Better

Organizations need to communicate the purpose and benefits of data governance more effectively to mitigate these negative perceptions. It's essential to emphasize that governance is not about imposing unnecessary controls, but about enabling better data management practices that ultimately lead to more informed decisions and business success. Rather than focusing on the rules and restrictions, the conversation should highlight how governance supports the organization's goals by ensuring that data is accurate, accessible, and secure.

One approach is to draw parallels between governance and stewardship, rather than government. Stewardship implies care, responsibility, taking care of something for somebody else, and proactive management—qualities that are inherently positive and less likely to evoke thoughts of bureaucracy. By framing data governance through data stewardship, organizations can shift the focus from control to care, from restriction to responsibility. This subtle change in language can make a big difference in how the organization perceives and embraces governance.

NIDG plays a crucial role in clarifying this relationship by focusing on the integration of governance into the everyday activities of the organization. By positioning governance as an enabler rather than a controller, NIDG helps reframe the governance conversation. It emphasizes the importance of making governance a part of the organization's culture, which is seen as a supportive and essential element of data management rather than an external force imposing restrictions. This approach fosters a more positive perception of governance and encourages broader acceptance and participation.

NIDG helps reframe the governance conversation.

Is There a Better Term?

So, is "data governance" the best term, or could there be a better one? While "data stewardship" is certainly a compelling alternative, it might not fully capture the comprehensive nature of governance, which includes policymaking, enforcement, and compliance in addition to care and responsibility. Another possible term could be "data enablement," which emphasizes processes and practices that allow an organization to unlock the full potential of its data. Enablement involves making data accessible, understandable, and usable for all stakeholders, ensuring that data is available in the right format, at the right time, and with the right quality to support decision-making, innovation, and business operations.

In the end, while "data governance" may not be a perfect term, it is widely recognized and understood within the industry. The key is not necessarily to change the term but to change how it is communicated and implemented within organizations. By focusing on the positive aspects of governance—such as protection, quality assurance, and responsibility—and downplaying the more bureaucratic elements, organizations can foster a culture where governance is seen as an enabler rather than an obstacle.

NIDG supports the idea that while the term "data governance" might not be perfect, it is effective when implemented correctly. NIDG's approach to governance focuses on embedding governance practices into existing workflows and making them a natural part of the organization's culture. This non-invasive approach ensures that governance is not seen as a separate or external force but as an integral part of how the organization operates. By adopting NIDG, organizations can ensure that governance is effective and positively perceived, regardless of terminology.

NIDG's approach to governance focuses on embedding governance practices into existing workflows and making them a natural part of the organization's culture.

Conclusion

To wrap this up, while there are similarities between data governance and government, this analogy can be both a strength and a weakness. Governance is necessary to ensure that data is managed properly, but it must be communicated to avoid the negative connotations associated with government. Companies can create a more positive and effective governance culture by reframing data governance as stewardship and emphasizing its role in supporting organizational goals. Ultimately, whether or not the term "data governance" is ideal, the focus should be on how it is implemented and understood within the organization.

NIDG provides a framework for implementing data governance in a way that supports these goals. By focusing on integration, flexibility, and cultural alignment, NIDG ensures that governance is effective, well-received, and aligned with the organization's overall objectives. This approach helps minimize the government analogy's potential downsides and ensures that governance is seen as a valuable and necessary component of successful data management.

Informal to Formal Data Governance

Organizations often find themselves overwhelmed by the sheer volume of data they collect, store, and analyze. While many companies start with informal data governance practices—often a patchwork of guidelines and ad-hoc procedures— there comes a time when moving to a more formal, structured approach is essential for sustained success.

This transition doesn't have to be disruptive. By following the Non-Invasive Data Governance (NIDG) approach, organizations can smoothly shift to formal data governance without overhauling existing processes. Here's how to make that move effectively.

Step 1: Assess Your Current State

Begin by taking a close look at your current data governance practices. What's working? What's not? Identify who is responsible for data management tasks and how decisions are made regarding data quality, security, and usage. This assessment will help you understand the gaps in your current approach and provide a foundation for developing a more structured plan.

Conduct this assessment non-invasively by engaging with key stakeholders to gather their perspectives and document current processes. This collaborative approach ensures that the transition builds on what already works well while addressing any gaps and inefficiencies. By involving those who are already managing data in some capacity, you can capture practical insights and foster a sense of ownership, making the transition smoother and more effective.

Step 2: Define Clear Roles and Responsibilities

In informal settings, roles related to data governance are often vague or distributed among various individuals without clear accountability. Moving to formal governance means defining specific roles such as data stewards, data custodians, and data owners. Data stewards ensure the accuracy and integrity of data within their domains, while data custodians manage the technical environment in which data resides.

Integrate these roles into existing job functions and processes without significant disruption. Engage with employees to understand their current responsibilities and identify how these new roles can align with and enhance their existing duties. This approach helps maintain productivity and fosters a sense of ownership and collaboration, ensuring that formal governance practices are embraced and effectively implemented.

Step 3: Develop Policies and Procedures

Formal data governance requires well-documented policies and procedures that everyone in the organization can follow. These should cover key areas such as data quality standards, access controls, data classification, and data lifecycle management. Clear policies help mitigate risks, ensure compliance with regulations, and maintain high standards of data integrity and security.

To achieve this in a non-invasive way, involve key stakeholders in the policy development process to gather input and ensure the policies are practical and relevant—to them as well as yourself. Use existing frameworks and guidelines as a foundation, making incremental adjustments rather than sweeping changes. This approach ensures that new policies are seamlessly integrated into current workflows, reducing resistance and encouraging widespread adoption and adherence.

Step 4: Implement Appropriate Tools and Technologies

While technology alone isn't the solution, it plays a crucial role in supporting formal data governance. Invest in tools that facilitate data cataloging, metadata management, data quality monitoring, and access control. These tools help automate and enforce governance policies, making it easier to maintain consistency and compliance across the organization.

To stay non-invasive, select tools that integrate seamlessly with your existing systems and processes. Conduct pilot tests to ensure compatibility and gather feedback from users to fine-tune implementations. This approach minimizes disruption and encourages user acceptance, ensuring that technological enhancements support your data governance objectives effectively and efficiently.

Step 5: Educate and Train Your Team

Transitioning to formal data governance involves more than just new policies and tools; it requires a cultural shift. Educate your employees about the importance of data governance and their roles in maintaining data quality and security. Provide training on new tools and procedures to ensure everyone is equipped to follow the new governance framework effectively.

To stay non-invasive, integrate training sessions into existing meetings and use familiar communication channels. Offer on-demand resources and hands-on workshops that align with current workflows. This approach ensures that training is practical, relevant, and minimally disruptive, fostering a culture of continuous learning and commitment to data governance without overwhelming your team.

Step 6: Establish Metrics and Monitor Progress

Establish metrics to monitor compliance and performance to ensure your formal data governance efforts are effective. Regularly review these metrics to identify areas for improvement and make necessary adjustments. This continuous monitoring and refinement process helps maintain the relevance and effectiveness of your data governance framework.

To continue in a non-invasive manner, incorporate these metrics into existing reporting structures and review cycles. Use tools and dashboards that your team is already familiar with to track and visualize data governance performance. This approach ensures that monitoring becomes a natural part of your ongoing operations, making it easier to identify trends, address issues promptly, and continuously enhance your data governance practices without imposing additional burdens on your team.

Step 7: Foster Continuous Improvement

Formal data governance is not a one-time project but an ongoing process. Encourage feedback from stakeholders and continuously refine your policies and procedures to adapt to changing business needs and technological advancements. By fostering a culture of continuous improvement, you can ensure your data governance practices remain robust and effective over time.

To stay non-invasive, establish regular check-ins and feedback loops using existing communication platforms and meetings. Create a simple, accessible process for stakeholders to share their insights and suggestions. This method ensures continuous improvement is seamlessly integrated into daily operations, allowing for adaptive and responsive data governance that evolves without causing significant disruptions.

Conclusion

Moving from informal to formal data governance is a significant step that can bring immense benefits to your organization. By adopting the Non-Invasive Data Governance approach, you can achieve this transition smoothly and effectively, ensuring that data governance enhances rather than hinders your operations.

Start with a thorough assessment, define clear roles, develop robust policies, leverage appropriate technologies, and invest in training and continuous improvement. This structured approach will help you harness the full potential of your data, driving better decision-making and long-term success.

Why IT Needs Data Governance

In the grand scheme of things, Information Technology (IT) has been the heavyweight champion of the organizational landscape for decades. Led by the CIO, IT has traditionally held the reins of data management, carrying the bulk of the responsibility—and the budget. However, if we're honest, the ROI from all that shiny tech has often been more of a whisper than a roar. Now, with AI investments piling onto the heap of tech infrastructure, there's more pressure than ever to show some tangible results. Meanwhile, in the opposing corner, here comes the Non-Invasive Data Governance (NIDG) function, led by a Chief Data Officer (CDO), Chief Data Analytics Officer (CDAO), or Chief Data, Analytics, and Innovation Officer (CDAIO)—or even nestled within a broader Data Strategy Office. And suddenly, IT realizes they've got some company in the data space. But this isn't just some turf war; it's about getting the organization to finally unlock the value of its data.

The beauty of Non-Invasive Data Governance is right there in the name: *non-invasive*. It doesn't come in with the heavy hand of policy police, forcing everyone to fill out forms and hold endless meetings. Instead, NIDG works quietly, often behind the scenes, guiding the organization to handle data responsibly without disrupting the day-to-day flow of work. The CDO and their team aren't there to make life harder for IT or anyone else. In fact, they're there to ensure that all those data-related investments work in harmony with what the business actually needs. Because let's be real: buying new technology doesn't mean much if the data itself isn't governed and usable.

The ideal arrangement between NIDG and IT requires mutual respect and a healthy dose of collaboration. IT, typically led by the CIO, has been doing the heavy lifting in terms of infrastructure, networks, security, and storage for years. They know the ins and outs of the organization's tech stack better than anyone. But they've traditionally been more focused on the technology itself than on ensuring the data flowing through those systems is aligned with business outcomes. That's where the CDO and the NIDG function step in.

Rather than stepping on IT's toes, NIDG complements IT's technical focus by ensuring that the data is being treated as a business asset, not just a byproduct of the tech. The CDO and their team are the stewards of the organization's data strategy, ensuring that the data is accurate, compliant, and ready to support decision-making. They do this by establishing a framework of rules, standards, and best practices that are easy to follow—yes, even for the IT folks—and integrated into the business's existing operations.

But the question remains: Why hasn't IT, with all its funding, delivered the ROI that organizations expect? Well, it turns out that throwing money at technology doesn't necessarily solve the real problem. Without governance, the data running through those high-tech systems is often chaotic, inconsistent, and untrustworthy. It's like installing a state-of-the-art kitchen and then realizing you have no ingredients to cook with. Sure, the tech is flashy, but what good is it if the data is a mess?

Without governance, the data running through those high-tech systems is often chaotic, inconsistent, and untrustworthy.

This is where NIDG adds real value. The CDO or CDAO, working with the IT team, ensures that the data feeding into those systems is well-governed, reliable, and aligned with the business's goals. The CIO continues to manage the technology, but NIDG ensures that the data itself is actually delivering on its promise. Together, they can start turning those AI and tech investments into tangible business value.

And let's not forget AI, which has now joined the lineup of IT's big promises. The buzz around AI is deafening, but once again, the technology is only as good as the data feeding it. Without proper data governance in place, AI investments will produce lackluster results at best, and outright disasters at worst. AI needs clean, governed, and well-understood data to provide accurate insights and drive automation. This is where the partnership between NIDG and IT becomes essential: IT provides the platforms and NIDG ensures the quality of the data.

In the ideal setup, the CIO and CDO work in tandem, understanding that both functions are critical to the success of the data strategy. IT keeps the systems running smoothly, while NIDG ensures that the data flowing through those systems is fit for purpose. It's a balance of technical excellence and strategic oversight, with NIDG ensuring that data governance is woven into the fabric of every business process—without slowing things down or creating unnecessary bureaucracy.

Conclusion

The days of IT shouldering the entire data burden are over. While IT continues to play an essential role, it's time to recognize that managing data is more than just a technical challenge. It's a business challenge. And that's where the CDO and the NIDG function shine, ensuring that data is treated as the valuable asset it is. Together, IT and NIDG can deliver the ROI that's been missing from years of tech investment. And let's face it, if we've learned anything from decades of watching money go into tech with little to show for it, it's that data governance isn't just a nice-to-have—it's the missing piece that finally makes the whole system work.

Why Information Governance Needs Data Governance

This essay is directed at all of my friends that focus on Information Governance (but not Data Governance) within organizations around the world. There are many of you ... including members of ARMA, AIIM, and the KM community, ... and lots of you were in the field years before Data Governance became something people were even talking about. You may not have called it Information Governance throughout the years (it *is* relatively new jargon). You may have used (or may still use) the labels of records management, content management, document management, and similarly toned names. I don't need to explain this to you, but your focus has been on the formal governance of all of your organization's data that is often severely different than the data found in information systems and databases across your organization.

When you think of "governance," your mind likely jumps to Information Governance—the governance of this unstructured data, records, content, and more. It's been a critical function for organizations dealing with massive amounts of information in all shapes and forms. But here's the kicker: many of those focused solely on Information Governance are missing a significant opportunity. As AI and machine learning sweep through industries, organizations must ensure that 100% of the data feeding these systems is governed effectively—including both structured and unstructured data. Enter Non-Invasive Data Governance (NIDG), a discipline and program that offers a comprehensive approach to governing data, structured and unstructured, without disrupting day-to-day operations.

The Scope of Data: It's Bigger Than You Think

Information Governance focuses largely on unstructured data—documents, emails, PDFs, videos, and so forth. And while that's a massive chunk of the organizational data pie, it's not the whole pie. Structured data, the stuff in databases, spreadsheets, and Enterprise Resource Planning (ERP) systems, needs just as much care and attention as your unstructured records. And with the rise of AI, every single piece of data (structured or not) is being thrown into the mix. AI doesn't care if it's a neatly categorized database entry or an obscure email attachment—it's all fuel for the machine. That's where Non-Invasive Data Governance steps in.

Non-Invasive Data Governance isn't about disrupting existing practices, but it's about ensuring that every corner of your data, from the most mundane database to the messiest folder of email archives, is governed appropriately and properly. If your AI is making decisions based on incomplete or poorly managed data, you can bet those decisions won't hold up to scrutiny. A well-integrated governance strategy covers all the bases, ensuring that your Information Governance efforts don't operate in a vacuum.

Integration is the Key: Uniting Data Governance and Information Governance

Here's a question: Why should people who focus on Information Governance be invested in a broader data governance strategy like NIDG? Simple. Because unstructured data doesn't live in a separate universe from structured data—it's all interconnected. The best AI solutions are those that can seamlessly blend data from multiple sources, including structured and unstructured content. If your Information Governance framework isn't integrated with a broader Data Governance strategy, you risk leaving gaps in how your data is managed, accessed, and, more importantly, audited.

AI systems thrive on data but are only as good as the data they consume. Without formal governance of the data, it's like building a house without a solid foundation—you might end up with something functional for a time, but cracks will show eventually. Non-Invasive Data Governance ensures that every piece of data, whether a structured database entry or a scattered email thread, is accounted for, managed, and, most importantly, auditable. This auditable trail is crucial, especially in industries with regulatory requirements or compliance needs, as AI outputs often need to be explained and justified.

Why AI Makes Governance Essential, Not Optional

AI is not a trend that's going to fade away—it's the future, and it's growing faster than many organizations can keep up with. Companies are turning to AI to gain insights, automate processes, and make smarter decisions, but those decisions are only as good as the data behind them. Without appropriate and formal governance of the data, there is no assurance that the data feeding your AI systems is reliable, accurate, or compliant. The integration of both structured and unstructured data into AI models means you need governance that covers both sides of the data spectrum.

A formal governance program like NIDG allows organizations to maintain control over how data flows into AI models, ensuring that the output isn't just accurate but auditable. And let's face it—auditing is no longer a nice-to-have; it's a requirement in industries where AI is making decisions that impact customers, finances, or legal compliance. Without governance, you're flying blind, and no one wants to explain to a regulator that your AI made a poor decision because of bad data management.

Conclusion

It's clear that Information Governance specialists need to think bigger. Focusing exclusively on unstructured data is only part of the equation. AI solutions require 100% data governance coverage, which means embracing a broader data governance strategy. Integrating your Information Governance practices with a formal NIDG program ensures that your data, structured or unstructured, is managed, monitored, and auditable. It's not about reinventing the wheel but about ensuring all your data feeds into your AI systems properly so you can trust their results.

Non-Invasive Data Governance provides the framework to govern all data across your organization without the heavy lifting or disruption that traditional governance models can bring. If you're serious about maximizing the potential of your AI initiatives, it's time to consider how a unified, auditable governance program can drive the future success of your organization.

The Human Element
in Data Governance

Data governance may be about managing information, but at its core, it's truly about managing people and their relationship to data. Chapter 2, *The Human Element in Data Governance*, dives deep into the critical role that individuals and teams play in making governance effective and sustainable. With the book's subtitle, *Empowering People to Govern Data and AI*, in mind, this chapter underscores that governance isn't about control or bureaucracy—it's about collaboration, awareness, and accountability.

The chapter begins with *Data Governance Equals People Governance*, a powerful reminder that governance is inherently tied to guiding human behavior. This essay, drawing on insights from Len Silverston, explores why governance is fundamentally about empowering individuals to understand and fulfill their roles in managing and protecting data effectively.

Next, *Shifting Paradigms in Data Stewardship* highlights the evolution of stewardship from a rigid, title-based role to a more dynamic and inclusive concept. By advocating for a shift in mindset, this essay illustrates how organizations can create a more collaborative and engaged governance culture.

Become Woke About Your Data is a call to action for organizations to rethink their relationship with data and approach it with a renewed sense of purpose and awareness. This essay focuses on how a deeper understanding of data's value can inspire individuals to take responsibility and engage meaningfully in governance efforts.

The chapter takes a direct tone in *Dear Executive, Pay Attention to Data Governance*. Addressing senior leadership, this essay emphasizes the importance of executive buy-in and accountability in driving governance success. It lays out the case for why leaders must not only support governance initiatives but actively champion them.

Data Governance for the Unwilling speaks to those who may resist governance efforts, outlining practical ways to turn skepticism into commitment. By addressing common objections and misconceptions, this essay provides strategies to engage even the most reluctant participants in governance.

Balancing "Data" and "Digital" navigates the often-blurred line between data governance and digital governance. This essay provides clarity on how these disciplines intersect and why aligning them is essential for organizations to thrive in the modern digital age.

In *Data Stewardship By the People and For the People*, the chapter emphasizes the democratic nature of stewardship, advocating for a model where governance is not imposed but embraced by individuals at all levels. This essay ties back to the idea of empowerment, showing how stewardship can be a unifying force within organizations.

Finally, the chapter closes with *Everybody is a Data Steward. Get Over It—Again!*, a reminder that stewardship is not confined to a specific group or department. By reinforcing the idea that everyone who defines, produces, or uses data has a role to play, this essay ties the chapter's themes together, demonstrating how governance can—and should—be a shared responsibility.

This chapter weaves together these essays to present a holistic view of the human element in data governance, making a compelling case for why empowering people is the key to governing AI and data successfully. It challenges organizations to embrace the full potential of their teams, ensuring that governance becomes not just a process, but a culture.

Data Governance Equals People Governance

A good friend of mine once told me that we should not call our beloved discipline "Data Governance" and that "People Governance" was a more appropriate label. His reasoning: "The data does what we tell it to do, and it is truly people's behavior that must be governed." That statement made a lot of sense when he shared it with me then and still resonates with me today. I didn't name my friend because, ultimately, he does not remember making that comment. Either way, there is truth in the idea of People Governance. Let me explain.

Data governance has emerged as an axis around which many business operations and strategic decisions revolve. However, at its core, the effectiveness of data governance hinges not on the sophistication of technologies deployed or the rigidity of policies legislated but on the engagement, commitment, and collaboration of the people within the organization. This essay explores how data governance, in essence, equates to People Governance, with a spotlight on stewardship and leadership engagement under the guidance of Non-Invasive Data Governance (NIDG) best practices.

Non-Invasive Data Governance is a methodology that emphasizes the engagement of existing organizational roles and responsibilities in governing data. Unlike traditional data governance frameworks that often impose new structures and roles, NIDG works within the existing fabric of the organization, making the NIDG Framework inherently people-centric. It acknowledges that data governance is not merely about managing data but about governing the people who use, manage, and make decisions based on that data.

People-Centric Approach

At the heart of this people-centric approach are the data stewards. These individuals are not assigned in an ad hoc manner but are recognized based on the data-related roles they already play within their day-to-day functions. The NIDG approach empowers these stewards with the authority, responsibility, and tools they need to ensure data is managed effectively, efficiently, and ethically. By aligning their roles with data governance objectives, stewards become pivotal in bridging the gap between high-level governance policies and ground-level operational practices.

Leadership engagement, on the other hand, is the linchpin that secures the data governance structure firmly within the organizational culture. Leaders, from executives to department heads, play a critical role in championing the cause of data governance. Their commitment is instrumental in fostering a culture that values data as a strategic asset and recognizes the importance of its governance. By actively participating in data governance initiatives, setting clear expectations, and embodying the principles of NIDG, leaders inspire trust and enthusiasm across all levels of the organization.

Adopting NIDG best practices requires a shift in perspective—from viewing data governance as a series of mandates to seeing it as a cultural philosophy that infuses every facet of the organization. This involves clear and continuous communication about the value and objectives of data governance training and education to ensure everyone understands their role in it, as well as the creation of a collaborative environment where ideas and challenges can be shared openly.

Community of Practice

The inclusion of a Data Governance Community or Center of Practice (CoP) significantly amplifies the "Data Governance Equals People Governance" narrative, especially under the NIDG approach. This addition nurtures a holistic environment where data governance transcends mere policy enforcement, embedding itself into the cultural fabric of the organization through collective wisdom, shared practices, and mutual learning.

A Data Governance Community of Practice, when aligned with NIDG principles, serves as a vibrant ecosystem where stakeholders across the organization—data stewards, IT professionals, business users, and executives—converge to share knowledge, experiences, and best practices. This collaborative platform enables the democratization of data governance, making it a shared responsibility rather than a top-down mandate. Within this community, we realize the true essence of people governance, as it fosters a sense of belonging, participation, and ownership among its members.

The CoP acts as a catalyst for cultural change, facilitating the transition towards a data-informed organization. By engaging members through regular meetings, workshops, and forums, the community ensures that data governance is continuously aligned with evolving business objectives and technological advancements. This dynamic engagement helps in maintaining the relevance and effectiveness of data governance initiatives, ensuring they adapt to internal and external pressures.

Moreover, the CoP under NIDG promotes a non-invasive integration of data governance into daily operations. It respects and utilizes the existing organizational structure, minimizing resistance and fostering a positive perception of data governance. Through the community, data governance becomes less about compliance and more about enhancing business performance, data quality, and decision-making. The non-invasive nature of NIDG, combined with the supportive environment of the CoP, empowers individuals at all levels to contribute to and benefit from effective data governance practices.

The community also plays a crucial role in identifying and addressing the training and development needs of its members. Tailored educational programs and resources ensure that everyone, from seasoned data professionals to those new to data governance, can enhance their understanding and skills. This continuous learning environment not only elevates individual competencies, but also strengthens the organization's collective data governance capabilities.

In essence, the Data Governance Community or Center of Practice (or Excellence) embodies the spirit of people governance within the realm of NIDG.

It provides a structured yet flexible framework for collaboration, innovation, and shared responsibility. Through its activities, the community not only advances the organization's data governance objectives, but also cultivates a culture where data is recognized as a pivotal asset for achieving strategic goals. By fostering an inclusive, informed, and engaged community, organizations can ensure that their data governance initiatives are not only effective but also enduring and aligned with the broader objectives of people governance.

Conclusion

The implementation of NIDG highlights the importance of recognizing and leveraging the informal networks and relationships that exist within organizations. By harnessing these existing connections and governing people's behavior in addition to the data itself, data governance initiatives can be more effectively disseminated and ingrained within the organization. This approach fosters a sense of ownership and accountability among all stakeholders, making data governance a shared responsibility.

The essence of effective data governance lies in its ability to govern people and their interactions with data. Through the principles of Non-Invasive Data Governance, organizations can cultivate a data governance framework that is not only effective and sustainable, but also deeply integrated into the organizational culture. Steward and leadership engagement are paramount in this endeavor, as they embody the human elements that drive the success of data governance initiatives. By prioritizing people over processes and technologies, organizations can unlock the full potential of their data, guiding their journey toward data-driven excellence with wisdom, foresight, and collective effort.

Shifting Paradigms in Data Stewardship

I have been writing a lot in recent days about data stewards and data stewardship. I have written about rules for becoming a data steward, stewardship in the age of AI, and even about how data stewards are the gardeners in a data landscape. The reason for this abundance of new content is the resounding importance of stewards as one of the backbones of data governance programs in which I am involved.

In data governance, the role of the data steward is vital. However, not all approaches to data governance involve their data stewards in the same way. In my work and through my advocacy for Non-Invasive Data Governance (NIDG), I have emphasized the need for a distinctive understanding of different stewardship strategies. Let's explore the contrasts and nuances between assigning data stewards, identifying data stewards, and recognizing data stewards, and how these models align with various governance approaches.

Assigning Data Stewards: The Command-and-Control Approach

The assignment of data stewards is often a part of what I refer to as the "Command-and-Control" approach. This approach is characterized by its top-down nature, where data stewardship roles are explicitly designated by management. Here, stewards are formally assigned specific responsibilities and tasks related to data governance. The responsibilities of the data steward are presented as "not optional" and the assignment often is interpreted as being "over-and-above" a person's present responsibilities. Typically, this model is used in organizations where data governance is in its nascent stages or where there is a need for rapid and controlled responses to data issues.

While this approach ensures clear accountability and direct oversight, it can be quite invasive. It often involves significant changes to job roles and may require considerable effort to enforce and maintain. In the "Command-and-Control" model, stewards might feel that their roles are thrust upon them, which can lead to resistance or lack of engagement. While effective in certain contexts, this approach often misses tapping into the intrinsic motivation and existing knowledge of the workforce.

In the "Command-and-Control" approach, the association with data stewardship roles often aligns with hierarchical positions within the organization. This model typically assigns stewardship roles based on job titles, departmental functions, or perceived authority in data-related matters. While this ensures clear lines of responsibility and accountability, it may not fully leverage the depth of knowledge and experience available within the organization. Moreover, this approach can create a sense of imposition among the assigned stewards, possibly leading to a lack of genuine engagement and ownership in data governance activities.

Identifying Data Stewards: The Traditional Approach

Identifying data stewards is a step away from the "Command-and-Control" approach, moving towards what I call the "Traditional" approach. This tactic is akin to the famous line from the Academy-award nominated movie, *Field of Dreams*: "If you build it, they will come." Here, the organization creates a formal data governance framework and then identifies individuals who naturally fit the role of data stewards based on their existing interaction with data.

This method is less invasive than assigning roles directly. It acknowledges the existing dynamics and workflows within the organization. However, it still relies on the formal identification of stewards, which can sometimes lead to gaps in coverage or engagement. While this approach is more inclusive and considers the natural data flow within an organization, it may not fully realize the potential of informal data governance activities happening at various levels.

The "Traditional" approach to associating individuals with data stewardship roles takes into consideration the existing roles and interactions employees have with data. This model identifies stewards based on their current involvement with data within their functional areas. It respects and builds upon the natural flow of data within the organization, thus making the transition into formal stewardship roles more seamless and less disruptive. However, it can sometimes be limited in its reach, overlooking potential stewards who may not be as prominently visible in their data interactions but nonetheless hold valuable insights and skills.

Recognizing Data Stewards: The Non-Invasive Approach

Recognizing data stewards is the cornerstone of my Non-Invasive Data Governance model. This approach is based on the premise that stewardship, in the form of *informal* accountability, is already occurring within organizations. People are already responsible for defining, producing, and using data as part of their everyday jobs. It's about acknowledging and leveraging the natural relationships that employees have with data. In this approach, instead of assigning or identifying stewards, we recognize and empower those who already demonstrate stewardship in their daily work.

This approach is the least invasive and most aligned with fostering a culture of data responsibility. It's predicated on the belief that individuals, when recognized for their natural interactions with data, are more likely to be engaged and take ownership of data governance. Recognizing stewards is about enhancing what is already working well and formalizing the informal stewardship activities. This method promotes a sense of ownership and pride in data management and leads to a more sustainable and ingrained data governance culture.

The "Non-Invasive" approach, which I strongly advocate, fundamentally shifts the paradigm by recognizing and empowering individuals who naturally exhibit stewardship behaviors in their day-to-day activities. This approach does not rely on formal assignments or identifications; instead, it acknowledges and cultivates the inherent data management skills and expertise found across various levels of the organization. It promotes a culture where data stewardship is seen as a collective responsibility and an integral part of every employee's role, encouraging a broader and more engaged participation in data governance efforts.

Comparative Analysis: Efficacy and Cultural Fit

Each of these approaches has its place and effectiveness depending on the organizational context and maturity of data governance practices. The "Command-and-Control" model, while more invasive, can be effective in establishing initial governance structures or in situations requiring stringent control. The "Traditional" approach, on the other hand, offers a balance between formal structure and natural flow, suitable for organizations with some level of data governance maturity.

However, the "Non-Invasive" approach, which I promote, aligns most closely with building a lasting and self-sustaining data governance culture. It leverages the existing knowledge and practices within an organization, minimizes resistance, and promotes widespread engagement. This approach fosters a sense of collective responsibility, where data governance becomes an integral part of everyone's role.

Conclusion

Understanding the differences between assigning, identifying, and recognizing data stewards is critical for effective data governance. While the "Command-and-Control" and "Traditional" models have their merits in certain situations, the "Non-Invasive" approach of recognizing data stewards aligns best with fostering a culture of data responsibility and stewardship across the organization. It's about creating a governance ecosystem that is organic, sustainable, and deeply rooted in the organization's culture. As we move forward, embracing this holistic view of data stewardship will be key to thriving in the complex and data-driven world of today.

Become Woke About Your Data

The world is undergoing a significant shift, and with it, the meaning of being "woke" is changing dramatically. What once was a badge of awareness and consciousness has, in many circles, become a controversial or even derisive term. I will not address why that change is taking place in this writing.

The Merriam-Webster dictionary defines the term "woke" as "becoming aware of and actively attentive to important facts and issues." In today's fast-paced world, where data is more valuable than gold, it's time to wake up—no, scratch that—it's time to become woke about your data. But what does it mean to be woke about your data? It's about awareness, responsibility, and a collective effort to ensure that data is used, governed, and improved in ways that benefit the entire organization. Let's quickly dive into the key reasons and steps your organization must take to get there.

First, let's talk about awareness. Data is everywhere and growing faster than we can keep up. But not all data is created equal. To get the most out of it, your organization needs to recognize data's value and treat it as a vital asset. This isn't just about the folks in IT or the data scientists in the back room crunching numbers. It's about everyone—from the intern to the CEO—understanding that the data they touch is part of a much bigger picture. That email you sent? Data. That customer interaction? Data. That spreadsheet you can't find? Yep, data. Becoming woke about your data starts with realizing how deeply it's embedded in everything you do.

Now, here is where it gets interesting. There is a non-invasive approach to governing your data. You heard that right—*non-invasive*. It's not about coming in with a sledgehammer and making drastic changes that disrupt everyone's work. Instead, it's about integrating data governance practices into your existing processes in a way that feels natural and, dare I say, easy. This approach respects the way your organization already operates while gradually guiding it towards better data practices. Think of it as gently steering a ship rather than turning it on a dime. The result? A smoother ride with fewer bumps along the way.

But here's the kicker: becoming woke about your data isn't a solo journey. It's a collective effort that requires everyone's participation. This means that every single person in your organization plays a role in data governance. Yes, *everyone*.

Whether you're entering data into a system, analyzing it for insights, or making decisions based on it, you are part of the governance process. When everyone understands their role and takes ownership, the whole organization benefits. It's like a well-choreographed dance—when everyone is in sync, it's a beautiful thing.

Finally, and perhaps most importantly, you need to understand that data doesn't improve on its own. You can't just leave it to chance and hope for the best. Without formal governance, data becomes a mess—disorganized, inaccurate, and ultimately useless. Imagine a garden left untended: weeds grow, plants wither, and what was once a beautiful space becomes an eyesore. The same goes for your data. Formal governance is like the gardener, tending to your data, ensuring it's healthy, accurate, and ready to be used when you need it.

Conclusion

In summary, becoming woke about your data is about recognizing its value, adopting a non-invasive approach to governance, ensuring everyone in the organization contributes, and acknowledging that data doesn't take care of itself. It's a journey, but one that's well worth the effort. So, wake up, get involved, and start treating your data like the valuable asset it is. After all, in this data-driven world, staying woke is the key to staying ahead.

Dear Executive, Pay Attention to Data Governance

Sometimes it takes a bold move to elevate your position and carve out your niche as somebody who demonstrates significant value for your organization. Have you ever considered writing a letter to your Senior Executives with the hopes of getting them to wake-up and take notice of something that has been right in front of their noses for a long time? What would a letter like that look like? Here it is.

Dear Senior Executive,

I hope this letter finds you well. I am writing to address a matter of strategic importance that holds the potential to significantly enhance our organization's efficiency, decision-making, and competitive edge: the implementation of a formal Non-Invasive Data Governance (NIDG) program.

Before you shrug off the idea as something you've heard before, I was hoping that you will take three minutes to learn about why this time, and this method, may be different than your previous discussions.

While the organization leans into leveraging AI and digital technology through a strategy that supports our overall business strategy, it is crucial to acknowledge that our organization is *already governing* the data that will feed AI in many ways, albeit informally. Across various departments, individuals are making decisions about the definition, production, and usage of *their* data. Individuals decide who can access their data, and they determine the acceptable level of quality of *their* data.

However, these efforts, while commendable, are often uncoordinated and inconsistent, and lack the formal accountability that can drive true enterprise data-driven success. This informal approach leads to inefficiencies, inconsistencies, and missed opportunities that can hinder our overall performance and strategic objectives. And beyond all of that, there is the recognition that *these issues will not resolve itself*.

A formal NIDG program offers a structured and sustainable way to manage our most critical data assets. Unlike traditional top-down and command-and-control data governance models, NIDG focuses on formalizing accountability rather than assigning additional work. This approach leverages existing roles and responsibilities, integrating data governance into the natural workflows of our employees. By doing so, we ensure that data governance becomes an inherent part of our organizational culture without overburdening our staff.

The Pot of Gold at the End of the Rainbow

One of the key benefits of the NIDG approach is the formalization of accountability. This does not mean adding more tasks to everyone's already busy schedules. Instead, it involves recognizing and formalizing the data-related activities that are already being performed. This formalization ensures that everyone understands their role in maintaining data quality and integrity, leading to more consistent and reliable data practices across the organization.

For example, our marketing team already collects and analyzes customer data to inform campaign strategies. By formalizing data governance in this area, we can ensure that the data used is accurate, up-to-date, and compliant with privacy regulations. This not only improves the effectiveness of our marketing efforts but also protects our reputation and builds trust with our customers.

Supporting and Sponsoring Data Governance

Your support and sponsorship are critical to the success of this initiative. As senior leaders, your endorsement sends a powerful message about the importance of data governance to the entire organization. Here are a few key reasons why your support is vital:

- **Strategic Alignment:** Data governance aligns with our strategic goals by ensuring that data is managed as a valuable asset. This alignment helps drive business performance and supports our long-term objectives.

- **Risk Mitigation:** A formal data governance program helps mitigate risks related to data breaches, compliance issues, and poor data quality. This proactive approach protects the organization from potential legal and financial repercussions.

- **Improved Decision-Making:** Reliable and high-quality data is the foundation of informed decision-making. By ensuring data accuracy and consistency, we empower our leaders to make better, data-driven decisions.

- **Operational Efficiency:** Data governance streamlines processes and reduces redundancies. This leads to increased efficiency and productivity, allowing us to do more with our existing resources.

Understanding the Role of Data Governance

To fully support this initiative, it is important for you to understand the role that formal data governance will play in our success. Data governance is not just an IT function; it is a business imperative that involves collaboration across all departments. Here's how we can achieve this:

- **Education and Awareness:** We will provide comprehensive training and resources to help all employees understand the principles and benefits of data governance. This will ensure that everyone is on the same page and committed to the initiative.

- **Stakeholder Engagement:** We will involve key stakeholders in the development and implementation of the data governance framework. Their input and feedback are essential to creating a program that meets the needs of the entire organization.

- **Clear Communication:** We will communicate the goals, expectations, and progress of the data governance program regularly. Transparency will help build trust and maintain momentum.

- **Resource Allocation:** We will allocate the necessary resources, including time, budget, and personnel, to support the data governance program. This investment will pay off in the form of improved data quality and business performance.

To conclude, the implementation of a formal Non-Invasive Data Governance program is a strategic move that will drive our organization towards greater efficiency, better decision-making, and enhanced competitive advantage. By recognizing and formalizing the data-related activities already taking place, we can achieve significant improvements without overburdening our staff. Your support and sponsorship are critical to the success of this initiative, and I am confident that, with your backing, we can make data governance a cornerstone of our organizational strategy.

Thank you for your attention to this important matter. I look forward to working with you to make our data governance program a resounding success.

Sincerely,

Phil Inurname

Data Management Advocate Extraordinaire

Your Organization Name Goes Here

Data Governance for the Unwilling

Organizations are increasingly recognizing the importance of data governance. However, not everyone within these organizations is equally enthusiastic about adopting new data governance initiatives, particularly when such efforts are perceived as intrusive or burdensome. This essay is for you—the reluctant data consumers, the skeptical stakeholders, and the cautious members of the workforce who are yet to be convinced of the benefits that data governance can bring to your specific performance and the broader organizational health.

Here, we'll explore how a Non-Invasive Data Governance (NIDG) approach can transform your apprehension into advocacy by emphasizing benefits that directly impact you without the disruptive overhaul you might fear.

Understanding Non-Invasive Data Governance

At its core, Non-Invasive Data Governance focuses on enhancing data management and governance through existing roles, responsibilities, and processes rather than introducing disruptive new systems or protocols. This approach respects the natural flow of work and leverages the inherent knowledge and expertise within the organization, making it a more agreeable proposition for those wary of change.

This methodology implicitly acknowledges the value and efficiency of leveraging what already works within an organization, subtly weaving data governance into the fabric of daily activities without the friction typically associated with new implementations. It's a recognition that the path to improved data stewardship doesn't have to be paved with upheaval but can instead be achieved by enhancing and elevating existing processes and knowledge bases.

By doing so, Non-Invasive Data Governance not only mitigates resistance from those who are hesitant to adopt new practices but also accelerates the adoption and effectiveness of governance initiatives. This approach cultivates a culture where data governance is not seen as an external imposition but as a natural extension of existing roles, making it fundamentally more sustainable and impactful in the long run.

Data Governance Is Not About Overhaul But About Enhancement

For those suspicious of data governance, it's crucial to understand that NIDG isn't about tearing down and rebuilding from scratch but rather about recognizing and formalizing the good practices already in place. This means your daily routines are not upended; instead, they're streamlined and optimized. This approach mitigates the fear of disruption, highlighting that data governance is an ally in improving performance, not an obstacle.

The essence of Non-Invasive Data Governance lies in its ability to subtly refine and elevate the data-handling practices that individuals and teams already perform well. It's about taking the informal, often unrecognized, data management efforts and giving them structure and visibility without imposing additional burdens. This refinement process includes identifying areas where small adjustments can yield significant benefits in data quality, accessibility, and security. By focusing on enhancement rather than overhaul, NIDG fosters a sense of ownership and pride in data practices, encouraging a more engaged and proactive stance toward data governance from those who may initially be reluctant.

Your Expertise Is Valued and Essential

NIDG leverages the existing expertise within the organization. Your knowledge about your data, your insights into its quirks and qualities, and your understanding of its flow and function are invaluable. This approach involves formalizing your role in data governance, acknowledging your contribution, and empowering you with greater control and clarity over the data you handle. This recognition not only enhances your sense of ownership but also directly contributes to improving the quality and reliability of organizational data assets.

Recognizing and utilizing the expertise of individual data handlers enables a richer, more subtle approach to data governance. By involving those who take action with data daily, organizations benefit from a ground-up perspective that ensures policies and practices are not only theoretically sound but practically applicable. This collaborative approach bridges the gap between high-level data governance objectives and the on-the-ground realities of data management, ensuring that governance frameworks are both effective and thoughtfully aligned with the needs and experiences of those who manage and depend on the data.

This empowerment leads to a more engaged workforce, where individuals are more likely to take the initiative in identifying and resolving data issues, contributing to a culture of continuous improvement and data excellence.

Data Quality Directly Impacts Your Work Quality

One of the primary goals of data governance is to ensure data quality and integrity. For the skeptical stakeholder, it's important to realize how high-quality data directly benefits you. Accurate, timely, and reliable data can significantly reduce the time spent verifying or correcting information, streamline decision-making processes, and increase confidence in the outcomes of your work. By getting onboard with NIDG efforts, you contribute to and benefit from the enhanced quality and reliability of the data you rely on.

The relationship between data quality and work quality is not merely additive; it's transformative. High-quality data acts as a catalyst for innovation, allowing for more accurate predictions, insightful analyses, and strategic planning. In a Non-Invasive Data Governance environment, where improvements in data handling and management practices are achieved without overhauling your daily activities, you play a critical role in this transformation.

Your participation in ensuring data quality does more than just enhance your immediate work outcomes; it elevates the organization's overall data literacy and capability, fostering a culture where data-driven decisions are the norm, not the exception. This culture shift, driven by improved data quality, leads to better business outcomes, enhanced customer satisfaction, and a competitive edge in the market.

Mitigating Risks and Enhancing Compliance

In an era of rigorous regulatory requirements, data governance is no longer an option but has become a necessity. For those concerned about the implications of compliance on their work, NIDG offers a pathway to ensuring that data handling practices meet regulatory standards without adding undue burden. By embedding compliance into everyday data practices, NIDG minimizes the risk of non-compliance and its associated penalties, protecting both you and the organization.

Following this approach includes compliance becoming an integrated part of the workflow rather than an external, often disruptive, requirement. This integration allows for a seamless adherence to legal and regulatory obligations, turning what can often be seen as an impediment into an advantage. It fosters a proactive rather than reactive compliance culture within the organization, where you are equipped with the knowledge and tools needed to anticipate and address compliance issues before they arise. This empowerment not only mitigates risks but also instills a greater sense of accountability and ownership over the data, contributing to a stronger, more compliance-conscious work environment.

Improving Collaboration and Reducing Silos

Data silos are a common challenge, leading to inefficiencies and errors. NIDG promotes a culture of collaboration and shared responsibility for data, breaking down these silos. For the reluctant data consumer, this means easier access to the data you need, when you need it, and in a form you can trust. By participating in a non-invasive data governance framework, you contribute to a more collaborative, efficient, and effective data environment.

This approach encourages an ecosystem where information flows freely between departments, enhancing both individual and organizational performance. When barriers are removed and data is shared openly (yet securely), you no longer have to waste time hunting for information or reconciling discrepancies between different versions of the truth. This not only accelerates project timelines but also fosters a sense of unity and purpose across the organization. By being an active participant in this culture, you help to create a more transparent, agile, and responsive environment where informed decisions are made swiftly and innovation thrives.

Conclusion

For those yet to be convinced of the value of data governance, consider the Non-Invasive Data Governance approach as a gateway to understanding how strategic data management can improve not just organizational performance but your daily work life. By engaging with NIDG efforts, you help shape a data governance framework that respects your expertise, enhances your performance, and contributes to a culture of data excellence. Remember, improving your data situation doesn't require a leap into the unknown but a step forward with the knowledge and practices you already possess.

The NIDG approach allows you to actively participate in a process that not only respects your current role within the organization but also seeks to elevate your contribution towards achieving data excellence. This involvement offers a unique blend of personal development and organizational growth, where your understanding and handling of data directly influence the success of governance initiatives. Through this engagement, you become a pivotal part of an evolving data culture that values continuous improvement, collaboration, and shared success.

As you contribute your expertise and learn from the collective knowledge within the organization, you are not only advancing your career but also playing a crucial role in steering the organization towards a future where data-driven decisions are the norm, and excellence in data governance is a shared achievement.

Balancing "Data" and "Digital"

In today's corporate environments, the words "data" and "digital" are often used interchangeably, but they carry distinct meanings and implications depending on the context. Understanding how these terms are related—and where they diverge—can have a significant impact on how organizations approach their business and data strategies. Let's look at four different perspectives on how "data" and "digital" are used, especially as companies focus on data management, governance, analytics, AI, and AI governance.

First, there's the technological perspective, where "digital" often refers to the tools and platforms that transform analog processes into electronic, automated workflows. Here, "data" is viewed as the raw material fueling these digital systems. For many organizations, this transformation means digitizing legacy systems and ensuring that data is properly captured, stored, and processed. Companies are heavily investing in "going digital," which is often equated with moving to the cloud or automating tasks, but without a focus on the underlying data, digital efforts can lack direction. Without reliable, well-governed data, the success of these digital initiatives is in jeopardy.

From this perspective, while "digital" is typically about the technology enabling business operations, "data" is the element that provides value to these digital systems. The power of digital tools depends entirely on the quality of the data they process. This means that an organization's ability to optimize its digital transformation is directly linked to how well it handles data. Poor data quality can undermine even the most advanced digital platforms, turning them from innovation drivers into costly burdens. For a true digital transformation, organizations must prioritize data from the outset, treating it not as an afterthought but as an essential building block for their digital tools.

Second, from a data governance perspective, especially through the lens of Non-Invasive Data Governance (NIDG), the terms "data" and "digital" take on a different relationship. Here, data is treated as an asset that must be governed effectively, and "digital" represents the environment where that data is used, managed, and shared. In this case, "data" is central to the conversation, and "digital" is the ecosystem within which data governance policies must operate. Companies that take the NIDG approach understand that they can implement governance within existing digital workflows, ensuring data quality, security, and compliance without disrupting the digital systems already in place.

In this view, governance doesn't have to disrupt digital processes—it can complement them. By recognizing that "data" and "digital" are interconnected but separate, NIDG helps organizations implement governance policies that work seamlessly within their digital environments. This approach ensures that digital initiatives don't get bogged down with bureaucratic governance processes. Instead, governance happens naturally, in the background, as part of digital operations. It allows organizations to reap the benefits of digital transformation while maintaining full control over their data, ensuring that the integrity of the data is preserved, even as the technology around it evolves.

A third perspective is the data analytics angle. When organizations talk about becoming "digital-first," they're often referring to their ability to leverage data for insights and decision-making. Here, "data" is the foundational element that drives "digital" efforts. Without high-quality data, the analytics and dashboards that power digital business models fall flat. In these cases, the interplay between "data" and "digital" becomes critical—digital platforms generate the data, but it's the data itself that drives innovation, customer insights, and operational efficiency. Analytics sits at the intersection, ensuring that the data flowing through these digital systems is actionable and insightful.

Looking deeper, the relationship between "data" and "digital" in the context of analytics is one of continuous feedback. Digital systems generate a vast amount of data from every interaction, which analytics tools then process to provide insights. But without robust analytics, the digital data remains raw and largely useless. This highlights the need for organizations to invest in both sides—digital infrastructure to gather data and advanced analytics to turn that data into actionable intelligence. It's not just about collecting data anymore—it's about having the right tools to transform it into something that drives decision-making and business value.

Finally, there's the perspective of AI and AI governance. When people talk about "digital transformation" today, AI often plays a major role. But the success of AI hinges on data—good data. Without well-managed, accurate, and governed data, AI models fail to perform as expected. This makes AI governance a critical part of the digital strategy, ensuring that the AI systems behaving autonomously in these digital environments are ethical, fair, and transparent. AI is often the final stage of a company's digital journey, but the road to AI success is paved with good data governance practices that start long before AI enters the picture.

The relationship between "data" and "digital" in AI governance goes beyond just feeding clean data into AI systems. AI governance also involves ensuring that the algorithms within these digital systems operate ethically and responsibly. As AI grows more autonomous, organizations must take care that their digital platforms are transparent in how they handle data, ensuring that the decisions made by AI are explainable and fair. The link between data quality and AI governance is crucial—without trustworthy data, AI systems can quickly become unreliable, and without governance, they can become unaccountable.

Conclusion

In conclusion, while "data" and "digital" are often used together in corporate settings, the nuances between them matter. The semantics of these words—how and when they are used—can influence a company's strategy. Whether it's through governance, analytics, or AI, organizations need to be intentional in distinguishing between "data" and "digital" in order to create effective, data-driven digital ecosystems that support their business goals. The right understanding of these terms ensures that businesses don't just become digital—they become data-informed, and that's where the real value lies.

Data Stewardship By the People and For the People

In today's increasingly data-driven world, effective data governance is more important than ever. Yet, the challenge lies not just in managing data but in making governance and stewardship practical, meaningful, and beneficial to those who use data daily. This is where the concept of "Data Stewardship By the People and For the People" comes into play. By leveraging Non-Invasive Data Governance (NIDG), this approach emphasizes that the governance and stewardship of data must be provided "by the people" who already have relationships with and recognized formal accountability for that data. At the same time, it ensures that data governance is "for the people," helping them in their daily jobs by making their work easier and more efficient.

The traditional approach to data governance often places the responsibility squarely on the shoulders of IT departments. However, NIDG recognizes that the real data experts are the business people who handle data daily, such as marketing managers, financial controllers, and HR professionals. These individuals are uniquely positioned to ensure data quality and proper usage because they interact with and understand the data intimately. By recognizing and formalizing their existing roles as data stewards, the Non-Invasive approach aligns stewardship responsibilities with natural workflows instead of imposing new burdens.

Formal accountability means that those who already handle specific types of data in their roles are formally recognized as being responsible for the quality and management of that data. For instance, marketing managers are naturally accountable for customer data quality, financial controllers steward and ensure accurate financial records, and HR professionals safeguard employee data privacy. By empowering these individuals, we create a collaborative environment where data governance becomes practical, relevant, and aligned with existing responsibilities.

The Non-Invasive approach emphasizes that governance should not disrupt existing workflows. Instead, it should seamlessly integrate into the daily operations of business professionals. Marketing managers, for example, continue to focus on customer insights while also ensuring that customer data is accurate and consistent. Financial controllers maintain the integrity of financial data as part of their routine responsibilities. This alignment allows data governance to be naturally embedded into everyday work.

One of the key elements of this approach is the power of relationships. By leveraging the relationships between data stewards and their respective teams or departments, we foster collaboration between IT and business units. This synergy enhances data quality and consistency while ensuring that stewardship remains practical and relevant.

But what about the benefits? What does data governance "for the people" look like in practice? First, effective governance leads to improved data quality and accuracy. When individuals are formally accountable for the data they handle, its quality becomes a shared priority, reducing errors and inconsistencies. Clear data standards and definitions also ensure that everyone speaks the same language, reducing confusion and misinterpretation.

Another significant benefit is enhanced decision-making. High-quality data that is well-organized and accurate leads to better business insights. Employees can confidently base decisions on data, knowing that it's reliable and up to date. Streamlined compliance is another outcome. With formal stewardship roles, compliance becomes less of a burden because people know what data they're responsible for and how it should be managed. Automated data lineage tracking simplifies regulatory audits and reporting, reducing the stress of meeting compliance requirements.

Efficiency and productivity also increase when data governance is done right. Reduced data duplication and fewer errors mean less time wasted on cleaning and correcting data. Business users can access accurate, well-documented data faster, improving productivity. Additionally, better collaboration and communication arise from a shared understanding of data definitions and ownership. Cross-functional teams can communicate more effectively, leading to innovative solutions and shared best practices.

To implement "Data Stewardship By the People and For the People," organizations can follow a series of practical steps. First, recognize and formalize data stewards across business units, ensuring that their roles align with their existing responsibilities. Next, establish clear data standards and definitions that everyone can understand and use. This step will foster a shared language around data governance. Additionally, create a collaborative environment by bridging the gap between IT and business units, enabling them to work together seamlessly on data-related projects.

Training, awareness, and data literacy programs can further empower data stewards by providing them with the skills and knowledge needed to excel in their roles. Finally, implement tools and technologies that support data governance, such as automated data lineage tracking and data catalogs.

Conclusion

"Data Stewardship By the People and For the People" following the Non-Invasive Data Governance approach offers a practical and inclusive approach to managing data. By recognizing and empowering the business people who already handle data daily, organizations can improve data quality, enhance decision-making, and streamline compliance while fostering a culture of collaboration and efficiency. Ultimately, it's about making data governance a part of the natural workflow, benefiting both the organization and its people.

Everybody is a Data Steward. Get Over It—Again!

Back in January 2018, I published an essay in The Data Administration Newsletter (TDAN.com) titled *Everybody is a Data Steward; Get Over It!* The essay was both popular and controversial. The two stated criticisms were 1) that it wasn't nice to tell people to "get over" anything, and 2) that if everybody is a data steward then nobody is a data steward. In response to 1) I apologize if I came across as being rude. And 2) I outright disagree.

The assertion that "... nobody is a data steward" fails to hold water within the framework of Non-Invasive Data Governance (NIDG). This approach pivots on the premise that anyone who interacts with data in any capacity—whether defining, producing, or using it—is inherently a steward of that data. This broad definition of stewardship is deliberate, aiming to foster a culture where data management responsibilities are universally recognized and integrated into everyday job functions.

Under NIDG, the formal accountability for data associated with an individual's role ensures that data stewardship is not an abstract, assigned duty but a concrete, personalized responsibility. Rather than diluting the importance of data stewardship by making everyone a steward, NIDG emphasizes and clarifies the role each person plays in maintaining the integrity and utility of data, making the governance process more inclusive and effective.

By recognizing each individual's interaction with data as a form of stewardship, NIDG promotes a widespread accountability framework that enhances overall data governance without the need for stringent control measures typically seen in traditional governance models. This approach ensures that data stewardship is not seen as a special designation for a select few but as a standard aspect of professional conduct for all. This broad participation helps in embedding data quality and compliance into the operational fabric of the organization, driving collective efforts towards data accuracy, legality, and usefulness. The NIDG approach inherently counters the notion that universal stewardship diminishes the role's importance; instead, it strengthens and specifies the role each employee plays in safeguarding data as a valuable organizational asset.

Paradigm Shift

The Non-Invasive Data Governance (NIDG) approach offers a compelling paradigm shift compared to the Command-and-Control or Traditional approaches. That shift is the idea that everyone in an organization who interacts with data is, by virtue of their interaction, a steward of that data. This concept extends beyond the confines of traditional data governance models, which often limit stewardship to specific roles or individuals designated under more rigid Command-and-Control or traditional frameworks. NIDG democratizes the responsibility of data stewardship, fundamentally altering how organizations perceive and manage their data.

The NIDG approach operates on the principle that anyone who defines, produces, or uses data has an inherent accountability for its accuracy, privacy, and overall management. This accountability isn't assigned or imposed from the top down, as seen in the Command-and-Control approach, nor is it a label simply attached to individuals as part of their job description, as often happens in traditional governance models. Instead, recognition as a data steward in NIDG is a natural extension of an individual's daily interactions with data. This recognition is crucial as it shifts the perception of data governance from being a mandated task to an integral part of everyone's job.

Recognition Over Assignment

Recognizing individuals as data stewards based on their relationship with data, rather than assigning these roles, has several advantages. First, it ensures that data governance is deeply embedded into the operational fabric of the organization. Employees become more naturally inclined to consider the implications of their data handling, leading to improved data quality and compliance as they understand their direct impact on the outcomes. This approach encourages a culture of accountability and transparency, as individuals recognize their part in the broader data ecosystem and see their contributions as critical to the organization's data integrity.

The NIDG framework fosters a more engaged and proactive workforce. Since stewardship is linked to daily data-related activities, employees are more likely to take the initiative in identifying and resolving data issues. This proactive engagement can lead to faster resolution of data quality problems, more innovative ideas for using data effectively, and a greater sense of ownership and pride in the organization's data-driven achievements.

The Impact at Levels

In the NIDG approach, there are two levels of data stewards. The role of data domain stewards at the tactical level and operational data stewards is recognized not by imposition but through the acknowledgment of the natural data responsibilities that individuals already hold. Data domain stewards are those who oversee subject areas of data that span across multiple business functions. They are recognized for their expertise and accountability in managing the integrity, usability, and security of data within a particular domain, such as customer information, product data, or financial metrics.

These stewards play a pivotal role in setting data-related policies and standards that align with both organizational objectives and regulatory requirements. By anchoring their stewardship in the NIDG approach, domain stewards facilitate a seamless integration of governance practices across various departments, ensuring that data policies enhance rather than hinder operational effectiveness.

Operational data stewards, on the other hand, are typically those individuals embedded within specific business functions or processes, accountable for the handling of data within their daily operations. In a NIDG setting, these stewards are recognized based on their direct interactions with data—whether in processing, maintaining, or reporting it. This recognition is crucial as it empowers them to take ownership of data quality and compliance at the grassroots level, making data governance a part of their routine activities rather than an additional burden. Operational data stewards ensure that the standards and policies devised at the domain level are practically applied, addressing the unique challenges and needs of their specific areas.

The NIDG approach thus ensures that data governance is embedded into the fabric of everyday business processes, enabling a culture where every data interaction is guided by governance principles, driven by the stewards at both the domain and operational levels.

Minimize Resistance

The NIDG approach minimizes the resistance often encountered with the introduction of new governance structures. By integrating stewardship into existing roles and responsibilities, organizations can avoid the pitfalls of disruptive changes, making the transition to comprehensive data governance smoother and more acceptable to all involved. Employees do not feel burdened by additional tasks; instead, they continue their regular duties with an enhanced focus on the quality and utility of the data they handle.

In essence, the NIDG approach to data stewardship brings numerous benefits. It empowers all employees to act as stewards of the data they interact with, enhancing the overall data culture within the organization. It breaks down silos by fostering cross-departmental collaboration and understanding of data processes, enriching both the data itself and the insights derived from it. Ultimately, recognizing rather than assigning data stewardship roles makes data governance a shared responsibility and a common goal, aligning it more closely with the strategic objectives of the organization.

Conclusion

By embracing the notion that everyone is a data steward, organizations can harness the collective power of their workforce to enhance data management practices and drive more effective, data-informed decisions. This is not just a shift in strategy but a cultural evolution towards greater data maturity and responsibility—a change that everyone in the organization should get over, again!

AI and Data Governance

Artificial Intelligence (AI) has become the new frontier of innovation, but its success is inherently tied to how well the data feeding these systems is governed. Chapter 3, *AI and Data Governance*, dives into the intricate relationships between AI, data governance, and the people who steward these efforts. Through the lens of the book's subtitle, *Empowering People to Govern Data and AI*, this chapter underscores that achieving sustainable, ethical, and high-performing AI depends on building a foundation of effective governance.

The chapter begins with *A Comparison of Data Governance Vs. AI Governance*, which provides clarity on the intersection and distinctions between these two disciplines. It explains how AI governance extends beyond data to include algorithm accountability and ethical decision-making while still relying on robust data governance as its backbone. This essay lays the groundwork for understanding why a unified approach to governance is critical in the age of AI.

In *The Risk and Promise of AI*, the narrative explores AI's dual nature: its capacity to drive extraordinary progress and its potential to exacerbate risks when improperly governed. This essay provides an honest evaluation of both sides of AI, urging organizations to embrace the promise of AI while addressing its inherent vulnerabilities.

The Risk of AI Solutions with Ungoverned Data sharpens the focus by examining the dangers of unleashing AI on ungoverned datasets. Highlighting real-world scenarios, this essay demonstrates how poor data governance can lead to biased models, inaccurate predictions, and reputational risks, making the case for proactive governance as a prerequisite for AI success.

In *What's the Difference Between an AI Model and a Large Language Model?*, the chapter takes a more technical turn, exploring how governance must adapt to different AI frameworks. This essay explains the unique requirements of governing data for general AI models versus the intricacies of managing the vast datasets that fuel large language models, shedding light on why tailored governance strategies are necessary.

Data is Key to Sustainable Gen AI zooms out to emphasize the long-term perspective. It argues that the sustainability of generative AI depends on a steady stream of high-quality, well-governed data. This essay encourages organizations to view governance not as a one-time effort but as a continuous practice that ensures AI remains relevant, reliable, and responsible.

The chapter crescendos with *Connect AI and Data Governance! You Won't Be Sorry (Unless You Don't)*, which passionately advocates for a closer alignment between AI initiatives and data governance frameworks. This essay emphasizes that organizations ignoring this connection risk inefficiencies, non-compliance, and missed opportunities, while those prioritizing integration are better positioned to thrive.

In *AI Will Not Render You Obsolete, However ...*, the focus shifts to a reassuring yet realistic perspective for data professionals. The essay debunks the myth that AI will eliminate jobs, instead highlighting how data governance expertise is becoming more critical as organizations navigate the complexities of AI-driven transformation.

Artificial vs. Augmented Intelligence takes a philosophical turn, discussing the distinction between machines that replace human tasks and those that amplify human potential. This essay argues for a balanced approach where governance ensures AI systems augment human decision-making rather than replace it outright.

Finally, the chapter concludes with *What Comes After AI for Data Professionals*, which imagines the evolving landscape of data and AI governance. This essay challenges data professionals to prepare for the future, emphasizing that governance will remain a cornerstone of innovation as AI technologies mature.

Together, the essays in this chapter provide a robust exploration of AI and data governance, illuminating the ways they intersect and complement each other. By weaving together technical insights and strategic guidance, Chapter 3 demonstrates that empowering people to govern data and AI is the key to unlocking AI's transformative potential while minimizing its risks. This chapter is not just about adapting to AI—it's about thriving in a world where governance and innovation go hand in hand.

A Comparison of Data Governance Vs. AI Governance

In today's hyper-connected, data-fueled, constantly artificial intelligence-this and artificial intelligence-that world, organizations are increasingly relying on both Data Governance and AI Governance to maintain control over their digital assets and technologies. These two forms of governance are essential but differ in their scope, focus, and implications for business and society. Data Governance has been a long-standing practice aimed at ensuring data quality, security, and accessibility, while AI Governance is a relatively new field concerned with the ethical use and regulation of artificial intelligence systems.

What makes this comparison particularly interesting is the way these governance frameworks overlap and diverge, especially when considering the Non-Invasive Data Governance (NIDG) approach I've developed. NIDG integrates governance into the natural flow of an organization without creating friction, while AI Governance often involves setting up new layers of oversight specifically tailored to managing the risks and ethical concerns associated with AI technologies. Both approaches, though rooted in governance, serve distinct purposes—one is about ensuring data can be trusted and used effectively, while the other safeguards the decisions made by autonomous systems.

While both forms of governance aim to manage risks, AI introduces complexities that are more difficult to predict and manage compared to data. With data, we can focus on securing, organizing, and ensuring that people are held accountable for its quality and accessibility. But AI systems act on data, sometimes making autonomous decisions that can impact business operations, consumers, and even society at large. This makes AI Governance a much broader concept that requires deep ethical consideration, rigorous oversight, and transparency that goes beyond the typical concerns of Data Governance.

The Evolution of Governance

Historically, Data Governance emerged as organizations began to recognize data as a critical asset. The need to ensure that data was accurate, secure, and compliant with regulations became paramount. Data Governance, in its simplest form, is about creating accountability for data and ensuring that it is managed and used effectively. With NIDG, the goal is to make this process non-intrusive, meaning that people are not burdened with extra tasks, but rather recognized for their existing roles and relationships with data. This approach encourages seamless integration into everyday activities, making data governance feel like a natural extension of the work.

AI Governance, on the other hand, is a more recent development, spurred by the rise of AI and machine learning technologies. AI systems, by their very nature, operate autonomously, making decisions based on algorithms and data inputs. This introduces new risks, particularly around bias, transparency, and accountability. The stakes are high because AI doesn't just manage data—it interprets it, makes decisions, and can potentially act on those decisions without human oversight. This requires a distinct governance framework that goes beyond just ensuring data quality—it needs to ensure that AI systems are ethical, fair, and aligned with societal values.

As AI continues to evolve, AI Governance must also adapt, covering broader implications like algorithmic accountability, explainability, and human oversight. This means ensuring that organizations understand how their AI systems arrive at decisions, how they can be audited, and what impact they have on the people affected by those decisions. While traditional Data Governance focuses on keeping data accurate and secure, AI Governance takes on the challenge of making sure AI operates in ways that align with not just business goals but also broader ethical and societal standards.

Where Data Governance and AI Governance Intersect

At first glance, you might think that Data Governance and AI Governance are entirely separate concepts. But in reality, they are deeply interconnected. AI systems are only as good as the data they are fed. Poor data quality can lead to biased or inaccurate AI outcomes, making robust Data Governance essential to the success of any AI initiative. While the focus of Data Governance is on managing the integrity and use of data, its practices directly influence the effectiveness of AI Governance by ensuring that the inputs into AI systems are reliable and free from bias.

For example, in an organization where NIDG is implemented, data is meticulously managed across its lifecycle, ensuring that it is accurate, complete, and secure. This level of oversight helps minimize the risks of bias or error when that data is used to train an AI system. However, once the AI system is operational, AI Governance kicks in, ensuring that the algorithms themselves behave ethically, transparently, and without bias. In essence, while Data Governance ensures the quality and security of the data, AI Governance ensures that the AI system using that data behaves in a way that aligns with both business objectives and ethical standards.

Furthermore, as AI systems become more ingrained in day-to-day operations, AI Governance must ensure that these systems remain adaptable and auditable. While Data Governance sets the foundation, ensuring that high-quality, compliant data is used, AI Governance steps in to manage the lifecycle of the AI models themselves. This includes monitoring how AI evolves with new data and ensuring that ongoing adjustments to the models don't compromise the ethical standards or fairness of the AI system's outcomes.

The Key Differentiators Between Data and AI Governance

When you look closely at how Data Governance and AI Governance function, you'll find several key differentiators, each critical to their respective roles.

Key Differentiator	Data Governance (NIDG)	AI Governance
Scope of Governance	Focuses on the quality, security, and compliance of data across its lifecycle. Governance is tied to how data is created, managed, and used by people in their everyday roles.	Encompasses not only the data used by AI but also the ethical management of AI models, ensuring they behave transparently and without bias in their decision-making.
Risk Management	Manages risks related to data accuracy, privacy, and security. NIDG takes a formal yet non-intrusive approach by embedding data stewardship into existing workflows.	Focuses on ethical risks, such as biased algorithms, transparency, and unintended consequences of AI decision-making. There's a need for higher scrutiny due to AI's autonomy and impact.

Key Differentiator	Data Governance (NIDG)	AI Governance
Compliance and Regulations	Primarily about adhering to data privacy regulations like GDPR and ensuring data is protected and governed properly. Compliance is achieved through formal data policies and standards.	Focuses heavily on regulatory and ethical compliance, especially around AI ethics, bias mitigation, and transparency, with evolving guidelines from governments and AI watchdogs.
Accountability and Roles	In NIDG, everyone who interacts with data is accountable for its governance, and their roles are based on their existing relationships to data (definers, producers, users).	Requires specific roles, such as AI ethicists, data scientists, and legal experts, to manage the development and deployment of AI, ensuring that the models align with ethical standards.
Decision-Making and Impact	Data Governance is about ensuring that data is accurate, reliable, and available for decision-making, which directly impacts business operations and strategies.	AI Governance is broader in scope, ensuring AI-driven decisions are fair, ethical, and explainable. AI impacts not only operations but also societal issues like fairness, justice, and trust.

The Complexity of AI Governance

One of the most significant differences between Data Governance and AI Governance is the level of complexity involved. While Data Governance focuses on ensuring that data is accurate, accessible, and protected, AI Governance introduces a range of ethical considerations that are much harder to measure and control. For instance, how do you ensure that an AI system is fair? What does transparency look like when you're dealing with complex machine learning models that even the data scientists who build them don't fully understand?

These are tough questions, and they highlight the need for AI-specific governance frameworks that go beyond traditional data management. AI Governance involves not just data scientists but also ethicists, legal experts, and compliance officers, all working together to ensure that AI systems are behaving as they should. The goal is to ensure that AI aligns with societal norms, business values, and regulatory requirements, while also fostering innovation.

In addition, AI Governance requires ongoing monitoring and adjustment. Unlike data, which is relatively static once it's collected and stored, AI models can evolve, learn, and adapt over time, which means that their governance must be flexible and continuous. This makes it vital to have clear guidelines on how AI models are trained, tested, and deployed, and how they are monitored for performance and fairness long after they go live.

Data Governance as the Foundation

Even though AI Governance introduces new challenges, it's important to remember that Data Governance remains the foundation for any successful AI initiative. Without clean, well-governed data, AI systems can't function properly. In fact, many of the high-profile failures of AI systems—such as biased hiring algorithms or flawed facial recognition technologies—can be traced back to poor data governance. If the data fed into an AI system is incomplete, biased, or inaccurate, the AI model will produce flawed results.

That's why a solid Data Governance program, like Non-Invasive Data Governance (NIDG), is crucial. By embedding governance into everyday activities, organizations can ensure that the data they collect and use is of the highest quality, free from bias, and managed securely. This, in turn, provides a strong foundation for AI Governance, making it easier to develop ethical, transparent, and effective AI systems.

Moreover, the feedback loop between Data Governance and AI Governance is vital. Data informs AI, but AI also generates new insights and data, which in turn needs governance. Organizations that get this balance right will not only mitigate risks but also unlock new opportunities, using both their data and AI systems more strategically and ethically.

Conclusion

As AI technologies become more integrated into business processes, the lines between Data Governance and AI Governance will continue to blur. Organizations will need to develop comprehensive governance frameworks that address both the quality of the data and the ethical implications of AI. As AI systems evolve and generate more data, businesses will need to ensure that governance covers both traditional data assets and AI-driven insights, managing them with the same rigor and responsibility.

In the future, we can expect AI-driven data governance tools to emerge, where AI helps manage the data governance process itself—automating tasks like data quality checks, compliance monitoring, and anomaly detection. These AI-driven tools will create a self-sustaining governance loop where data helps improve AI systems, and AI improves the governance of data.

The goal will be to create governance systems that are flexible enough to manage the evolving landscape of AI technologies while maintaining the accountability and security that are the hallmarks of traditional data governance. For companies to remain competitive and responsible in this rapidly changing landscape, harmonizing Data Governance and AI Governance will be key. The successful organizations of tomorrow will be those that can balance data management with ethical AI practices, ensuring that their AI systems are trustworthy, transparent, and impactful.

In the end, both Data Governance and AI Governance are about building trust—trust in the quality and security of data, and trust in the fairness and transparency of AI systems. Together, they form the foundation of a well-governed, data-driven organization, enabling businesses to innovate responsibly while maintaining control over their most critical assets: data and technology.

The Risk and Promise of AI

AI is rapidly reshaping our world, influencing everything from the way we work to the way we live. It's like a double-edged sword, offering incredible potential while also posing significant risks. At the heart of this transformation lies data, the fuel that powers AI systems. How we manage this data can determine whether AI will be a boon or a bane for society. Governed data, maintained through Non-Invasive Data Governance (NIDG), can help us minimize the risks while maximizing the promise of AI.

Understanding the Risks of AI

One of the main concerns surrounding AI is the potential for misuse. AI systems, if trained on biased or poor-quality data, can perpetuate discrimination or reinforce harmful stereotypes. For instance, facial recognition systems have been criticized for their inability to accurately identify individuals from different ethnic backgrounds. This bias often stems from datasets that lack diversity.

Another significant risk is data privacy. AI algorithms require massive amounts of data to learn and make predictions, which raises concerns about how personal information is collected, stored, and used. If data is not governed properly, sensitive information could be exposed, leading to identity theft, data breaches, or unethical surveillance.

There's also the issue of transparency. AI systems often function as "black boxes," making decisions that are difficult to understand or explain. Without proper governance, this opacity could lead to decisions that are unfair or unaccountable, especially in critical areas like healthcare, finance, or criminal justice.

Beyond these immediate concerns, there's the overarching challenge of regulatory compliance. Different countries have varying standards regarding data privacy, security, and ethical use, such as the General Data Protection Regulation (GDPR) in Europe and the California Consumer Privacy Act (CCPA) in the United States. Navigating this complex landscape requires organizations to have a thorough understanding of regional regulations, which can be especially tricky when working with global datasets.

The problem of AI misuse extends to malicious actors who could weaponize AI for cyberattacks. Deepfakes, for example, are increasingly used to create convincing yet fake videos that can spread misinformation or manipulate public opinion. Furthermore, hackers could exploit AI algorithms to bypass security systems or automate large-scale attacks, amplifying the damage.

The transparency challenge is further complicated by the rapid advancement of machine learning techniques like deep learning. These models are often so complex that even their developers struggle to explain how they arrive at specific decisions. This lack of interpretability can have significant consequences, particularly in sectors where ethical and legal accountability is paramount.

Finally, there's the broader societal concern about the impact of AI on employment. As AI systems become more capable, they could automate roles traditionally held by humans, leading to widespread job displacement. This disruption could exacerbate economic inequality if appropriate reskilling and policy measures aren't in place.

The risks surrounding AI are multifaceted and require a proactive approach. Properly governed data, anchored in principles like privacy-by-design and transparency, can mitigate these risks. Non-Invasive Data Governance offers a practical path forward by embedding governance practices into everyday workflows without overwhelming data professionals. By ensuring that data is accurate, secure, and ethically managed, organizations can harness the transformative power of AI while safeguarding against potential pitfalls.

The Promise of AI

Despite these risks, AI holds tremendous promise. In healthcare, AI systems can analyze medical images faster and with greater accuracy than humans, leading to the early detection of diseases. In agriculture, AI-powered drones and sensors can monitor crops, optimizing irrigation and reducing pesticide use. And in finance, AI algorithms can detect fraudulent transactions in real-time, safeguarding our money.

The potential benefits of AI are endless: improving efficiency, reducing costs, and solving problems that once seemed insurmountable. But to fully unlock this promise, we need high-quality, well-governed data.

In manufacturing, AI-driven predictive maintenance helps companies avoid costly downtime by identifying equipment issues before they lead to breakdowns. This technology enables factories to schedule repairs and replacements efficiently, saving both time and money. Additionally, AI can optimize production lines by analyzing workflow patterns, reducing waste, and improving overall productivity.

In education, AI is transforming how we learn and teach. Intelligent tutoring systems can adapt to individual learning styles, providing personalized lessons that help students grasp complex concepts. Automated grading systems enable educators to spend less time marking papers and more time engaging with students, fostering a more supportive learning environment.

Transportation is another area where AI is making significant strides. Self-driving vehicles are poised to revolutionize the automotive industry by reducing traffic accidents and improving fuel efficiency. In logistics, AI algorithms can optimize delivery routes, reducing shipping times and costs. This not only benefits businesses but also leads to a more environmentally friendly transportation network.

AI's potential for environmental conservation is also remarkable. Climate models powered by AI can predict weather patterns and natural disasters with unprecedented accuracy, giving governments and organizations the insights they need to prepare and respond effectively. In wildlife conservation, AI can analyze satellite images to monitor deforestation or poaching activities, providing critical data to protect endangered species.

The entertainment industry is seeing the creative side of AI as well. From generating realistic visual effects in movies to composing music and writing scripts, AI is becoming an essential tool for creators. Streaming platforms utilize AI to offer personalized recommendations, enhancing user engagement and satisfaction.

However, realizing these promises hinges on having high-quality, well-governed data. NIDG plays a pivotal role in this by embedding governance practices into everyday workflows without creating additional burdens for data professionals. By ensuring that data is accurate, secure, and ethically managed, NIDG enables organizations to harness the transformative power of AI responsibly.

The Role of Governed Data

Governed data plays a crucial role in managing the risks and realizing the promise of AI. High-quality data, free from bias and errors, ensures that AI systems make fair and accurate decisions. Privacy-focused data governance practices protect personal information, fostering trust among users.

Transparency is another area where governed data shines. By clearly documenting data sources, processing methods, and decision-making criteria, organizations can make their AI systems more explainable and accountable. This transparency builds confidence in AI decisions, especially in critical applications like healthcare or finance.

Beyond fairness and transparency, governed data also promotes compliance. With evolving data privacy regulations like the GDPR and CCPA, organizations need to handle personal information responsibly. Governed data ensures that AI systems comply with these regulations by anonymizing sensitive information and tracking how data is collected, processed, and used. This compliance not only reduces legal risks but also builds public trust in AI technologies.

Governed data helps streamline collaboration between data scientists, engineers, and business teams. By providing a clear framework for data usage and quality standards, data governance makes it easier for cross-functional teams to share and utilize data effectively. This collaboration is crucial for developing AI systems that align with business objectives while adhering to ethical guidelines.

Data governance also fosters scalability. As organizations expand their AI initiatives, managing growing volumes of data becomes increasingly challenging. A robust data governance framework helps organizations maintain data quality at scale, ensuring that AI models continue to perform accurately as they grow. This scalability is essential for organizations looking to leverage AI across different departments and geographies.

Governed data improves decision-making by enhancing data lineage. Understanding where data originates, how it is transformed, and how it's used provides valuable insights into data quality and relevance. This lineage enables organizations to trace errors back to their source and refine their data pipelines, leading to better decision-making and more reliable AI models.

Governed data supports continuous improvement. Regular audits, data quality assessments, and feedback loops ensure that data governance practices evolve with changing business needs. This iterative approach allows organizations to refine their AI systems continually, reducing bias, improving accuracy, and enhancing transparency.

NIDG integrates these principles seamlessly into everyday workflows. It minimizes disruption while embedding governance practices at every stage of the data lifecycle. By prioritizing collaboration and aligning governance practices with organizational goals, NIDG ensures that data remains a valuable asset in the pursuit of responsible and transformative AI.

Conclusion

Governed data is fundamental to managing AI's risks and realizing its promise. It ensures fairness, transparency, compliance, and collaboration, providing a solid foundation for organizations to innovate confidently. Non-Invasive Data Governance offers a practical approach to achieving these goals, enabling organizations to harness AI responsibly and ethically.

Artificial intelligence is transforming our world in ways we couldn't have imagined just a few decades ago. It holds the power to solve some of humanity's greatest challenges, but it also carries significant risks. Governed data, maintained through Non-Invasive Data Governance, can help us navigate these challenges. By embedding governance practices into everyday workflows, NIDG minimizes the risks and maximizes the promises of AI, ensuring that this powerful technology serves humanity's best interests.

The Risk of AI Solutions with Ungoverned Data

The sensation (!) and adoption of AI are growing at an unprecedented rate. Organizations are increasingly turning, or planning to turn, toward AI to gain insights, automate processes, and enhance decision-making. However, the success of AI initiatives heavily depends on the quality and governance of the data being used.

This essay explores the core differences between AI Governance and Data Governance, why it is crucial to distinguish between the two, and ultimately, the risks associated with implementing AI solutions with ungoverned data, plus the next steps you can take to integrate Data Governance into an AI Governance Strategy.

Core Differences Between AI Governance and Data Governance

AI Governance and Data Governance, while interconnected, serve different purposes and focus on distinct aspects of data management and utilization. Data Governance primarily deals with ensuring that data is accurate, consistent, secure, and available. It encompasses aspects like data quality, which ensures data is accurate, complete, and reliable; data security, which protects data from unauthorized access and breaches. It includes data management, which defines policies for data lifecycle management, including storage, archiving, and deletion—and data compliance, which ensures adherence to legal and regulatory requirements related to data handling and privacy.

On the other hand, AI Governance focuses on the ethical, transparent, and accountable use of AI technologies. It includes ensuring that AI systems are designed and used ethically, avoiding biases and unfair practices. It includes making AI algorithms and decision-making processes understandable and explainable. It also includes defining who is responsible for AI decisions and their outcomes and ensuring that AI systems comply with relevant laws and regulations. These distinct focuses highlight the necessity of having both governance frameworks in place to support each other and to ensure robust and ethical data and AI practices.

Why It Is Important to Differentiate AI Governance and Data Governance

Understanding the distinction between AI Governance and Data Governance is essential for several reasons. Each governance type focuses on different aspects, with Data Governance ensuring data integrity and AI Governance ensuring ethical and responsible AI use. Blurring these lines can lead to inadequate oversight in both areas. Differentiating them allows organizations to develop specific policies and procedures tailored to the unique needs and challenges of data management and AI deployment. This tailored approach ensures that each governance framework can address its specific requirements without interference.

Clear differentiation also aids in resource allocation. For instance, data stewards can focus on data quality and compliance, while AI governance teams can work on ethical AI use and transparency. This separation of duties ensures that both areas receive the attention and resources they need to be effective. Lastly, understanding the differences helps identify and mitigate risks specific to data handling and AI usage, ensuring a more robust governance framework. By having clear boundaries and responsibilities, organizations can better manage the complexities associated with data and AI governance.

Risks Associated with AI Solutions with Ungoverned Data

Implementing AI solutions without formally governed data poses significant risks. Data quality issues are a major concern, as ungoverned data may be incomplete, inaccurate, or inconsistent, leading to poor AI model performance and unreliable outputs. Security vulnerabilities also arise, as without proper data governance, sensitive data may be exposed to security breaches, risking unauthorized access and data leaks. Compliance risks are another major issue, as failure to comply with data protection regulations can result in legal penalties and damage to the organization's reputation.

Bias and unfairness are significant risks associated with AI solutions using ungoverned data. AI systems built on ungoverned data are more likely to incorporate biases, leading to unfair and unethical decisions. Lastly, operational inefficiencies can result from poor data governance, as it can lead to data silos, making it difficult to access and integrate data, thereby reducing the efficiency of AI initiatives. These risks highlight the critical importance of having well-governed data as a foundation for any AI solution to ensure ethical, reliable, and efficient AI practices.

The lack of data governance can severely impact the scalability of AI solutions. As organizations expand their AI capabilities, the volume and variety of data increase exponentially. Without a robust data governance framework, managing this influx becomes challenging, leading to potential bottlenecks and inefficiencies. Scalability issues can stymie AI projects, resulting in increased costs and delayed time-to-market for AI-driven innovations.

In addition to scalability concerns, the absence of data governance hampers the ability to conduct meaningful audits and ensure accountability within AI systems. Auditing AI processes and outputs is essential for maintaining transparency and trust. Without clear data governance, tracing data lineage and understanding how data has influenced AI decisions becomes nearly impossible, making it difficult to address errors, biases, or compliance issues. This lack of accountability can erode stakeholder confidence and limit the adoption of AI technologies within the organization.

Conclusion

Differentiating between AI Governance and Data Governance is crucial for building robust, ethical, and compliant AI solutions. Ensuring well-governed data is foundational to the success of any AI initiative, as it directly impacts the quality, security, and reliability of AI systems. Organizations must invest in both data governance and AI governance frameworks to mitigate risks and harness the full potential of AI technologies.

To integrate data governance into their AI Governance Strategy, organizations can take several simple yet effective actions. First, establish clear data governance policies that outline data quality standards, security protocols, and compliance requirements. This includes defining roles and responsibilities for data stewardship to ensure accountability. Second, implement regular data audits and validation processes to maintain data integrity and identify any discrepancies early on. Third, foster a data-driven culture by providing training and resources to employees, emphasizing the importance of data governance in AI initiatives. And last but not least, leverage automated tools for data cataloging, lineage tracking, and monitoring to streamline governance processes and ensure continuous oversight. By taking these steps, organizations can create a solid foundation for their AI projects, ensuring they are built on reliable and well-governed data.

What's the Difference Between an AI Model and a Large Language Model?

AI is revolutionizing the way organizations operate, and at the heart of this revolution are AI Models and Large Language Models (LLMs). AI models are mathematical algorithms designed to perform specific tasks by learning patterns from data. These models, ranging from decision trees and support vector machines to more complex neural networks, are used in various applications such as image recognition, predictive analytics, and anomaly detection. LLMs, on the other hand, are a specialized subset of AI models focused on understanding and generating human language. Models like ChatGPT, BARD, PaLM, and Gemini are based on deep learning architectures and trained on vast amounts of text data to mimic human-like text generation and comprehension.

While AI models and LLMs share common foundational principles, their applications and complexities differ, offering unique capabilities that can transform organizational processes and decision-making. AI models and LLMs can be integrated to create powerful AI systems that leverage the strengths of both types of models. By understanding the distinct roles and functionalities of AI models and LLMs, organizations can better leverage these technologies to address their specific needs and challenges, ultimately driving innovation and efficiency.

Similarities and Differences

AI models and LLMs share the fundamental principle of machine learning, which involves training algorithms on data to recognize patterns and make predictions. However, their applications and scale set them apart. AI models are broadly applied across various domains, such as image recognition, robotics, and recommendation systems. They can handle structured data efficiently and are integral in automating processes and making data-driven decisions. LLMs are designed specifically for natural language processing tasks, such as translation, summarization, and conversational agents. The size and complexity of LLMs, with billions of parameters, require extensive computational resources and vast datasets for effective training.

These models excel at understanding context, generating coherent text, and providing human-like responses, making them invaluable for tasks that involve unstructured text data. Together, AI models and LLMs can offer comprehensive solutions that address both structured and unstructured data needs within an organization. By combining these models, organizations can enhance decision-making processes, offering deeper insights and more accurate predictions. For instance, an AI model can identify a sales trend, while an LLM can provide context by analyzing customer sentiments from reviews and social media posts.

How They Work Together

AI models and LLMs can be integrated to create powerful AI systems that leverage the strengths of both types of models. An organization might use general AI models for predictive analytics to identify trends and patterns in structured data, providing insights into customer behavior, market trends, and operational efficiencies. Simultaneously, they can employ LLMs to analyze and interpret unstructured text data, such as customer feedback, social media interactions, and internal documents. This synergy allows for a comprehensive understanding of both quantitative and qualitative aspects of the data.

By combining these models, organizations can enhance decision-making processes, offering deeper insights and more accurate predictions. For instance, an AI model can identify a sales trend, while an LLM can provide context by analyzing customer sentiments from reviews and social media posts. This integrated approach ensures that decisions are informed by a holistic view of all available data, ultimately leading to more effective strategies and outcomes.

Steps for Successful Early Implementations

Implementing AI and LLMs in an organization requires a strategic approach to ensure success, especially in the early stages. The first step is to identify specific use cases where these models can add value, such as improving customer service with chatbots, enhancing data-driven decision-making, or automating routine tasks. It is crucial to invest in the necessary infrastructure, including computational resources and data storage, to support the training and deployment of these models. Equally important is fostering a culture of data literacy within the organization, ensuring that all employees understand the potential and limitations of AI technologies.

This involves providing training and resources to help staff become comfortable with AI tools and techniques. Additionally, developing a clear AI strategy that aligns with organizational goals is essential. This strategy should outline the objectives, expected outcomes, and metrics for success, ensuring that AI initiatives are targeted and measurable. Regularly reviewing and adjusting this strategy based on feedback and results will help maintain momentum and address any challenges that arise.

	AI Models	Large Language Models (LLMs)
Applications	AI models are mathematical algorithms designed for specific tasks such as image recognition, predictive analytics, and autonomous driving. Broad applications across domains (e.g., computer vision, robotics).	Specialized AI models for understanding and generating human language, capable of performing tasks like translation, summarization, and sentiment analysis. Focused on natural language processing tasks.
Scale	Handles structured data efficiently, often requiring specialized training data sets tailored for the specific application. Designed to perform a wide range of tasks but typically one at a time.	Processes unstructured text data, capable of understanding context and generating coherent responses in multiple languages. Typically involves vast amounts of data and computational resources for training.
Data Handling	Operates on structured data, processing inputs to make predictions or classifications based on trained patterns. Focus on data quality and relevance for specific tasks.	Operates on large volumes of unstructured text, requiring advanced techniques for managing and preprocessing data to ensure relevance and accuracy. Utilizes context to generate human-like text.

	AI Models	Large Language Models (LLMs)
Use Cases	Used in various industries for automating processes, improving accuracy, and generating insights (e.g., medical diagnosis, financial forecasting).	Widely used in applications such as chatbots, virtual assistants, content generation, and customer support.
Ethical Considerations	Ethical use involves ensuring models are free from biases and that their deployment does not result in unfair treatment or decisions. Continuous monitoring for fairness, accountability, and transparency.	Ethical AI use involves ensuring transparency, avoiding biases, and maintaining user privacy. Regular audits and reviews are essential to uphold ethical standards.
Governance	Data governance frameworks ensure that AI models are used responsibly, with policies in place to manage data quality, security, and compliance. Governance integrates with existing systems to support ethical use and data integrity.	AI governance frameworks promote transparency and accountability, ensuring that LLMs are used ethically and responsibly. Policies are aligned with broader data governance efforts to support consistent and ethical AI use.

Non-Invasive Data Governance and the NIDG Framework

To effectively utilize AI and LLMs, it is widely recognized that organizations must adopt robust data governance practices. This is where Non-Invasive Data Governance (NIDG) and the NIDG Framework come into play. NIDG focuses on integrating governance seamlessly into existing workflows, minimizing disruption while maximizing effectiveness. It involves defining clear roles and responsibilities, establishing processes for data management, and ensuring continuous communication across all levels of the organization. By embedding these practices into the fabric of daily operations, organizations can maintain high data quality, enhance compliance, and foster accountability.

NIDG emphasizes using existing structures and tools, reducing the need for significant changes or additional resources. This approach not only makes it easier to implement but also ensures that governance practices are sustainable and scalable. By integrating NIDG with AI governance, organizations can ensure that their AI systems are developed and deployed responsibly, adhering to ethical standards and regulatory requirements.

Leveraging NIDG for AI Governance

AI governance is an extension of data governance, focusing specifically on the ethical and responsible use of AI technologies. The NIDG Framework provides a structured approach to AI governance, ensuring transparency, fairness, and accountability in AI applications. It involves setting guidelines for AI development and deployment, monitoring AI systems for biases and inaccuracies, and regularly auditing AI models to ensure they align with organizational values and regulatory requirements. By integrating AI governance within the broader NIDG Framework, organizations can mitigate risks and build trust in their AI systems.

This approach ensures that AI initiatives are not siloed but are part of a cohesive strategy that considers all aspects of data management and governance. Regular audits and reviews help identify and address potential issues early, ensuring that AI systems remain aligned with organizational goals and ethical standards. Training programs and workshops can further support this integration by raising awareness and building skills across the organization.

Conclusion

The integration of AI models and Large Language Models offers immense potential for organizations to enhance their operations and decision-making processes. However, achieving success requires a thoughtful approach that includes identifying strategic use cases, investing in the right infrastructure, and fostering a culture of data literacy. By adopting Non-Invasive Data Governance and the NIDG Framework, organizations can ensure that their AI initiatives are built on a foundation of high-quality, well-governed data. This not only enhances the effectiveness of AI models and LLMs but also ensures that their deployment is ethical, transparent, and aligned with organizational goals.

As we navigate the complexities of AI and data governance, it is clear that a non-invasive, integrated approach is key to unlocking the full potential of these transformative technologies. Organizations that embrace this approach will be well-positioned to leverage AI's benefits while mitigating risks and ensuring sustainable success. This holistic strategy will help organizations build trust, drive innovation, and achieve their strategic objectives in an increasingly data-driven world.

Data is Key to Sustainable Gen AI

Earlier today, I came across the following press release from Gartner: *Gartner Predicts 30% of Generative AI Projects Will Be Abandoned After Proof of Concept By End of 2025* (https://www.gartner.com/en/newsroom/press-releases/2024-07-29-gartner-predicts-30-percent-of-generative-ai-projects-will-be-abandoned-after-proof-of-concept-by-end-of-2025). Before I read the release, I was not certain what to think. Was 30% a high or low number? The statement primarily focused on realizing the business value and calculating the business impact of generative AI.

As usual, my thoughts immediately turned to the data. I wanted to dive into the role data plays in whether or not a generative AI PoC ever gets past the "Proof" phase. More specifically, the actions data practitioners and data leadership can take to increase the odds that generative AI will be successful and sustainable. That is the topic of this essay. Don't be surprised that data governance is right in the middle.

In the rapidly evolving landscape of generative AI, many organizations find themselves stuck at the proof of concept phase, unable to scale their initiatives to full production. Achieving success requires more than just innovative technology; it demands robust data governance practices. By focusing on key governance actions, organizations can ensure the longevity and effectiveness of their AI projects. This essay explores the top data governance-oriented actions that are essential for extending the potential of generative AI beyond initial experiments, paving the way for sustainable and impactful AI implementations.

Embrace Data Quality Management

Ensuring high-quality data is paramount for the success of generative AI initiatives. Organizations must implement rigorous data quality management practices to guarantee that the data feeding into AI models is accurate, complete, and relevant. Poor data quality can lead to flawed AI outputs, diminishing trust in AI systems and hindering their adoption beyond the proof of concept phase.

*Organizations prioritizing data quality can build
robust AI models that deliver reliable and actionable insights,
thus fostering confidence in their AI initiatives.*

To achieve high data quality, organizations should establish data profiling, cleansing, and enrichment processes. Data profiling involves analyzing data to understand its structure, content, and quality, while data cleansing identifies and corrects errors or inconsistencies. Enrichment enhances data by integrating additional information from external sources, making it more comprehensive and useful. These practices ensure that data is robust and reliable, providing a solid foundation for AI models.

Continuous data quality monitoring is essential. Implementing automated data quality checks and alerts helps organizations detect and address issues in real time, ensuring that data remains accurate and relevant. Regular audits and assessments of data quality processes can also identify areas for improvement, enabling organizations to refine their practices and maintain high standards. By embedding data quality management into their operations, organizations can enhance the reliability and effectiveness of their AI initiatives.

Establish Clear Data Governance Policies

Clear and comprehensive data governance policies form the backbone of any successful AI initiative. These policies should outline data ownership, access controls, privacy standards, and compliance requirements. By having well-defined governance frameworks, organizations can ensure that data is managed consistently and ethically. This not only helps maintain data integrity but also helps comply with regulatory standards, thereby reducing the risk of legal and financial repercussions. Clear governance policies enable smoother transitions from proof of concept to full-scale AI deployments.

Developing data governance policies involves identifying key data assets and defining roles and responsibilities for managing them. This includes specifying who owns the data, who can access it, and under what conditions. Implement access controls to ensure that only authorized personnel can view or modify sensitive data, protecting it from unauthorized use or breaches. Establish privacy standards to safeguard personal information and comply with regulations, such as GDPR or CCPA.

Organizations should create data usage guidelines that specify using data within AI models. These guidelines should address ethical considerations, such as avoiding bias and ensuring transparency in AI decision-making processes. Organizations can foster responsible AI practices and build trust among stakeholders by setting clear expectations and boundaries for data usage.

Comprehensive data governance policies provide a framework for managing data effectively, supporting the successful deployment and scaling of AI initiatives.

Foster Cross-Functional Collaboration

Generative AI initiatives often require the expertise and input of various departments within an organization. Encouraging cross-functional collaboration between data scientists, IT professionals, compliance officers, and business stakeholders is crucial. This collaborative approach ensures that AI models are not only technically sound, but also aligned with business objectives and compliant with governance standards. By fostering a culture of teamwork, organizations can leverage diverse perspectives to enhance their AI initiatives, making them more robust and scalable.

To facilitate cross-functional collaboration, organizations should establish regular communication channels and meetings where team members can share updates, discuss challenges, and brainstorm solutions. Creating interdisciplinary teams that bring together individuals from different departments can also promote collaboration and knowledge sharing. These teams can work together to define project goals, develop AI models, and ensure they meet technical, business, and compliance requirements.

Organizations should provide training and development opportunities to help employees from different departments understand AI and its implications. This can include workshops, seminars, and online courses that cover topics, such as AI fundamentals, data governance, and ethical considerations. By building a common understanding of AI across the organization, teams can collaborate more effectively and contribute to the success of AI initiatives. Cross-functional collaboration not only enhances the quality and impact of AI models but also ensures that they are developed and deployed in a responsible and ethical manner.

Invest in Scalable AI Infrastructure

To move beyond the proof of concept phase, organizations must invest in scalable AI infrastructure. This includes advanced data storage solutions, powerful processing capabilities, and robust security measures. Scalable infrastructure ensures that AI models can handle increasing data volumes and computational demands as they transition to production. Investing in the right technology infrastructure allows organizations to support ongoing AI development and deployment, thereby maximizing the potential of their generative AI initiatives.

A critical component of scalable AI infrastructure is cloud computing. Cloud platforms offer flexible and scalable resources that can accommodate the growing demands of AI workloads. Organizations can leverage cloud services to store and process large datasets, run complex AI algorithms, and deploy models in a cost-effective manner. Additionally, cloud-based infrastructure provides the scalability needed to handle spikes in demand, ensuring that AI systems remain responsive and efficient.

Another important aspect is data security. Since AI initiatives often involve sensitive and valuable data, organizations must implement robust security measures to protect against breaches and unauthorized access. This includes encryption, access controls, and regular security audits. Ensuring data security not only safeguards the organization's assets but also builds trust with customers and stakeholders. By investing in scalable and secure AI infrastructure, organizations can support the long-term success and growth of their AI initiatives.

Monitor and Measure A Performance

Continuously monitoring and measuring AI performance is essential to ensure ongoing success and improvement. Organizations should implement metrics and KPIs to track the effectiveness and impact of their AI models. Regular performance reviews help identify areas for improvement, address potential biases, and ensure that AI outputs remain aligned with business goals. By establishing a culture of continuous improvement, organizations can refine their AI models and processes, driving sustained success beyond the initial proof of concept phase.

Key performance indicators (KPIs) for AI initiatives might include accuracy, precision, recall, and F1 score, which measure the performance of AI models in making correct predictions. Monitoring these metrics helps organizations assess the quality of their models and make necessary adjustments. Additionally, tracking model drift and data drift can identify changes in model performance over time, allowing for timely updates and retraining of AI models to maintain their accuracy and relevance.

Organizations should implement bias detection and mitigation strategies to ensure fairness and ethical AI practices. This involves regularly auditing AI models for biases and taking corrective actions to address any identified issues. By continuously monitoring and measuring AI performance, organizations can ensure that their AI initiatives are effective, fair, and aligned with their strategic objectives. This proactive approach to performance management fosters trust in AI systems and supports their successful scaling and deployment.

Conclusion

To summarize, the potential of generative AI initiatives can be significantly enhanced by focusing on these top data governance-oriented actions. Ensuring data quality, establishing clear governance policies, fostering cross-functional collaboration, investing in scalable infrastructure, and continuously monitoring AI performance are crucial steps. These actions not only build a strong foundation for AI initiatives but also enable organizations to scale and sustain their AI efforts, ultimately driving innovation and competitive advantage. By following these best practices, organizations can move beyond the proof of concept phase and fully realize the benefits of their generative AI initiatives.

Connect AI and Data Governance!
You Won't Be Sorry (Unless You Don't)

Personal note: As a professional deeply invested in this field, I find it troubling that many organizations are rapidly advancing their AI and AI governance strategies with little regard for the vital role of data and data governance. It is concerning that, even in this digital age, the critical connection between data governance and AI's value and risk management is still overlooked. I often find myself contemplating how to bridge this gap more effectively. If your thoughts differ from what I'll share here, I would love to hear them.

The linkage of AI and data governance is not just a strategic advantage but an **absolute** imperative. Integrating these two elements can be **THE key** to unlocking immense value from data while ensuring ethical, reliable, and effective AI applications. Here are ten compelling examples of how AI and data governance should be tightly integrated, highlighting a prime opportunity for executives to support formal data governance programs.

First and foremost, the formation of an AI & Data Executive Steering Committee can permanently link and ensure that strategic decisions are made with a holistic understanding of both AI capabilities and data management and governance needs. This committee, composed of leaders from various departments, can drive alignment between AI initiatives and data governance policies, ensuring that AI projects are grounded in high-quality, well-governed data.

By bringing together diverse perspectives from across the organization, an AI & Data Executive Steering Committee can provide comprehensive oversight and strategic direction. This collaborative approach ensures that AI initiatives are not only technologically sound but also aligned with the organization's broader goals and compliance requirements. The committee can prioritize projects, allocate resources effectively, and address any cross-departmental issues that arise, thereby fostering a more cohesive and efficient implementation of AI technologies.

Secondly, appointing an AI & Data Governance Administrator is crucial. This role serves as the linchpin between AI developers and data stewardship, ensuring that data used in AI models adheres to governance standards. By having a dedicated person oversee this intersection, organizations can maintain data integrity and enhance the reliability of AI outputs.

The AI & Data Governance Administrator is pivotal in bridging the gap between technical teams and data management experts. This person ensures that data governance policies are consistently applied across all AI projects, mitigating risks associated with data quality and compliance. They can also provide training and support to teams, helping them understand and implement best practices in data management and AI development. This role is essential for maintaining high standards and building trust in AI systems.

Another reason for this integration is the emphasis on governed data as a core part of AI and AI governance strategies. Governed data means data that is accurate, consistent, and secure—essential qualities for training robust AI models. Without governed data, AI systems risk producing unreliable or biased results, leading to poor decision-making and loss of trust.

When data is well-governed, AI models can be trained on datasets that are clean, comprehensive, and representative of real-world scenarios. This reduces the likelihood of bias and errors in AI outputs, leading to more reliable and trustworthy AI applications. Additionally, governed data provides a clear audit trail, making it easier to validate and explain AI decisions. This transparency is critical for gaining executive support and ensuring regulatory compliance.

Data governance frameworks can help manage the ethical use of AI. By enforcing policies that ensure data privacy and compliance with regulations, organizations can mitigate risks associated with AI, such as data breaches or misuse of sensitive information. This ethical oversight is critical in maintaining public and stakeholder trust in AI systems.

Ethical AI use is a growing concern, and data governance frameworks provide the necessary structure to address these issues. By implementing strict data privacy and security measures, organizations can protect sensitive information and ensure that AI systems operate within legal and ethical boundaries. This not only helps prevent potential legal and financial repercussions but also builds confidence among users and stakeholders, who can trust that their data is being handled responsibly.

Integrating AI with data governance also enables better data quality management. Data governance ensures that data is clean, complete, and relevant, which is vital for the success of AI models. High-quality data leads to more accurate AI predictions and insights, driving better business outcomes.

High-quality data is the backbone of effective AI models. Data governance frameworks provide the tools and processes needed to manage data quality, from initial collection and processing to ongoing maintenance and monitoring. This ensures that AI models are trained on datasets that accurately reflect the realities they are intended to represent. As a result, organizations can rely on their AI systems to deliver precise and actionable insights, improving decision-making and operational efficiency.

Fostering a culture of data literacy within the organization is another key benefit. When AI and data governance are intertwined, employees at all levels are encouraged to understand and value the importance of data management. This cultural shift can lead to more informed decision-making and a greater appreciation for the strategic role of data.

Data literacy empowers employees to make data-driven decisions and to understand the implications of using data in their work. Organizations can create a more knowledgeable and capable workforce by promoting data literacy through integrated AI and data governance initiatives. Employees who understand the value of data governance are more likely to follow best practices, reducing the risk of data misuse and enhancing the overall effectiveness of AI applications.

Data governance provides a structured approach to data access and security. By implementing clear policies and controls, organizations can ensure that only authorized personnel have access to sensitive data, reducing the risk of data leaks and enhancing overall data security. This controlled access is vital for maintaining the integrity of AI systems.

Controlled access to data is essential for maintaining both security and compliance. Data governance frameworks establish policies and procedures that dictate who can access specific data sets and under what conditions. This not only protects sensitive information from unauthorized access but also ensures that data is used appropriately and ethically. Secure data access is a foundational element of trustworthy AI systems, helping to prevent breaches and ensuring that AI models are built and operated within secure environments.

Another advantage is the enhancement of transparency and accountability in AI projects. Data governance frameworks require thorough documentation of data sources, usage, and lineage. This transparency allows for better tracking of data flows and ensures that AI models can be audited and validated, which is essential for accountability.

Transparency and accountability are critical for the successful implementation of AI technologies. Data governance frameworks provide detailed records of data provenance and usage, making it easier to track how data is transformed and utilized within AI models. This level of documentation supports audits and compliance checks, helping organizations verify the integrity and accuracy of their AI systems. By ensuring that AI processes are transparent and accountable, organizations can build trust with stakeholders and regulators.

Connecting AI and data governance helps streamline data integration processes. Many AI projects require data from multiple sources. Data governance ensures that these sources are integrated seamlessly and consistently, reducing the time and effort needed to prepare data for AI applications.

Data integration is a common challenge in AI development, especially when dealing with diverse and disparate data sources. Data governance frameworks provide standardized processes for integrating data, ensuring that it is combined in a consistent and reliable manner. This streamlining of data integration not only accelerates AI development but also enhances the quality of the resulting models. By reducing the complexity and time required to prepare data, organizations can focus more on innovation and less on data wrangling.

Finally, executive support for formal data governance programs can be significantly bolstered by demonstrating the direct benefits of AI initiatives. Executives are more likely to invest in data governance when they see how it enhances AI capabilities, drives innovation, and provides a competitive edge. This support can lead to more resources and attention dedicated to building robust data governance structures.

Securing executive support is crucial for the success of both AI and data governance initiatives. By clearly articulating the benefits of integrated AI and data governance, such as improved data quality, ethical AI use, and enhanced decision-making, organizations can make a compelling case for investment.

When executives understand the strategic advantages
and potential ROI of these initiatives, they are more likely to
allocate the necessary resources and champion the cause,
leading to stronger and more effective governance practices.

Conclusion

To sum this all up, the integration of AI and data governance is not just a beneficial strategy but a critical one. From forming executive committees to appointing dedicated administrators and emphasizing data quality, the connection between AI and data governance can drive better business outcomes, enhance ethical standards, and secure executive backing. By embracing this integration, organizations can fully leverage their data assets and AI technologies, positioning themselves for success in the digital age.

By aligning AI initiatives with robust data governance practices, organizations can unlock the full potential of their data and AI investments. This holistic approach ensures that AI systems are built on a foundation of high-quality, well-governed data, leading to more accurate, reliable, and ethical outcomes. As the digital landscape continues to evolve, the integration of AI and data governance will be essential for maintaining competitive advantage and fostering innovation.

AI Will Not Render You Obsolete, However ...

The rise of AI often raises concerns about job security and the future of various professions. In particular, data governance and data management practitioners may worry about AI's potential to automate their roles.

The truth is that AI will not render these professionals obsolete. Instead, the individuals who grasp the dynamics, impacts, benefits, and ways to utilize AI effectively will thrive and replace those who do not adapt.

The truth is that AI will not render you obsolete.

Let's acknowledge that AI is a powerful tool that can significantly enhance data governance and management practices. AI can automate repetitive tasks, such as data entry, cleansing, and validation, freeing up valuable time for practitioners to focus on more strategic activities. This automation can lead to improved accuracy and efficiency, allowing organizations to manage their data more effectively. However, the expertise of data professionals is still crucial for interpreting results, setting data policies, and ensuring compliance with regulations.

AI excels in handling large volumes of data and identifying patterns that might be invisible to the human eye. Yet, it lacks the nuanced understanding and contextual awareness that human practitioners bring to the table. Data governance involves making informed decisions about data usage, privacy, and security—areas where human judgment is indispensable. Professionals who can combine their domain knowledge with AI capabilities will be better equipped to make strategic decisions and guide their organizations through the complexities of data governance.

The real challenge lies in the ability to understand and harness the full potential of AI. Those who invest time in learning about AI, its applications, and its limitations will find themselves at a significant advantage. They will be able to leverage AI tools to enhance their work, leading to more innovative and efficient data management practices. Conversely, those who resist or ignore these advancements risk being left behind.

The landscape is shifting and staying informed and adaptable
are key to remaining relevant.

AI also brings about new opportunities for data governance and management practitioners. With AI-driven insights, professionals can uncover trends and insights that were previously unattainable. This capability allows for more proactive and strategic decision-making, helping organizations to anticipate and respond to market changes more swiftly. Data professionals who can interpret these insights and translate them into actionable strategies will become invaluable assets to their organizations.

The ethical implications of AI in data governance cannot be overlooked. AI systems are only as good as the data they are trained on and the algorithms that drive them. Ensuring that AI operates fairly, transparently, and ethically is a critical responsibility that falls on human practitioners. Those who understand the ethical dimensions of AI and can navigate these challenges will play a crucial role in shaping the future of data governance.

The integration of AI into data governance and management is not about replacing humans but rather augmenting their capabilities. It is a partnership where AI handles the heavy lifting of data processing, and humans provide strategic oversight, ethical considerations, and contextual understanding. This synergy creates a more powerful and effective data governance framework.

My opinion is that AI will not render data governance and data management practitioners obsolete. Instead, it will elevate the profession, offering new tools and insights that enhance their work. The individuals who truly understand and embrace the dynamics, impacts, and benefits of AI will be the ones who thrive and lead the way. By staying informed, adaptable, and proactive, data professionals can ensure their continued relevance and importance in this rapidly evolving field. AI is not the end of the road but a stepping stone to a more advanced and efficient future in data governance.

Artificial vs. Augmented Intelligence

Terms like AI and augmented intelligence are often used interchangeably. However, they represent fundamentally different approaches to utilizing technology, especially when it comes to data governance. Understanding these differences is crucial for organizations looking to implement non-invasive and effective data governance frameworks. This essay explores the distinctions between artificial intelligence and augmented intelligence, focusing on their roles in data governance and how they can be leveraged without disrupting existing workflows.

What Is Artificial Intelligence?

AI refers to the development of computer systems capable of performing tasks that typically require human intelligence. These tasks include understanding natural language, recognizing patterns, solving problems, and making decisions. AI systems operate autonomously, using algorithms and vast datasets to learn and improve over time. In data governance, AI can automate processes such as data classification, anomaly detection, and policy enforcement, significantly reducing the need for human intervention.

Benefits and Challenges of AI in Data Governance

The primary benefit of AI in data governance is its ability to handle large volumes of data with speed and accuracy. AI systems can quickly identify patterns and inconsistencies that human analysts might miss. For example, AI can automatically flag data entries that do not comply with established standards, ensuring data quality and consistency. Additionally, AI can enhance compliance by continuously monitoring data activities and ensuring they adhere to regulatory requirements.

However, the implementation of AI in data governance is not without challenges. One of the main concerns is the potential for disruption. AI systems often require significant changes to existing workflows and processes, which can be met with resistance from employees. Moreover, the autonomous nature of AI can lead to a lack of transparency and accountability, as decisions made by AI systems may not always be easily understood or explained by humans. This "black box" issue can be problematic in highly regulated industries where accountability and auditability are critical.

What Is Augmented Intelligence?

Augmented intelligence, on the other hand, takes a more collaborative approach. Instead of replacing human intelligence, it aims to enhance it by providing tools and insights that support human decision-making. Augmented intelligence leverages AI technologies to process and analyze data, but it keeps humans in the loop, allowing them to make the final decisions. This approach is particularly beneficial in data governance, where human expertise and contextual understanding are invaluable.

Practicality of Augmented Intelligence in Data Governance

The primary advantage of augmented intelligence is its non-invasive nature. Integrating AI tools into existing workflows minimizes disruptions and leverages the expertise of individuals already in positions of authority and subject matter expertise. For instance, data stewards and analysts can use AI-powered tools to gain insights and identify data quality issues, but they remain responsible for interpreting the results and taking appropriate actions.

Augmented intelligence fosters a culture of collaboration and continuous improvement. Empowering employees with advanced tools enhances their ability to manage and govern data effectively. This approach not only improves data quality and compliance but also promotes a sense of ownership and accountability among employees. Furthermore, by keeping humans involved in the decision-making process, augmented intelligence ensures transparency and traceability, which are essential for maintaining trust and meeting regulatory requirements.

Implementing Augmented Intelligence in Data Governance

Consider an organization that needs to improve its data quality and compliance but wants to avoid the disruptions associated with a full-scale AI implementation. By adopting augmented intelligence, the organization can integrate AI tools into its existing data governance framework. These tools can assist data stewards in identifying data quality issues, generating reports, and suggesting remediation actions. However, the data stewards retain control over the final decisions, ensuring that the governance processes remain aligned with the organization's goals and regulatory requirements.

In this scenario, the organization benefits from the speed and accuracy of AI while maintaining the critical human oversight needed for effective data governance. The data stewards can focus on high-value tasks, such as interpreting data insights and making strategic decisions, rather than getting bogged down in manual data processing.

Comparing AI and Augmented Intelligence in Data Governance

When comparing artificial intelligence and augmented intelligence in the context of data governance, it is essential to consider their respective impacts on workflows and employee roles. AI's ability to automate complex tasks can lead to significant efficiency gains, but it can also result in resistance due to the changes it necessitates. In contrast, augmented intelligence's collaborative approach ensures a smoother integration with existing processes, making it a more practical choice for organizations looking to enhance data governance without causing major disruptions.

Augmented intelligence aligns more closely with the principles of Non-Invasive Data Governance (NIDG), which emphasizes leveraging existing roles and responsibilities rather than imposing new structures. This alignment makes augmented intelligence an attractive option for organizations that value employee engagement and seek to minimize the upheaval associated with technological change.

The Future of Data Governance

As technology continues to evolve, the distinction between artificial intelligence and augmented intelligence will become increasingly important for data governance. Organizations will need to carefully consider their goals, existing workflows, and regulatory requirements when choosing between these approaches. While AI offers powerful capabilities for automation and efficiency, augmented intelligence provides a balanced approach that enhances human decision-making and maintains transparency and accountability.

In the future, we can expect to see more organizations adopting hybrid models that combine the strengths of both AI and augmented intelligence.

By doing so, they can achieve the benefits of automation while ensuring that human expertise and oversight remain integral to the data governance process. This hybrid approach will likely become the norm, providing organizations with the flexibility and adaptability needed to navigate the complex landscape of data governance.

Conclusion

Understanding the differences between artificial intelligence and augmented intelligence is crucial for effective data governance. While AI offers significant advantages in terms of automation and efficiency, its implementation can be disruptive and may lack transparency. Augmented intelligence, on the other hand, enhances human decision-making and integrates seamlessly with existing workflows, making it a more practical and non-invasive approach. By leveraging the strengths of both approaches, organizations can improve data quality, compliance, and overall governance while maintaining the essential human element in the decision-making process. As we move forward, the successful integration of AI and augmented intelligence will be key to navigating the evolving challenges of data governance.

What Comes After AI for Data Professionals

At a time when every conversation in tech seems magnetically drawn to the topic of AI, it is essential to peer beyond the horizon and consider what's next. While AI continues to reshape countless aspects of our lives and work, data management and data governance professionals are arriving at a pivotal moment.

In this essay, I quickly explore the key trends poised to take center stage once the spotlight on AI dims, offering insights into how to prepare for the next tectonic shifts in data's crust.

When the enthusiasm surrounding AI begins to stabilize, data management and data governance professionals will be poised at an interesting juncture. The rapid integration of AI into various business processes and decision-making frameworks has underscored the value of robust data governance and management.

However, as we look to the future beyond the peak of the AI craze, several emerging trends and technologies promise to shape the next chapter in the data landscape. Understanding and preparing for these advancements will be crucial for professionals in the field to stay relevant and effective.

Decentralization and Blockchain

To begin with, the decentralization of data through technologies like blockchain is gaining momentum. Blockchain offers a transparent, assured ledger that is ideal for managing data across disparate entities while ensuring data integrity and traceability. For data governance professionals, this means adapting policies to govern data that is not stored centrally but distributed across multiple nodes, each requiring synchronization and compliance with data standards and regulations.

The shift towards blockchain necessitates a fundamental rethinking of data governance frameworks to accommodate the decentralized nature of data storage and management. Data governance professionals must develop new protocols for access control, data validation, and consensus mechanisms that are specific to blockchain technology.

As blockchain enables more secure and transparent transactions, professionals must also focus on leveraging this technology to enhance data provenance and auditability, thereby reinforcing trust and compliance in digital interactions. This evolution in data governance will play a crucial role in enabling organizations to harness blockchain's full potential in various industries, from finance and healthcare to supply chain management and beyond.

Internet of Things (IoT)

Another significant trend is the proliferation of Internet of Things (IoT) devices, which are generating vast amounts of data from diverse sources at an unprecedented scale. The challenge here lies not only in managing the sheer volume of data, but also in ensuring that data from sensors and devices are reliable and processed in real-time. Data governance frameworks will need to evolve to address the complexities of IoT data management, focusing on privacy, data quality, and interoperability issues.

As IoT continues to expand into everyday applications, data governance professionals must tackle the increased risks associated with data breaches and cyberattacks. The interconnected nature of IoT devices means that a single vulnerability can lead to systemic failures, making robust security protocols a critical component of data governance.

With IoT data often involving personal and sensitive information, ensuring compliance with global data protection regulations becomes more challenging yet imperative. Professionals will need to establish more dynamic and responsive governance models that can adapt to the fast-paced evolution of IoT technology and its data management needs.

Quantum Computing

Quantum computing, though still in its emerging stages, is set to revolutionize how we process data. With the potential to perform complex calculations that are beyond the reach of current computers, quantum computing could greatly enhance AI capabilities and enable new data analytics methodologies. For data professionals, understanding quantum computing's implications for data encryption and security will be critical, as traditional encryption methods may become obsolete.

The advent of quantum computing introduces a paradigm shift in data management strategies, especially in the realm of cybersecurity. Data governance frameworks must be redesigned to anticipate the quantum future, where quantum-resistant encryption becomes standard to secure sensitive data against quantum attacks.

The sheer computational power of quantum computers offers new avenues for optimizing big data processing, necessitating updates to data handling protocols and infrastructure to leverage these advanced capabilities effectively. For data professionals, staying ahead means engaging with ongoing quantum computing research, participating in simulations, and planning transitions to quantum-safe practices well ahead of the curve.

Data Privacy and Ethics

The increasing focus on data privacy and ethics, fueled by more stringent regulations like the GDPR in Europe and CCPA in California, is leading to a demand for greater transparency in data processes. Data governance professionals will need to ensure that their organizations are not only compliant, but also that they maintain the trust of their customers by handling data responsibly and ethically.

As the landscape of data privacy continues to evolve, the role of data governance professionals becomes increasingly complex and vital. They must navigate between regulatory compliance and the ethical considerations of data usage, which includes not only how data is collected and stored but also how it is analyzed and shared.

The implementation of ethical guidelines that go beyond legal requirements will be a crucial step in building a sustainable trust relationship with users. This ethical framework should address emerging concerns such as bias in data analysis, the right to data portability, and the implications of data monetization, ensuring that privacy and user rights are upheld in every aspect of data handling.

Augmented Analytics

Finally, the rise of augmented analytics, which uses machine learning to automate data analysis processes, is something to keep an eye on. This technology can help uncover insights more quickly and with less human intervention, which could shift the role of data professionals from managing and analyzing data to interpreting and implementing data-driven strategies.

As augmented analytics mature, it will transform how organizations approach data-driven decision-making. The ability of augmented analytics to process and analyze vast datasets in real-time means that data professionals can focus more on strategic tasks such as interpreting complex patterns, making predictions, and providing actionable recommendations.

This shift will not only enhance the value that data professionals bring to their organizations but also require them to develop new skills in data science, machine learning, and strategic business analysis. This progression represents a significant opportunity for data professionals to lead in innovation and contribute to shaping business strategies that are deeply rooted in data-driven insights.

Conclusion

While AI continues to be a significant driver of innovation, the landscape of data management and governance is rapidly evolving with new technologies and challenges. Professionals in this field must stay informed about these trends and adapt their skills and strategies accordingly. The future will likely hold a blend of advanced technologies intermingled with enhanced data governance practices that not only address operational efficiency, but also ethical considerations, making the role of data management more integral than ever. As the AI craze settles, the real work of building a sustainable, data-driven future begins.

Practical Strategies and Tools

In the ever-evolving landscape of data and AI, organizations need actionable strategies and reliable tools to empower their teams and create lasting impact. Chapter 4, *Practical Strategies and Tools*, delivers exactly that—guidance designed to align with the book's central theme of *Empowering People to Govern Data and AI*. This chapter offers a deep dive into the tangible methods and approaches organizations can adopt to strengthen their governance practices while remaining agile and cost-effective.

The chapter begins with *How to Select Data Governance Use Cases*, a critical exploration of how organizations can prioritize their efforts to maximize impact. This essay provides a roadmap for identifying and selecting governance use cases that align with organizational goals, ensuring that data governance initiatives deliver measurable results and resonate with stakeholders at all levels.

In *Making Data AI-Ready*, the focus shifts to preparing data for the demands of artificial intelligence. This essay underscores that successful AI initiatives require more than technology; they depend on high-quality, well-governed data. It offers practical advice on how organizations can align their governance practices to create the foundation AI systems need to succeed, avoiding the pitfalls of incomplete or unreliable data.

Data Investor—A New Name for a Data Owner introduces a fresh perspective on traditional roles within data governance. By rebranding the "data owner" as a "data investor," this essay highlights the value of framing data ownership as an investment with clear returns. It challenges organizations to rethink accountability and engagement, fostering a sense of ownership that drives better stewardship and collaboration.

Governance doesn't have to break the bank, as demonstrated in *Strategies for Data Governance on a Limited Budget*. This essay provides creative and resourceful approaches to achieving governance goals without the need for significant financial investment. By leveraging existing tools, processes, and talent, organizations can make meaningful progress in their governance journeys, even when resources are constrained.

Federated Data Governance Without Clear Authority tackles one of the most complex challenges in governance: managing data in environments where authority is distributed or unclear. This essay offers pragmatic advice on creating frameworks and fostering collaboration in federated structures, ensuring that governance remains effective even when decision-making is decentralized.

Together, the essays in Chapter 4 present a comprehensive suite of practical strategies and tools that organizations can adopt to empower their people and govern their data with confidence. By emphasizing actionable insights and real-world solutions, this chapter reinforces the idea that effective governance doesn't require perfection—it requires commitment, creativity, and a clear focus on enabling success in both AI and data-driven initiatives.

How to Select Data Governance Use Cases

Selecting the "right" data governance use cases can seem daunting, but with the right approach, it becomes manageable and highly beneficial for any organization. By using the Non-Invasive Data Governance (NIDG) approach and applying the NIDG framework, organizations can identify and address specific issues and opportunities for improvement within their data governance and business practices. This essay provides a series of steps focused on effectively selecting and implementing data governance use cases using the NIDG approach.

Even before selecting data governance use cases, it is important to understand your organization's specific needs and pain points. This involves conducting a thorough assessment or analysis of current data practices and identifying areas where data quality, integrity, and accessibility are lacking. In other words, look for challenges to address and opportunities to improve. By engaging with stakeholders from various departments, you can gather insights into the most critical data issues that impact business operations and decision-making.

The NIDG approach emphasizes leveraging existing roles and processes, making it easier to integrate data governance practices without disrupting day-to-day activities. This means identifying use cases that align with current business processes and can be addressed using existing resources and expertise, ensuring a smoother and more efficient implementation.

The NIDG approach emphasizes leveraging existing roles and processes.

Understanding the Importance of Data Governance Use Cases

Data governance use cases are practical examples or scenarios where data governance principles and practices can be applied to solve real-world problems or improve processes. Selecting the right use cases is crucial because it ensures that the data governance efforts are focused on the most impactful areas, providing tangible benefits and demonstrating the value of data governance to the organization.

To identify the most effective use cases, it's essential to engage with key stakeholders across the organization to understand their data-related challenges and objectives. This engagement helps prioritize use cases that align with strategic goals and have the potential for significant impact.

It is important to consider the scalability and sustainability of these use cases, ensuring that the solutions can be maintained and expanded as needed. By focusing on high-impact areas and maintaining clear communication with stakeholders, organizations can build a strong foundation for successful data governance initiatives using the Non-Invasive Data Governance framework.

Step 1: Identifying Potential Use Cases

The first step in selecting the best data governance use cases is to identify potential areas where data governance can add value. This involves engaging with various stakeholders across the organization, including business units, IT, and particularly your executive leadership, to understand their pain points and data-related challenges. Common areas to consider include data quality issues, compliance requirements, data privacy concerns, and data access and usage inefficiencies.

In addition to these common areas, analyzing existing processes and systems is crucial to identify gaps where data governance can play a significant role. For example, assessing data lineage to uncover inconsistencies, examining data integration processes for potential improvements, and reviewing data security protocols to ensure compliance with regulatory standards.

By conducting a thorough analysis and involving a diverse group of stakeholders, organizations can uncover a wide range of potential use cases that may not be immediately apparent, thereby laying the groundwork for a comprehensive and impactful data governance strategy.

Step 2: Assessing and Prioritizing Use Cases

Once potential use cases have been identified, the next step is to assess and prioritize them. This can be done by evaluating each use case against specific criteria, such as:

- **Impact:** How significant is the impact of addressing this use case on the organization? Consider both short-term and long-term benefits.

- **Feasibility:** How feasible is it to implement a data governance solution for this use case? Consider the resources, time, and effort required.

- **Alignment:** Does the use case align with the organization's strategic goals and objectives? Ensure that the selected use cases support the broader business strategy.

- **Stakeholder Support:** Is there sufficient support from key stakeholders for this use case? Strong stakeholder backing is crucial for the success of any data governance initiative.

Prioritizing use cases helps focus efforts on the most critical areas that promise the highest returns. It also ensures that the organization is not overwhelmed by tackling too many issues at once, allowing for a more manageable and structured approach to improving data governance.

Step 3: Defining Specific Issues and Opportunities

After prioritizing the use cases, it's important to define the specific issues and opportunities within each use case. This involves a detailed analysis of the current state of data governance related to the use case, identifying gaps, and understanding the root causes of the issues. For instance, if data quality is a major concern, identify specific data quality problems, such as missing data, duplicate records, or inaccurate data entries.

To further refine this process, it's essential to map out the data flow and pinpoint where data governance controls may be lacking or ineffective. This can include evaluating data entry processes to ensure consistency, examining how data is stored and accessed to identify potential security risks, and reviewing data usage policies to ensure compliance with regulations.

By thoroughly defining these specific issues and opportunities, organizations can develop targeted interventions that address the root causes and lead to substantial improvements in their data governance practices. This approach not only helps in solving immediate problems, but also in establishing a robust framework that can adapt to future challenges.

Step 4: Applying the NIDG Framework

The Non-Invasive Data Governance framework is designed to integrate data governance practices into the existing organizational structure without causing major disruptions. Here's how to apply the NIDG framework to the selected use cases:

- **Data Component:** Ensure data governance practices are embedded in the data lifecycle. For example, if the use case involves improving data quality, implement data quality checks and validation processes at every stage of the data lifecycle.

- **Roles Component:** Identify and formalize accountability for data governance roles related to the use case. This includes defining the responsibilities of data stewards, data owners, and other stakeholders involved in managing the data, and that are articulated through your framework as part of your Operating Model.

- **Processes Component:** Develop and integrate data governance processes into the existing workflows. This might include establishing data quality monitoring processes, data access controls, and compliance checks.

- **Communications Component:** Ensure that there is clear and consistent communication about the data governance practices related to the use case. This involves educating stakeholders about their roles and responsibilities and keeping them informed about progress and outcomes.

- **Metrics Component:** Define and track key metrics to measure the success of the data governance initiative. For example, if the use case is about improving data quality, track metrics such as data accuracy, completeness, and consistency.

- **Tools Component:** Utilize appropriate tools to support data governance activities. This might include data quality tools, metadata management tools, and data governance platforms.

Step 5: Implementing the Solution

With the framework in place, the next step is implementing the data governance solution for the selected use case. This involves executing the defined processes, leveraging the identified tools, and ensuring all stakeholders actively participate in the data governance activities. It's important to monitor the implementation closely and address any issues that arise promptly.

During implementation, it is crucial to establish clear communication channels to keep all stakeholders informed and engaged. Regular updates and feedback loops should be instituted to identify and resolve any challenges quickly. In addition, staff training sessions can be beneficial to ensure everyone understands their roles and responsibilities within the new framework.

By maintaining a proactive approach and encouraging collaboration, the organization can ensure the solution is not only implemented effectively, but also sustainable in the long term, ultimately leading to improved data quality, compliance, and overall data governance maturity.

Step 6: Monitoring and Continuous Improvement

Data governance is not a one-time activity but an ongoing discipline. Continuously monitor the effectiveness of the data governance practices and make necessary adjustments based on feedback and performance metrics. Regular reviews and updates ensure that the data governance practices remain relevant and effective in addressing the identified issues and opportunities.

To facilitate continuous improvement, establish a structured process for collecting and analyzing feedback from stakeholders. Implement performance dashboards that track key metrics, such as data quality scores, compliance rates, and user satisfaction levels. Schedule regular meetings to review these metrics, discuss progress, and identify areas for enhancement. Encourage a culture of open communication where team members can share insights and suggestions for improvement.

By fostering an environment of continuous learning and adaptation, organizations can ensure their data governance practices evolve with changing business needs and technological advancements, leading to sustained success and value creation.

Conclusion

Selecting and implementing the best data governance use cases is crucial for maximizing the value of data governance initiatives. By using the Non-Invasive Data Governance approach and applying the NIDG framework, organizations can address specific issues and opportunities within their data governance practices effectively. This not only improves data quality, compliance, and efficiency, but also demonstrates the value of data governance to the organization, securing ongoing support and commitment from stakeholders. Remember, the key to successful data governance is continuous improvement and adaptation to the changing needs and challenges of the organization.

By focusing on the right use cases, engaging with stakeholders, and implementing a structured, Non-Invasive approach, organizations can achieve significant improvements in their data governance practices. The NIDG framework provides a practical, scalable, and sustainable methodology for embedding data governance into everyday operations, ensuring long-term success and value realization.

Making Data AI-Ready

These days, every data-focused conversation eventually leads to the topic of AI. I am often asked my thoughts on the impact of data governance on AI and the impact of AI on data governance. My thought process continues to evolve as the industry evolves. Many conversations with clients have started leaning toward the question of what it will take for data to become AI-ready. I am addressing my thoughts on this topic through this essay.

Creating a data environment primed for AI is a strategic imperative for organizations aiming to leverage the full potential of this transformative technology. Achieving AI readiness is not merely about amassing vast amounts of data or investing in the latest AI tools. AI-readiness is fundamentally about ensuring that data is managed, governed, and utilized in a way that aligns with the principles of clarity, quality, and accessibility. A non-invasive approach to data governance can play a pivotal role in this process, offering a pathway to prepare data for AI without the heavy-handed mandates that often stifle innovation and collaboration.

Leverage Existing Components

At its core, Non-Invasive Data Governance (NIDG) is about leveraging and formalizing the existing roles, responsibilities, and processes that manage data as an asset within an organization. This approach recognizes that every individual who interacts with data, whether in IT, analytics, or business roles, contributes to its governance. By acknowledging and empowering these contributions, organizations can create a culture where data governance is woven into the fabric of daily activities, thus ensuring that data is accurate, accessible, and ready for AI applications.

The beauty of NIDG lies in its ability to foster a sense of ownership and accountability among all data users, which is crucial for the integrity and reliability of data. By embedding data governance principles into the routine actions of data creators, users, and managers, NIDG facilitates the establishment of a data-first mindset. This mindset, in turn, primes data for AI by ensuring it's continuously maintained, categorized, and enriched in line with the organizational goals and AI requirements. Such an environment not only streamlines the pathway for AI adoption but also significantly reduces the time and resources required to prepare data for AI-driven analysis and decision-making.

NIDG facilitates the establishment of a data-first mindset. This mindset, in turn, primes data for AI by ensuring it's continuously maintained, categorized, and enriched in line with the organizational goals and AI requirements.

Make Data AI-Ready

Making data AI-ready begins with achieving a high level of data quality. AI and machine learning algorithms require clean, consistent, and well-structured data to function effectively. Under the NIDG framework, people who know the data best drive data quality initiatives—the business users, data analysts, and IT professionals who interact with data on a daily basis. By engaging these stakeholders in the process of identifying, cleaning, and maintaining data, organizations can ensure that their data meets the high standards required for AI. Tools and technologies that support data quality efforts should be integrated seamlessly into existing workflows, minimizing disruption and resistance.

This engagement not only elevates the quality of data but also cultivates a collaborative environment where the significance of data integrity is universally recognized and upheld. In this context, the Non-Invasive Data Governance approach acts as a catalyst, enabling organizations to harness the collective knowledge and expertise of their personnel toward the goal of data optimization for AI readiness.

Furthermore, establishing clear, accessible documentation and metadata under this framework ensures that the data is not only of high quality but also comprehensively understood. This detailed understanding of data resources accelerates the preparation phase for AI projects, ensuring that algorithms are fed with data that is not only clean but also richly annotated and contextually relevant, thereby maximizing the potential for insightful, actionable AI outcomes.

Address Data Accessibility

Data accessibility is critical for AI readiness. Data silos and access restrictions can severely limit the ability of AI systems to generate insights that span across the entire organization. The NIDG approach advocates for a governance model that promotes transparency and open access to data within the bounds of security and privacy regulations. By defining clear data ownership and stewardship roles in a non-invasive manner, organizations can ensure that data is shared and utilized effectively across departments and teams. This involves setting up data catalogs and metadata management practices that make it easy for users to find the data they need and understand its context and provenance.

Implementing an accessible data environment under NIDG principles involves more than just technology—it requires a cultural shift towards valuing and practicing open data sharing while maintaining a vigilant approach to data security and privacy. Such an environment encourages innovation and experimentation, which are critical components of successful AI initiatives. For instance, by utilizing centralized data catalogs that are meticulously curated and updated, organizations not only streamline the process of data discovery, but also foster a culture of knowledge sharing and collaboration.

This framework ensures that all stakeholders have equitable access to the organization's data assets, thereby democratizing data usage and unlocking new possibilities for cross-functional AI applications that drive forward the organization's strategic goals.

Emphasize Ethics and Privacy

Preparing for AI requires a strong emphasis on data ethics and privacy. As AI systems increasingly make decisions affecting customers and employees, ensuring data is used responsibly is paramount. The NIDG approach addresses these concerns by embedding ethical considerations and compliance with data protection regulations into the organization's data governance framework. This includes establishing guidelines for data usage, consent management, and impact assessments for AI projects, ensuring that AI applications are developed and deployed in a manner that respects individual rights and societal norms.

Incorporating ethical data use into the fabric of organizational culture demands active engagement and education at all levels. It's about fostering an environment where every stakeholder understands the importance of ethical considerations in data handling and AI implementation. Workshops, training sessions, and regular communication on ethical data use and privacy protection can build a strong foundation of awareness and commitment.

By creating a transparent mechanism for reporting and addressing ethical concerns and data misuse, organizations can demonstrate their commitment to ethical principles. This not only fortifies trust among consumers and employees but also safeguards the organization against potential legal and reputational risks associated with AI technologies.

Learn and Adapt

Finally, fostering a continuous learning and adaptation culture is essential for making data AI-ready. As AI technologies evolve, so too must the organization's data governance practices. The NIDG approach supports this by encouraging feedback loops, regular reviews of data governance policies, and the agile adaptation of roles and responsibilities in response to new challenges and opportunities presented by AI advancements. Investing in training and development programs to enhance the data literacy and AI skills of the workforce ensures that the organization remains at the forefront of AI innovation.

The journey to AI readiness is ongoing, requiring organizations to remain vigilant and responsive to technological shifts. Creating communities of practice within the organization can serve as a platform for sharing insights, best practices, and innovative solutions in AI applications and data governance. These communities foster a collaborative environment where learning is shared, and collective intelligence grows.

Partnering with external experts and academic institutions can bring fresh perspectives and cutting-edge knowledge into the organization, further fueling the cycle of learning and adaptation. This proactive stance on learning and development, underpinned by the principles of Non-Invasive Data Governance, prepares organizations to harness the full potential of AI, ensuring they not only keep pace with technological advances but lead the way in ethical, effective AI deployment.

Conclusion

To wrap things up, making data AI-ready is a comprehensive endeavor that extends beyond the technical aspects of data management. It requires a strategic approach to data governance that emphasizes collaboration, empowerment, and respect for data as a valuable organizational asset. By adopting a non-invasive approach to data governance, organizations can create a data ecosystem that is not only prepared for the demands of AI, but also conducive to innovation, efficiency, and ethical decision-making. In this way, NIDG becomes not just a method for governing data, but a catalyst for realizing the full potential of AI within the organization.

Data Investor—A New Name for a Data Owner

Let's put a fresh twist on a familiar concept in data governance. We've all heard the term "Data Owner" tossed around in boardrooms and governance meetings. It makes sense, right? Someone's got to own the data, manage it, and be accountable for it. But what if I told you that thinking of people as "Data Owners" might not be the best way to approach it? Instead, let's try something more forward-thinking: calling them "Data Investors." Now, before you roll your eyes and think this is just another trendy rebranding, let me explain why this shift could bring about real benefits, especially when viewed through the lens of Non-Invasive Data Governance (NIDG).

First, let's break down the term "Data Owner." It's been around for years and implies control, responsibility, and accountability over a specific dataset. While it gets the point across, it can sound possessive and even a bit invasive. Ownership implies that the data is a static asset to be kept and guarded, like a treasure chest hidden away from everyone else. In the context of Non-Invasive Data Governance, this mindset can create resistance because ownership also sounds a lot like another job title—one that gets dumped on someone without them asking for it. When people are "assigned" to be Data Owners, it can feel like a burden they never wanted, and worse yet, they might not even fully understand what they're supposed to do with it. Ownership comes with an implied exclusivity that doesn't necessarily align with the collaborative spirit of NIDG.

Now, let's consider the term "Data Investor." Doesn't that feel different already? It has a more proactive and engaged vibe to it. Instead of guarding data like a dragon protecting its stash, a Data Investor sees the potential for growth, value, and, yes, a return on investment (ROI) from how they manage, share, and enhance data. In the Non-Invasive Data Governance world, this shift in mindset aligns perfectly with how we emphasize accountability without adding unnecessary burden.

Data Investors aren't just responsible for the data they handle; they are actively contributing to its value within the organization.

They're aware that their "investment" in data management practices leads to better decisions, improved processes, and a stronger data culture overall. It's no longer about ownership in the possessive sense; it's about contribution and engagement. But there are two sides to every coin, right? The upside of calling people Data Investors is clear: it promotes a more dynamic, value-driven relationship with data. It encourages individuals to think beyond just holding and managing data and consider its broader implications. It frames their role as part of a collective strategy to unlock the value of data, which feels far more empowering and forward-looking. This fits beautifully with NIDG's philosophy of integrating governance naturally into existing roles and responsibilities without making people feel overwhelmed or burdened by the title of "Owner."

On the flip side, however, not everyone might immediately buy into the idea of being a "Data Investor." For some, this might feel like just another buzzword, or worse, something that adds more pressure. They might think, "Now I have to invest in this?!" In reality, the concept behind the term doesn't ask for anything more than what's already expected in a good data governance framework—it simply reframes the way we think about it. But let's not pretend: rebranding a job or responsibility can sometimes lead to confusion, no matter how well-intentioned. Some folks might still prefer the old-school clarity of "ownership" because it's straightforward, even if it's not as inspiring.

Conclusion

In the end, the goal remains the same whether you call someone a Data Owner or a Data Investor: ensuring that data is managed, governed, and used effectively across the organization. Non-Invasive Data Governance is all about embedding these responsibilities into existing processes in a natural and non-disruptive way. So, the next time you're talking about data governance, ask yourself this:

Do you want people to feel like they own a piece of the data puzzle, or do you want them to invest in its value and future?

In my approach to data governance, the latter sets a more engaging tone for the journey ahead.

Strategies for Data Governance on a Limited Budget

Implementing effective data governance programs, especially Non-Invasive Data Governance (NIDG) programs, on a limited budget requires a strategic and resource-conscious approach. While larger organizations might have dedicated budgets for comprehensive governance initiatives, smaller organizations or those with financial constraints can still achieve meaningful governance outcomes. Let's discuss several suggestions for implementing NIDG on a limited budget.

Leverage Existing Structures

Leveraging existing structures is a pragmatic approach to initiate Non-Invasive Data Governance. Identify individuals contributing to data quality informally, acknowledging and formalizing their roles in the NIDG framework. This not only recognizes their efforts but also establishes a foundational structure for a comprehensive and cost-effective governance strategy.

To further reinforce this foundation, conduct awareness programs and training sessions. Empower these recognized contributors with the necessary knowledge and tools, ensuring a smooth transition into their more formalized roles. Encourage open communication channels to gather insights from these individuals, promoting a collaborative environment. This proactive engagement not only enhances the effectiveness of NIDG but also nurtures a culture of shared responsibility and continuous improvement within the organization.

Form a Cross-Functional Data Governance Team

Forming a cross-functional data governance team is a strategic move to ensure a comprehensive approach to NIDG. This team, consisting of members from diverse departments, collaborates to define data policies, standards, and practices. By incorporating representatives from various areas, you leverage a spectrum of perspectives, fostering a holistic and inclusive governance framework.

To maximize the effectiveness of the cross-functional team, establish clear communication channels and facilitate regular meetings. Encourage open dialogue and idea-sharing to harness the collective intelligence of team members.

This collaboration ensures that the defined data governance strategies align with the unique requirements and challenges of different departments. Empower team members with training sessions on NIDG principles, enhancing their understanding and commitment to the shared goals of the organization.

Promote Data Stewardship Across Departments

Promoting the concept of data stewardship across departments is a cost-effective strategy for instilling a culture of responsibility and accountability. Instead of creating new roles, organizations can leverage existing leadership structures. Encourage department heads and managers to champion data stewardship within their teams, emphasizing the importance of data quality and responsible usage.

This decentralized approach empowers individuals at various levels to take ownership of data-related activities within their respective areas, fostering a sense of accountability and contributing to the overall success of Non-Invasive Data Governance.

Utilize Open-Source Tools

Explore open-source data governance tools that can provide essential functionalities without the hefty price tag associated with commercial solutions. Open-source tools often have active communities, allowing organizations to benefit from continuous improvements and updates without substantial financial investments.

In addition to utilizing open-source tools, organizations can leverage the flexibility and adaptability offered by these solutions. Open-source data governance tools, supported by active communities, not only provide essential functionalities at a lower cost, but also allow for customization based on specific organizational needs.

Prioritize Critical Processes

Identify and prioritize the most critical data processes within the organization. Focus governance efforts on these processes to ensure that limited resources are directed where they can have the most significant impact. This targeted approach allows for effective governance without spreading resources too thin.

When prioritizing critical processes, conducting a thorough assessment is essential to determine their impact on organizational objectives. Collaborate with key stakeholders to gain insights into which processes contribute most significantly to data quality, integrity, and overall business success. By aligning data governance efforts with the strategic goals of the organization, you not only optimize the use of limited resources but also ensure that governance initiatives are closely tied to the areas that matter most.

Implement Incrementally

Implement NIDG incrementally, starting with foundational elements and gradually expanding. This phased approach enables organizations to demonstrate value early in the process, making it easier to secure additional support and resources as needed. It also allows for adjustments based on evolving organizational needs.

An incremental implementation of NIDG allows organizations to build momentum and showcase the tangible benefits of governance practices. Begin with a pilot project or a specific business unit, focusing on clear and achievable objectives. You garner support from key stakeholders by demonstrating a positive impact on data quality, decision-making, or operational efficiency in a controlled environment.

Employee Training and Awareness

Invest in cost-effective training programs to enhance data literacy across the organization. Online courses, workshops, or webinars can be relatively inexpensive and contribute to building a data-centric culture. An informed workforce is better equipped to contribute to governance efforts even without a significant budget.

Employee training and awareness are pivotal components of successful NIDG implementation on a limited budget. To conduct training sessions, leverage existing internal resources, such as subject matter experts or experienced team members. This not only reduces external training costs but also fosters a culture of knowledge-sharing within the organization. Additionally, explore free or low-cost online resources to supplement training initiatives.

Establish Clear Communication Channels

Effective communication is essential for successful governance. Establish clear and open communication channels to keep stakeholders informed about governance initiatives. Regular updates, newsletters, or internal forums can facilitate communication without requiring substantial financial investments.

Establishing clear communication channels is critical for NIDG success on a limited budget. Leverage existing communication tools within the organization, such as internal newsletters, company-wide emails, or collaborative platforms. Encourage an open dialogue where stakeholders can ask questions or provide feedback, fostering a sense of inclusivity in governance efforts. Additionally, consider utilizing low-cost or free communication tools available in the market to streamline information dissemination.

Leverage Cloud-Based Solutions

Consider leveraging cloud-based solutions for data governance. Cloud platforms often provide scalable and cost-effective options, allowing organizations to pay for the resources they use. This can be particularly advantageous for smaller organizations looking to manage costs while benefiting from robust governance capabilities.

Implementing NIDG on a limited budget can benefit significantly from leveraging cloud-based solutions. Cloud platforms offer scalable and pay-as-you-go models, enabling organizations to access advanced data governance functionalities without substantial upfront investments. Explore cloud-based data governance tools that align with organizational needs, ensuring flexibility, scalability, and cost-effectiveness.

Collaborate with Industry Groups

Engage with industry-specific or data governance-focused groups and forums. These communities often share best practices, templates, and valuable insights. Networking with peers facing similar challenges can provide guidance and support without incurring additional costs.

Collaborating with industry groups is a cost-effective strategy to enhance NIDG implementation. Joining forums and communities focused on data governance allows organizations to tap into a collective pool of knowledge. These platforms often offer valuable resources, best practices, and shared experiences, enabling learning without the need for substantial financial investments.

Conclusion

Implementing Non-Invasive Data Governance (NIDG) on a limited budget requires strategic yet resource-conscious approaches. Organizations can leverage existing structures and recognize individuals already contributing to data management by acknowledging and formalizing their roles within the NIDG framework. Forming a cross-functional team comprising representatives from various departments enables the collaborative definition of data policies, standards, and practices without necessitating additional resources. Promoting data stewardship across departments and encouraging department heads and managers to champion this concept empowers individuals to take ownership of data quality within their respective areas.

Organizations can explore open-source data governance tools for essential functionalities without the hefty price tag. Prioritizing critical processes ensures that limited resources are directed where they can have the most significant impact, and implementing NIDG incrementally allows for value demonstration and adjustments based on evolving needs. Employee training, clear communication channels, and cloud-based solutions offer cost-effective ways to enhance data literacy, facilitate effective governance communication, and leverage scalable options.

Collaborate with industry groups that provide access to shared knowledge and best practices, fostering a supportive environment for organizations to navigate the challenges of data governance without a substantial financial burden.

Federated Data Governance Without Clear Authority

Organizations are increasingly adopting a Federated Data Governance (FDG) model to manage and govern their vast and varied data assets. This model, particularly when combined with the principles of Non-Invasive Data Governance (NIDG), acknowledges the decentralized nature of modern enterprises where individual business units operate autonomously yet are required to adhere to collective data standards and policies. This essay explores the complexities of implementing FDG within the NIDG framework, focusing on the crucial challenge of policy (including guidelines and standards) enforcement in the absence of centralized authority.

This model champions a delicate balance between respecting the independence of each unit and ensuring their alignment with overarching governance standards. It poses a unique challenge:

How can an organization maintain consistent data quality and compliance standards across diverse and independent business units without a centralized authority to enforce these policies?

The answer lies in the NIDG approach and framework, which offers a flexible yet structured methodology to bridge this gap. This essay explores strategies within the NIDG Framework that facilitate the integration of a federated governance model, fostering a cohesive data culture that supports shared organizational goals while honoring the autonomy of individual departments.

The NIDG Framework focuses on the six core components of data governance success (data, roles, processes, communications, metrics, tools) as viewed from each organizational level. The components are used in the essay to highlight ways that organizations can address governing in a non-invasive and federated way without clear authority.

Data: The Foundation of Federated Governance

Under Federated Data Governance, data is viewed as a strategic asset at every organizational level. Executives concentrate on the overarching data landscape, aligning it with broader business objectives. Strategic efforts involve defining and categorizing data assets. Tactically, there's an emphasis on aligning data with specific business functions, while operationally, the focus is on day-to-day data management. At the support level, the goal is to ensure data is accessible and usable across the organization. To tackle the challenge of policy enforcement, a culture of shared data responsibility is cultivated, where different units understand their impact on the organization's data ecosystem and are motivated to adhere to established standards for data management and usage.

In situations where clear authority or accountability (stewardship) is lacking, the FDG approach necessitates a more collaborative and inclusive strategy. This involves establishing a governance council or committee with representatives from various business units, ensuring a diversified and comprehensive understanding of data-related issues and needs across the organization. This council is crucial in fostering consensus and shared responsibility, acting as a mediator and coordinator for data governance initiatives. It also works towards setting up a framework for shared stewardship, where responsibilities and accountabilities for data management and governance are collectively defined and agreed upon.

Regular meetings, workshops, and training sessions can reinforce this framework, ensuring all parties are informed, engaged, and aligned in their approach to data governance. This strategy not only addresses the gaps in authority and accountability, but also strengthens the overall governance structure by promoting a culture of collaboration and shared ownership of data.

Roles: Defining Responsibilities

In FDG, defining roles at each organizational level is critical. Executives must champion data governance as a strategic imperative, while strategic roles are centered on policy development and framework delivery. Tactical people and teams are responsible for addressing specific and often domain-focused governance needs, such as data quality or compliance. Operational roles are focused on the daily management and effective use of data. At the support level, roles are centered around providing the necessary tools and resources for effective data governance. To address the challenge of enforcement, clear lines of communication and responsibility are established, ensuring that individuals at all levels understand their roles in maintaining governance standards and the implications of failing to comply.

When facing a lack of clear authority or accountability, the FDG model advocates for creating a framework that explicitly defines stewardship through roles and responsibilities across all levels. Develop this framework in consultation with representatives from different departments to ensure it reflects the diverse needs and challenges within the organization. Establishing data stewards or governance champions within each department can help bridge the gap in authority, serving as points of contact for governance-related issues and acting as liaisons between their department and the central governance body.

Equip these stewards with the authority to enforce governance policies within their respective areas and be held accountable for their department's adherence to these policies. Regular training and awareness programs can further reinforce the importance of these roles and the responsibilities they entail, fostering a culture of accountability and shared responsibility for data governance.

Processes: Streamlining Data Governance

In Federated Data Governance, processes are essential for ensuring efficient data management across various departments. At the executive level, the emphasis is on setting governance priorities and ensuring alignment with business strategies. Strategic processes involve developing and standardizing data governance policies. Tactically, the focus is on implementing these policies across different business functions. Operationally, processes are more about the practical execution of these policies, and at the support level, it's about providing the infrastructure to enable these processes to function efficiently. To address enforcement challenges, processes are developed collaboratively, with input from stakeholders at all levels, ensuring broad buy-in and facilitating easier implementation across diverse units.

In scenarios where there is no clear level of authority or accountability, a structured approach to process management becomes vital. This involves creating a governance framework that clearly delineates the processes at each level, with defined checkpoints for oversight and compliance. Implementing a decentralized approach to governance, where each department has a defined role in the governance process, can ensure more effective adherence to standards and policies.

This decentralized approach should be supported by a central governance team coordinating efforts and maintaining an overview of governance activities across the organization. Regular audits and reviews of processes at each level can identify areas of non-compliance or inefficiency, leading to timely interventions. Additionally, leveraging technology such as workflow management systems can help monitor process adherence and identify bottlenecks, ensuring that governance processes are not only clearly defined, but also effectively executed across the organization.

Communications: Bridging the Gaps

In FDG, effective communication is crucial at every level. Executive-level communication sets the governance tone, strategic communications focus on policy dissemination, tactical communications facilitate cross-functional discussions, operational communications deal with guidelines and best practices, and support-level communications ensure comprehensive information dissemination across the organization. To address the challenge of policy enforcement, a continuous feedback loop is established, allowing for policy adjustments as necessary and ensuring that all levels remain consistently informed and aligned with governance objectives.

When authority and accountability are unclear, communication strategies need to be more proactive and encompassing. Emphasize creating and sustaining an open dialogue that permeates throughout the organization. This can involve regular town hall meetings, cross-departmental workshops, and open forums where concerns and ideas can be freely exchanged. These communication platforms not only disseminate necessary information but also serve to clarify roles, responsibilities, and expectations in the governance process. Leadership should actively engage in these communications, demonstrating commitment and openness to feedback.

This approach aids in building a culture of transparency and accountability, where the lack of formal authority is mitigated by collective understanding and cooperative efforts toward governance objectives. The use of collaborative tools and platforms can further facilitate this ongoing conversation, making it easier to reach and engage stakeholders across different organizational levels and geographies.

Metrics: Measuring Success

In Federated Data Governance, metrics play a critical role in assessing the effectiveness of data governance efforts. Executives rely on high-level metrics to evaluate overall alignment with business objectives, while at the strategic level, metrics might focus on compliance rates or data quality improvements. Tactical metrics are more granular, zooming in on the effectiveness of specific governance initiatives. Operational metrics are concerned with day-to-day data management activities, and support metrics evaluate the performance and usage of data governance tools and resources. To address the challenge of enforcement, metrics are employed not only to measure compliance, but also to identify areas needing additional support or training, thus facilitating adherence to governance standards.

In scenarios where there is no clear level of authority or accountability, metrics can be a powerful tool to drive self-regulation and peer accountability. By making metrics transparent and accessible to all levels within the organization, individuals and teams can see how their actions impact the overall data governance goals. Establishing key performance indicators (KPIs) that are relevant, realistic, and aligned with the organization's data governance objectives is essential. Implement regular reporting of these metrics to maintain visibility and drive continuous improvement.

Based on these metrics, incorporating elements of gamification or recognition programs can motivate teams and individuals to adhere to governance standards. This approach encourages a culture where the responsibility for data governance is shared, and compliance becomes a collective achievement rather than a top-down directive.

Tools: Enabling Efficient Governance

In FDG, tools are indispensable for managing and governing data across different departments. At the executive level, tools such as dashboards help oversee data governance initiatives. Strategic tools assist in policy development and data categorization. Tactical tools are essential for facilitating cross-functional collaboration, while operational tools focus on the nitty-gritty of data management and analytics. At the support level, tools ensure that all departments have access to the necessary technology to implement governance policies effectively. To address enforcement challenges, these tools are designed to be user-friendly and integrated, ensuring ease of adherence to governance policies and facilitating the monitoring of compliance.

When authority and accountability are not clearly defined, leveraging technology to automate and track compliance can be highly effective. Equip tools with features that track user activities and flag deviations from set governance standards. Automated alerts and notifications can serve as reminders and prompts for required actions, ensuring that governance policies are consistently followed. Furthermore, implementing role-based access control (RBAC) within these tools can help to implicitly enforce governance policies by restricting data access and actions based on predefined roles and responsibilities.

By embedding governance requirements directly into the tools that personnel use daily, adherence to governance policies can be enhanced, reducing reliance on explicit enforcement mechanisms. This approach subtly ingrains governance practices into daily operations, encouraging a culture of compliance and responsibility.

Conclusion

Implementing Federated Data Governance (FDG) within the context of the Non-Invasive Data Governance (NIDG) framework presents a paradigm shift in how organizations approach data governance, particularly in environments where clear authority is not centralized. This essay has articulated a strategy, underscoring the importance of a multifaceted approach that honors the autonomy of individual business units while weaving a cohesive and unified data strategy throughout the organization.

The key pillars of Data, Roles, Processes, Communications, Metrics, and Tools form the backbone of this approach, each playing a critical role in addressing policy enforcement challenges across various organizational levels. By embedding these elements within the NIDG framework, organizations are equipped to foster a culture of shared responsibility and collaborative stewardship of data. This approach not only ensures that data is leveraged as a strategic asset but also facilitates a governance framework that is both robust and adaptable to the dynamic nature of modern businesses.

The insights provided in this essay illuminate the pathway for organizations to navigate the complexities of federated governance without clear authority. By adopting the principles of NIDG, organizations can cultivate a data governance environment that is not reliant on centralized control but thrives on collective accountability and strategic alignment. This model serves as a blueprint for organizations seeking to harness the full potential of their data assets in a decentralized yet harmonious governance structure, thereby achieving strategic goals and maintaining competitive edge in an increasingly data-driven world.

Data Stewardship

At the heart of *Non-Invasive Data Governance Unleashed: Empowering People to Govern Data and AI* lies the principle that effective governance begins with recognizing the pivotal role people play in managing, defining, and protecting data. Chapter 5, *Data Stewardship*, dives into the critical concept of stewardship, exploring how organizations can empower individuals to take ownership of their data-related responsibilities. This chapter emphasizes that stewardship is not about assigning additional tasks, but about formalizing the accountability that already exists across an organization.

The chapter opens with *Don't Assign Data Stewards*, which challenges the traditional top-down approach of appointing stewards to roles they may not understand or embrace. Instead, it advocates for fostering stewardship naturally by aligning it with individuals' existing relationships to data. This essay sets the tone for a broader discussion on how to make stewardship both effective and sustainable.

Recognize Your Data Stewards continues this theme by highlighting the importance of acknowledgment. Rather than assigning roles, this essay emphasizes recognizing the contributions employees already make as definers, producers, and users of data. This approach fosters engagement and accountability without the resistance often associated with traditional methods.

In *Data Domains and Data Domain Stewards*, the focus shifts to organizing stewardship efforts by data domains. This essay provides a practical framework for identifying and empowering stewards based on specific areas of data responsibility, making stewardship more targeted and manageable. It's an essential read for organizations looking to implement a scalable stewardship model.

Data Stewards are Already in the Building reinforces the idea that organizations don't need to look far to find stewards—they're already within the workforce. This essay underscores how to leverage the knowledge and expertise of current employees to build a robust stewardship program. It's a powerful reminder that stewardship doesn't require hiring new resources; it requires recognizing and formalizing the roles that already exist.

The chapter takes a forward-looking perspective with *Democratizing Data Stewardship*, exploring how stewardship can become a shared responsibility across all levels of an organization. By making stewardship accessible and inclusive, this essay demonstrates how to create a culture of accountability that drives collaboration and innovation.

Finally, *Defining Stewardship in the Age of AI* ties the concept of stewardship to the rapidly evolving landscape of artificial intelligence. This essay explains why stewardship is more critical than ever in ensuring that AI solutions are built on high-quality, well-governed data. It also provides insights into how organizations can adapt their stewardship practices to meet the demands of AI and advanced analytics.

Chapter 5 serves as a guide for organizations aiming to empower their teams through stewardship, ensuring that accountability for data is not just assigned but embraced. By focusing on recognition, inclusion, and adaptability, this chapter offers a roadmap for embedding stewardship into the fabric of an organization, aligning with the overarching mission of empowering people to govern data and AI.

Don't Assign Data Stewards

Sometimes I catch myself scratching my head, wondering, "Why are we still assigning people to be data stewards like it's a role you apply for instead of acknowledging the obvious?" It's not like people suddenly decide, "Hey, today I'll be a data steward!" They already *are* stewards—whether they know it or not—simply by how they define, produce, and use data in their daily work. Yet, here we are, appointing Data Stewards as if that badge of honor suddenly grants them the power to do what they've already been doing. Maybe we should start giving out 'Breather of Air' awards too—because that's how natural data stewardship really is.

The Non-Invasive Data Governance (NIDG) approach has been telling us for years that data stewardship isn't about a title. It's about accountability. People are already accountable for the data they touch. They're accountable for how they define it, how they produce and use it, and for how well they manage it. The difference between someone just "handling data" and someone *governing data* lies in whether or not they formalize and consistently apply best practices. But here's the kicker: we don't need to assign anyone new to do this job!

The real secret sauce is getting people to realize they've been stewards all along and empowering them to formalize what they're already doing, just with more consistency and transparency.

So why are we still assigning the title? Is it because giving someone a fancy new title makes us feel like we're progressing in our data governance journey? Or is it because we think they'll magically do a better job by naming them Data Stewards? The spoiler alert is that they won't. The real change happens when you help people recognize that the accountability they've had all along is actually valuable, and they can improve by formalizing that accountability. It's like telling someone who's been managing household finances forever, "Congratulations, you're now officially the family CFO!" Does the title change the way they balance the checkbook? Probably not, but guiding them on how to manage finances consistently and strategically? Now, that's where the magic happens.

The NIDG approach shines because it doesn't rely on handpicking "data stewards." Instead, it focuses on formalizing the relationships people already have with data. That's a radical shift that doesn't create more work, stress, or, heaven forbid, bureaucracy. Imagine this: you're a business analyst, and every day you use, produce, and define data. You may not call yourself a data steward, but guess what? You're already acting like one. You know the ins and outs of that data better than anyone. The trick is getting you to acknowledge it and then giving you the tools and structure to manage it consistently across your team or organization.

And yet, we're still dispensing stewardship roles like candy, expecting people to act differently just because we've given them the title or appointed them the position. Meanwhile, the folks who are already interacting with data day in and day out remain blissfully unaware that they could formalize their actions and instantly level up their impact. It's like giving someone a chef's hat but never teaching them how to actually use the stove.

We should be empowering people who already know the data—those in finance, HR, marketing, and operations—because they've been responsible for that data from day one. They don't need a new job title; they need a better playbook. If we help them see that they can improve how they handle data by simply formalizing their approach, then boom—instant data governance, no awkward new title required. And the best part? You see the results quickly. A little structure here, a sprinkle of consistency there, and suddenly, data is flowing smoother, fewer errors are popping up, and teams are spending less time firefighting bad data.

So why do we keep assigning people as "official" data stewards when they could just become more effective by formalizing what they're already doing? Maybe it's because we're stuck in an old-school mindset that equates progress with new titles and responsibilities. But honestly, wouldn't it be better if we focused on making the roles people already have more powerful and effective, rather than adding another layer of complexity?

Here's what happens when you stop focusing on titles and start focusing on accountability: people begin to own the data they've always been responsible for, but now with clarity. They start asking the right questions, defining data properly, and using it with greater consistency. And guess what? You didn't need to disrupt anyone's workflow or hold a meeting to announce the "new sheriff in town." You just needed to remind them that they're already running the show—they just needed a roadmap to get from good to great.

Conclusion

Let's face it: we've all got more important things to do than reassign titles. Let's skip the theatrics, and instead of announcing a new "data steward" regime, let's focus on refining what's already in place. People are naturally stewards of their own data—let's just help them do it a little better, smarter, and with much less fuss. The NIDG way.

Recognize Your Data Stewards

Most data practitioners agree that the concept and practice of data stewardship are central to effective data governance. However, the approach to enlisting data stewards can shape the trajectory of an organization's data governance strategy. The Non-Invasive Data Governance (NIDG) approach offers a compelling alternative to traditional methods by emphasizing the recognition of data stewards, which stands in contrast to the more prescriptive practices of assignment or mere identification. Recognition aligns with individuals' existing roles and their intrinsic relationship with data, fostering a sense of ownership and responsibility that is crucial for the adoption and success of data governance initiatives. Being "recognized" as a data steward is akin to an organic endorsement of an individual's expertise and existing contributions to data management within their daily work. This recognition goes beyond just labeling someone with a title; it is an affirmation of their inherent value and authority in handling data. Such an approach can lead to greater acceptance and engagement as individuals realize that their actions are pivotal to the organization's overarching goals in data governance. It respects their professional acumen and leverages their intimate understanding of the data they oversee.

Unlike the rigidity of an "assigned" role, which can be perceived as an additional task or top-down mandate, recognition is integrative and empowering. It encourages individuals to see the role of data steward not as an external imposition but as a formal acknowledgment of their critical function within the data ecosystem.

Recognition as a methodology for finding your data stewards presents numerous advantages that help embed a sustainable and effective governance structure within the organization. When stewards are chosen from among those who naturally exemplify the qualities of good data governance, it leads to a form of leadership that is both inspirational and aspirational. These stewards, acknowledged for their meticulous approach to data quality and governance, become the standard-bearers, instilling best practices through their actions and influence. This creates a model of governance based on demonstrable competence, encouraging a peer-driven culture of compliance and advocacy that resonates more deeply than any policy could.

Embracing recognition within the NIDG approach enhances the organization's ability to capitalize on its existing knowledge and expertise. Recognized data stewards are typically well-acquainted with the specific needs and nuances of their data domains, enabling them to make informed decisions that align with both governance policies and operational efficiencies. This minimizes the need for extensive training or reorientation, allowing for a more seamless integration of governance initiatives into existing workflows. Such an approach also fosters a decentralized model of governance, where decision-making is informed by hands-on experience and departmental insights, leading to quicker and more nuanced responses to data-related challenges.

Inclusion and diversity are additional pillars strengthened by the recognition approach in NIDG. By acknowledging the varied interactions different individuals have with data, an inclusive framework for stewardship is established. This model values diverse perspectives and skills, understanding that each individual's relationship with data can contribute uniquely to its governance. It democratizes the stewardship process, ensuring that the full spectrum of data's potential is realized through a collective effort, which is indispensable for maintaining integrity and maximizing the utility of data assets.

To wrap up this short piece, the principle of recognition in the NIDG framework is not just a methodology—it is a philosophy that nurtures a robust data governance culture. It is built on the premise that when individuals are acknowledged for their data stewardship based on their existing roles and interactions with data, they are more inclined to accept and excel in these roles, leading to a thriving governance environment.

Conclusion

Recognition engenders a sense of pride and empowerment, which in turn catalyzes a shared commitment to data excellence. The collective stewardship that arises from this approach is what makes NIDG a transformative force in the world of data governance, one that unlocks the full potential of data as a key asset in any organization.

Data Domains and Data Domain Stewards

Data domains and data domain stewards play a pivotal role in the management and governance of data, acting as a structural and operational pillar that ensures data is accurately categorized, maintained, and utilized across an organization. By segmenting data into domains (basically business subject areas), organizations can effectively manage and govern their data, as each domain represents a specific area of expertise or a particular business function. This categorization simplifies the complex landscape of organizational data, making it more controllable and easier to manage.

Data domain stewards, who are subject matter experts within these specific areas, enrich the data governance program. They bring a deep understanding of their respective subjects, ensuring that the data within the subject area is not only accurately defined and managed, but also aligned with both the internal standards and external regulations. Their expertise facilitates the development of tailored governance policies and data management practices that are specific to the needs and nuances of each domain, thereby enhancing data quality, consistency, and reliability across the organization.

Including data domain stewards in data governance implementations transforms the governance framework from a top-down, policy-driven approach to a more collaborative, engaged process. These stewards act as the bridge between the governance body and the operational teams, advocating for the needs and requirements of their domains while ensuring adherence to overarching governance policies and standards.

---

*Data domain stewards act as the bridge between
the governance body and the operational teams.*

This collaborative approach fosters a culture of data stewardship throughout the organization, where data governance becomes part of the operational character rather than an external imposition. It also enables more agile and responsive governance practices, as stewards can quickly identify and address emerging data issues or opportunities within their domains. In essence, data domains and their stewards are crucial for creating a structured yet flexible framework for data management and governance, ensuring that data assets are effectively leveraged for strategic advantage while maintaining integrity, security, and compliance.

In the Non-Invasive Data Governance (NIDG) approach, the Data Domain Steward plays a critical role by serving as the subject matter expert and potentially the authoritative figure for their designated data domain. Their responsibilities include overseeing data quality, ensuring data compliance with relevant standards and regulations, and fostering a culture of data-driven decision-making within their domain.

Depending on their official role and standing within the organization, Data Domain Stewards may possess the authority to make binding decisions regarding the management, utilization, and governance of their specific area of data. This authority enables them to effectively implement governance policies, standards, and practices that align with the organization's overall data strategy and objectives, thereby enhancing the value and integrity of the data under their stewardship.

Implementing data domains with formal data domain stewards is an important step toward deploying the NIDG program, which emphasizes collaboration, knowledge sharing, and leveraging the expertise within an organization without imposing cumbersome rules or processes. This approach ensures that data governance is integrated seamlessly into daily operations, enhancing data quality, compliance, and strategic decision-making. Below are five important reasons why implementing data domains with formal data domain stewards is crucial for the success of a non-invasive data governance program:

Expert-Led Data Management

Data domain stewards are subject matter experts who bring a deep understanding of their specific data domains. Their expertise is invaluable in managing data effectively, ensuring that data is accurate, relevant, and consistently defined across the organization. These stewards can make informed decisions about data standards, policies, and procedures that are tailored to the nuances of their specific domain, leading to more effective and efficient data management practices.

The role of data domain stewards extends beyond mere data upkeep; they are instrumental in fostering a culture of data-driven decision-making within their domains. By having a comprehensive grasp of both the data and its business context, stewards empower their colleagues by providing them with high-quality, actionable data. This enables departments to make decisions based on reliable information, thereby reducing risks and enhancing outcomes.

These stewards act as liaisons between the technical and business sides of an organization, translating complex data concepts into actionable insights for business leaders. Their ability to manage data governance tasks, from the creation and implementation of data quality metrics to the execution of data cleansing projects, underscores their critical role in the successful operation and strategic initiatives of their organizations.

Enhanced Data Quality and Integrity

One of the primary goals of a NIDG program is to improve the quality and integrity of the organization's data. Formal data domain stewards play a crucial role in achieving this goal by overseeing data quality initiatives within their domains. They can identify and address data quality issues, such as inaccuracies, inconsistencies, and redundancies, ensuring that the data is reliable and trustworthy. This, in turn, supports better decision-making and operational efficiency.

Beyond the initial identification and remediation of data issues, data domain stewards also implement proactive data quality management strategies. These strategies include establishing continuous monitoring processes, developing data quality benchmarks, and creating feedback loops with data users to continually refine and improve data quality over time. By setting up a systematic approach to data quality, stewards ensure that improvements are not just one-time fixes but part of an ongoing effort to uphold high standards of data integrity.

This systematic approach facilitates a sustainable environment where data quality is constantly monitored, issues are promptly addressed, and the overall data ecosystem within the organization is continuously optimized for peak performance.

Facilitated Regulatory Compliance

As data privacy and protection regulations become increasingly stringent, organizations must ensure their data handling practices are compliant. Data domain stewards are instrumental in this aspect, as they have the domain-specific knowledge required to understand and implement the relevant regulatory requirements. By ensuring that data within their domains is managed in compliance with these regulations, stewards help mitigate the risk of non-compliance, which can lead to significant financial penalties and reputational damage.

The value of data domain stewards in facilitating regulatory compliance extends into the territory of dynamic regulatory landscapes. They are not only responsible for current compliance but also for staying abreast of changes in legislation and adapting data management practices accordingly. This forward-looking approach ensures that an organization is not only compliant today but prepared for tomorrow's compliance challenges as well. Stewards often work closely with legal and compliance teams to interpret new regulations and assess their impact on data practices. Their ability to translate these complex regulatory requirements into actionable data governance policies and procedures is critical in maintaining an agile and compliant data management framework, safeguarding the organization against the evolving nature of data privacy and protection laws.

Promoted Cross-Functional Collaboration

Implementing data domains with formal stewards encourages cross-functional collaboration within the organization. Since data often spans multiple departments and functions, stewards from different domains need to work together to ensure data consistency and interoperability. This collaborative approach fosters a culture of shared responsibility for data governance, breaking down silos and enhancing communication and cooperation across the organization.

This enhanced collaboration extends to aligning various departments with the organization's overall data strategy and objectives. By working together, data domain stewards can identify and leverage synergies between different areas of the business, leading to more innovative uses of data and the development of comprehensive solutions to complex challenges.

Regular cross-domain meetings and integrated governance frameworks help ensure that data-related decisions are made with a holistic view of the organization's needs and goals in mind. This not only improves the quality and utility of the data but also supports a more cohesive and unified organizational strategy, where data acts as a bridge rather than a barrier between different parts of the business.

Strategic Data Utilization

Last but not least, data domain stewards enable organizations to leverage their data more strategically. With deep knowledge of both their domain and the organization's strategic goals, stewards can identify opportunities to use data in ways that drive innovation and competitive advantage. They can champion projects that utilize data for new insights, products, or services, aligning data initiatives with business objectives and ensuring that data is a strategic asset for the organization.

The impact of strategic data utilization goes beyond immediate projects or products; it fosters a culture of innovation and continuous improvement within the organization. Data domain stewards play a key role in embedding data analytics and insights into the decision-making processes, encouraging teams to challenge assumptions and explore new ideas. This proactive approach to data strategy not only positions the organization to adapt to changing market conditions and customer needs but also empowers employees to think creatively about how data can solve complex problems and create value. As a result, the organization not only achieves its current strategic goals but also lays the groundwork for sustained growth and success in the future.

Conclusion

Implementing data domains with formal data domain stewards is pivotal in a non-invasive data governance program. It ensures that data governance is expert-led, enhances data quality and integrity, facilitates regulatory compliance, promotes cross-functional collaboration, and enables strategic data utilization. This approach not only optimizes the organization's data management practices, but also supports its overall strategic objectives, making it an essential element of modern data governance strategies.

Data Stewards are Already in the Building

In the world of data governance, a common delusion is that hiring data stewards will solve the governance challenges. While it may seem logical to bring in new people specifically for these roles, it is not a best practice, especially when following the Non-Invasive Data Governance (NIDG) approach. NIDG is designed to make governance a natural part of day-to-day operations by leveraging the roles that already exist within an organization. Rather than hiring additional staff, the NIDG approach encourages formalizing the accountability for data within the existing workforce.

Why is hiring dedicated data stewards not the best strategy in this approach? First, data stewardship is not a new role but a responsibility that people already perform. Think about it: individuals throughout an organization are already interacting with, defining, producing, and using data daily. They may be doing this as part of their business analysis, IT, operations, or even marketing roles. The NIDG approach recognizes this and builds upon these natural relationships with data, turning these existing responsibilities into formal stewardship roles. By doing this, data governance doesn't feel like a separate, external task requiring extra resources, but rather something people are already equipped to handle.

Another significant point is that hiring dedicated data stewards can lead to confusion. When you hire someone specifically for the stewardship role, there can be a disconnect between them and those who truly understand the data—those already working with it daily. These newly hired stewards might struggle to integrate with teams, or worse, their authority may be questioned by those who feel they have been doing the job all along. The NIDG approach avoids this by embedding accountability within the existing structure, ensuring that the right people are formally responsible for the right data. This reduces friction and aligns data governance more closely with the organization's natural workflows.

Finally, hiring new data stewards adds unnecessary costs and complexity. It introduces the need for new funding first, and then additional onboarding, training, and role integration, which can create delays in getting a governance program off the ground. On the other hand, by following the NIDG approach, organizations can move faster and more efficiently. Rather than incurring costs associated with hiring, they can focus on empowering current employees, providing them with the tools and frameworks they need to succeed in their governance roles.

Conclusion

To sum it up, NIDG champions a more practical, cost-effective, and seamless way to implement data governance. By leveraging existing roles and responsibilities, you can build a sustainable and resilient governance program without the need for new hires. This not only saves time and money but also ensures that governance becomes part of the organization's culture rather than something imposed from the outside. Hiring data stewards may seem like a quick fix, but the NIDG approach offers a far more sustainable and effective solution in the long run.

Democratizing Data Stewardship

The effective management and governance of data is crucial for organizational success. The concept of democratizing data stewardship, central to Non-Invasive Data Governance (NIDG), redefines traditional governance models by emphasizing that every individual who interacts with data is a steward of that data. This approach fosters a culture of shared responsibility, enhancing data quality and accessibility across the organization.

Broadening the Scope of Stewardship

The NIDG approach broadens the definition of a data steward to include anyone who defines, produces, or uses data within their role. This inclusive perspective recognizes that data stewardship is not just the responsibility of IT and business departments or data specialists. Instead, it is a critical aspect of every employee's job description. By formally recognizing each individual's interaction with data as an act of stewardship, organizations empower their workforce, encouraging a proactive attitude toward data management. This empowerment helps individuals understand the impact of their data handling, leading to more conscientious practices in data entry, maintenance, and usage.

Democratizing stewardship helps to break down the silos that often hinder effective data governance. When everyone is a steward, data flows more freely between departments, enhancing collaboration and innovation. Employees across different levels and functions begin to see how their contributions to data management support the organization's overall goals, leading to a more aligned and unified approach to governance.

Formal Accountability for Data

Under NIDG, the key to effective democratization lies in the formal accountability of each data steward's role. Accountability is established based on the nature of an individual's interaction with data. For example, a marketing analyst who analyzes consumer data is held accountable for the accuracy and ethical handling of that data. This accountability ensures that every steward is aware of the standards and policies governing their specific data interactions and is responsible for adhering to these guidelines.

Formalizing this accountability does not involve assigning roles. Rather, it involves recognizing people into roles. It requires a clear definition of expectations and responsibilities. Organizations need to provide the necessary training and resources to enable their stewards to manage their data effectively. This includes access to the right tools to maintain data integrity and the knowledge to implement best practices in data quality and compliance.

Benefits of a Democratized Stewardship Model

The benefits of democratizing data stewardship are profound. First, it leads to better data quality as more individuals are involved in ensuring the accuracy and reliability of the data they handle. This widespread involvement also speeds up the detection and correction of data issues, reducing the risk of data errors permeating through critical business processes.

A democratized approach to data stewardship enhances organizational agility. With more employees empowered to manage and utilize data effectively, organizations can respond more swiftly to market changes and opportunities. Decision-making becomes faster and more informed, driven by data that is comprehensively maintained and readily available across the organization.

Implementing Democratized Data Stewardship

To implement this model, organizations should start by clearly communicating the importance of data stewardship to all employees. This involves not only defining what data stewardship entails, but also explaining the specific impact of each role on the organization's data ecosystem. Leadership must also be committed to supporting this cultural shift through ongoing education, appropriate technological support, and recognition of good data governance practices.

Implementing a successful democratized data stewardship model requires regular monitoring and review. This ensures that the stewardship practices remain relevant and continue to align with evolving business needs and technological advancements. It also helps to sustain engagement and accountability among all stewards by providing feedback and opportunities for improvement in their data management practices.

Conclusion

In conclusion, democratizing data stewardship via Non-Invasive Data Governance transforms data management from a specialized task confined to certain roles, into a fundamental aspect of every employee's responsibilities. This shift not only improves the quality and accessibility of data but also fosters a stronger, more data-literate culture within the organization. By embracing this model, companies can harness the full potential of their data assets, driving innovation and maintaining a competitive edge in the digital age.

Defining Stewardship in the Age of AI

The role of data stewardship takes on an unprecedented level of importance in the AI landscape. As AI continues to become a part of every facet of our lives, from business operations to personal decision-making, the way we manage and govern data becomes critical. This essay explores the definition of the role of data stewards in the age of AI, based on the principles of Non-Invasive Data Governance (NIDG).

Data stewards have always been pivotal in managing and maintaining data quality, integrity, and accessibility. However, in the AI-driven world, their role expands significantly. AI systems feed on data—the quality, quantity, and relevance of this data directly influence the effectiveness and reliability of AI outcomes. Thus, the role of data stewards becomes not just important, but indispensable.

In my NIDG approach, data stewardship is not a designated position but a role that anyone who defines, produces, or uses data in an organization inherently assumes. This perspective becomes even more relevant in the context of AI. AI systems are not just another tool; they are entities that interact with data at every level of an organization. Therefore, it becomes imperative that every individual who interacts with these systems understands and embraces their stewardship role.

A key principle of NIDG is recognizing and formalizing the inherent data responsibilities that individuals hold. This concept is vital in AI environments. With AI's capability to process and analyze data at an unprecedented scale, ensuring that every data interaction is governed by principles of accuracy, consistency, and context becomes a necessity.

A key principle of NIDG is recognizing and formalizing the inherent data responsibilities that individuals hold.

The informal, often unnoticed, acts of data management that employees engage in daily, from data entry to analysis, directly feed into the AI ecosystem. By formalizing these acts, we ensure that the AI systems are being nurtured with data that is not just abundant, but also accurate, relevant, and ethically sourced.

Another aspect of stewardship in the AI era is understanding the implications of AI-driven decisions. In their expanded role, data stewards must be aware of how data biases and inaccuracies can lead to flawed AI outputs. This awareness is crucial in ensuring ethical AI practices. It's not just about feeding data into systems but also about understanding and mitigating the potential biases these systems might learn from the data. The stewards' role, therefore, extends to being guardians of not just data quality, but also of ethical data usage.

In this age of AI, data stewardship must also evolve to encompass a broader understanding of data privacy and security. With their vast data-processing capabilities, AI systems can potentially expose sensitive information or be exploited for malicious purposes. The NIDG approach emphasizes the need for every individual handling data to be aware of and accountable for the privacy and security implications of their actions. This becomes even more critical in AI contexts, where the stakes are exponentially higher.

The transition to AI-driven systems does not diminish the role of human data stewards—it elevates it. AI systems, for all their intelligence, lack the nuanced understanding and ethical judgment that humans bring. In the NIDG framework, stewardship is about imbuing AI with these human values. It's about ensuring that AI systems serve the organization's goals ethically and effectively, without losing sight of the human element that lies at the core of all data governance efforts.

Let's explore how organizations can utilize the NIDG-defined role of data stewards to demonstrate success in AI:

- **Embracing Comprehensive Data Accountability:** The NIDG approach advocates that anyone interacting with data—be it defining, producing, or using it—inherently assumes a stewardship role. This translates into a comprehensive accountability for data quality at every level in AI contexts. For instance, data entry personnel become crucial in ensuring the accuracy of AI inputs, while analysts play a key role in interpreting AI outputs within ethical and business contexts.

- **Formalizing Informal Data Practices:** Informal data management practices, often overlooked, are the bedrock upon which AI systems operate. The NIDG method involves recognizing and formalizing these practices. By doing so, organizations can ensure that the data feeding into AI systems is not just voluminous but also of high quality and relevance. This step is crucial for AI systems that rely on nuanced data for decision-making processes.

- **Ensuring Ethical AI through Stewardship:** Data stewards, in the NIDG framework, are tasked with understanding and mitigating potential biases in AI-driven decisions. This role is crucial for maintaining ethical AI practices. For instance, stewards must ensure diversity in data sets to prevent AI biases, thereby promoting fair and unbiased AI operations.

- **Enhancing Data Privacy and Security in AI:** The expansive data processing capabilities of AI systems raise significant privacy and security concerns. In the NIDG model, every individual handling data is made aware of and accountable for these concerns. This awareness is vital in AI contexts, where data breaches or unethical data usage can have far-reaching consequences.

- **Human-Centric AI Systems:** In the NIDG framework, human judgment and ethical considerations are paramount. This human-centric approach ensures that AI systems are not just technically proficient but also aligned with the organization's ethical standards and societal values. Data stewards, therefore, play a pivotal role in embedding these human values into AI systems, making sure that these technologies reflect organizational ethics and are used for the betterment of society.

- **Implementing AI with a Stewardship-First Approach:** Organizations can utilize the NIDG framework to implement AI systems with a stewardship-first approach. This involves engaging data stewards at every stage of AI development and deployment. For example, when developing an AI model, stewards can ensure the data used is accurate, relevant, and ethically sourced. During deployment, they can monitor the model's performance, ensuring it remains true to its intended purpose and ethical guidelines.

- **Continuous Education and Adaptation:** Given the rapidly evolving nature of AI, continuous education and adaptation become key for data stewards. Under the NIDG framework, organizations must invest in ongoing training for their data stewards, focusing not just on the technical aspects of AI, but also on its ethical, legal, and societal implications. This education ensures that stewards can capably oversee AI systems throughout their lifecycle, adapting to new challenges and technologies as they arise.

- **AI and Data Stewardship, A Collaborative Effort:** Success in AI is not solely a technological endeavor—it's equally about effective data governance. By leveraging the NIDG-defined roles of data stewards, organizations can ensure that their AI initiatives are underpinned by robust data management practices. This involves creating a culture where data stewards collaborate closely with AI developers, ensuring that AI systems are both technically sound and ethically responsible.

Data stewardship, as defined by the NIDG approach, is not just a responsibility; it's a strategic imperative. By embracing comprehensive data accountability, formalizing informal data practices, and ensuring ethical AI operations, organizations can harness the transformative power of AI. This approach ensures that AI systems are not only advanced in capabilities but also grounded in the principles of responsible data governance, paving the way for AI to be a force for positive, ethical change.

By embracing comprehensive data accountability, formalizing informal data practices, and ensuring ethical AI operations, organizations can harness the transformative power of AI.

Conclusion

As we step further into the age of AI, the concept of data stewardship, as defined in the NIDG framework, becomes more pertinent. It's about recognizing that every interaction with data, whether by a human or an AI system, needs to be governed by principles of accuracy, ethics, and responsibility. It's about ensuring that AI serves us and not the other way around. This perspective on data stewardship is not just a requirement for effective data governance; it's a cornerstone for ensuring that AI evolves as a tool for positive transformation and ethical progress.

Data Governance in Action

Chapter 6, *Data Governance in Action*, is where theory transforms into practice. With the subtitle of this book, *Empowering People to Govern Data and AI*, as its guiding principle, this chapter provides a hands-on exploration of how organizations can implement data governance that is not only effective but also engaging and sustainable. These essays bring to life the essential activities and considerations that make governance more than just a policy—it becomes an integral part of daily operations, driving meaningful results and empowering individuals at every level.

The chapter begins with *Don't Do Data Governance*, an intriguing title that challenges the conventional understanding of governance initiatives. This essay argues against the typical overcomplicated, one-size-fits-all approaches and instead advocates for tailored, practical strategies that integrate governance seamlessly into existing workflows. It's a rallying cry for rethinking how organizations approach governance to ensure it truly adds value.

"What Data Do We Have?" tackles one of the most fundamental questions organizations must ask. This essay emphasizes the importance of understanding the breadth and depth of an organization's data assets as a foundation for effective governance. Without clarity on what data exists, where it resides, and how it's used, governance efforts risk being misdirected or incomplete.

In *They Cannot All Be Critical: Governing CDEs*, the focus shifts to Critical Data Elements (CDEs) and how to prioritize them effectively. This essay provides guidance on distinguishing between data that's vital to the organization's mission and data that, while important, does not require the same level of governance attention. It's a practical roadmap for avoiding governance fatigue and ensuring that resources are directed where they matter most.

Measuring the Effectiveness of Data Governance Roles explores how to evaluate the performance and impact of governance roles across an organization. This essay outlines key metrics and strategies for assessing whether roles like data stewards, owners, and custodians are fulfilling their responsibilities effectively, ensuring accountability and driving improvements where needed.

Governance doesn't have to be boring, as *Make Data Governance Fun* demonstrates. This essay offers creative and engaging ways to bring energy and enthusiasm to governance initiatives, showing that fostering a positive culture around governance can significantly enhance participation and outcomes.

Communication's Crucial Role in Data Governance highlights the power of clear, consistent messaging in achieving governance success. This essay explains why communication is not just an operational necessity, but a strategic enabler that aligns stakeholders, reduces resistance, and fosters a shared understanding of governance goals.

Finally, *How to Make Data Governance More Memorable* focuses on strategies to embed governance principles into the organizational consciousness. From storytelling to visual aids, this essay provides actionable tips for ensuring governance remains top-of-mind and consistently applied across teams and departments.

Chapter 6 exemplifies the practical and empowering spirit of *Non-Invasive Data Governance Unleashed: Empowering People to Govern Data and AI*. It takes governance from theory to reality, equipping organizations with the tools and strategies they need to make governance a living, breathing part of their success story. Through these essays, the chapter offers a clear pathway to turning governance into a dynamic and indispensable asset.

Don't Do Data Governance

This is probably the last title you would expect for an essay that I write on data governance. Maybe the title should have read 'Don't "Do" Data Governance' instead. But that wouldn't have been as interesting of a hook to get you to read the essay.

There's something that grinds my gears every time I hear it: organizations saying they're "doing" data governance, "doing" data quality, or now, in the age of AI, "doing" artificial intelligence. What does that even mean? Seriously, we need to retire the verb "doing" when it comes to these critical disciplines. It's non-descript. It's lazy. And quite frankly, it demonstrates nothing about whether your organization is actually benefiting from your efforts. Saying you're "doing" AI is about as helpful as saying you're "doing" lunch. It doesn't describe the complexity, purpose, or impact of what's really going on—and it certainly doesn't imply success or mastery.

Let's take data governance (or even Non-Invasive Data Governance) as an example. "Doing" data governance? No, no, no. Data governance isn't something you *do*—it's something you establish, implement, and evolve. It's a program, a framework. It's an entire way of thinking and operating that needs to be baked into the culture of your organization. You don't just "do" it like you do laundry. If you're "doing" data governance, I'm guessing you've just got a checkbox on some project plan that says, "Yeah, we're good." But are you, really? Or are you just paying lip service to the concept without actually putting any formal structures or accountability in place?

The same goes for data quality. I've heard plenty of folks say, "Oh, we're doing data quality." Are you now? What does that even look like in practice? It sounds to me like you're just fiddling with some reports, cleaning up a few records, and calling it a day. Real data quality isn't a one-time action; it's a continuous process. It's a commitment to making sure the data feeding your systems is accurate, complete, and fit for purpose—every single day. You don't *do* data quality; you build systems that ensure quality, you establish rules and standards, and you create a culture that understands the importance of having reliable data. When you're serious about data quality, it's something that's embedded into the very fabric of your operations, not something you check off on a to-do list.

I'm also hearing more and more organizations proudly proclaiming that they're "doing AI" or "doing AI governance." Stop. Just stop. Artificial intelligence is not something you *do*; it's something you implement, integrate, and optimize. If all you're "doing" is playing around with an AI chatbot or setting up a machine learning model without a real strategy or governance plan, you're missing the boat. AI is a powerful tool that, when done right, can transform your business—but it's not just a checkbox or a buzzword to toss around in meetings.

If you're serious about AI governance, you're thinking about the ethical implications, the data flows, the biases in your models, and how to integrate AI in a way that supports your long-term goals. You're not "doing" AI governance just because you've read a couple of essays about it. You're implementing a formal program that guides how your organization leverages AI in a safe, effective, and compliant manner. You're putting rules in place, assigning accountability, and measuring outcomes. That's not "doing"—that's governing. That's leading.

In fact, none of these things—data governance, data quality, AI, or AI governance—should be lumped into the nebulous verb "doing." These are comprehensive, complex initiatives that require thoughtful planning, ongoing management, and executive buy-in. You can't just wake up one day and say, "Oh, look, we're doing data governance now!" No, you need a strategy, a framework, and a commitment to continuous improvement. You need clear roles and responsibilities, and you need metrics that tell you whether what you've implemented is actually working.

And that's another thing: implementation matters. Saying you're "doing" data governance or AI doesn't tell anybody anything about how well you've implemented these initiatives. Are you setting up policies? Are you defining roles? Are you ensuring that your data governance efforts align with your business objectives? Are you monitoring and refining your AI models to ensure they're delivering accurate, unbiased results? These are the questions that matter. Saying you're "doing" something just sweeps all that under the rug.

I think the use of "doing" here actually reflects a deeper problem. The leadership at too many organizations still sees these critical functions—data governance, data quality, and AI—as optional. They're things to "do" when you have time, or when the next audit is looming, or when someone in leadership says, "Hey, shouldn't we have some AI strategy?" But that's not how it works.

If you're serious about driving value from your data, you don't just "do" governance; you build it, you sustain it, and you lead with it.

So, if you're tempted to say you're "doing" any of these things, stop yourself. Ask instead:

Are we leading our organization with a formal data governance framework? Are we ensuring quality at every step of the data lifecycle? Are we implementing AI in a way that aligns with our goals and mitigates risks?

If you can't confidently answer those questions, you're not "doing" anything that will matter in the long run.

Conclusion

And remember, the next time someone tells you they're "doing" data governance, just smile and ask them, "Really? How's that going for you?" Because if they're only "doing" it, chances are it's not going as well as they think.

"What Data Do We Have?"

While organizations are swimming in a sea of information, one of the most fundamental questions remains: *What data do we have?* Understanding and managing your data is critical for leveraging it effectively, but many organizations struggle to answer this seemingly simple question. This is where deploying a comprehensive Data Asset Inventory comes into play. A Data Asset Inventory is not just a list of databases or tables; it's a structured and well-maintained catalog that details every piece of data your organization holds. This includes internal data, external data sources, reports, and any other data assets that play a role in your business operations. Accurately defining and cataloging your data assets lays the groundwork for informed decision-making, compliance, and business agility.

A Data Asset Inventory serves as the backbone of your organization's data management strategy, providing visibility into all data resources. Without a clear inventory, businesses risk data redundancy, inefficiencies, and compliance failures. The inventory not only helps in tracking data assets, but also plays a critical role in data governance and strategic planning. It enables better resource allocation and helps identify gaps in data coverage, ensuring that the organization can respond quickly to new business needs and regulatory changes. By knowing exactly what data is available, where it is stored, and how it is used, companies can more effectively manage and utilize their data, turning it into a valuable asset rather than a potential liability.

Defining a Data Asset

The first step in creating a Data Asset Inventory is clearly defining what constitutes a data asset. This is more complex than it might seem. A data asset is typically any piece of data that holds value to the organization and is used in the course of business. However, this definition can vary greatly depending on the context. For some organizations, a data asset might only include structured data in databases, while for others, it could also encompass unstructured data like emails, reports, and even externally sourced data. The key is to have a clear, organization-wide understanding of what qualifies as a data asset. This definition should be broad enough to capture all valuable information but specific enough to avoid overwhelming the inventory with irrelevant details. By establishing a clear definition, you ensure that all stakeholders are on the same page and that the inventory accurately reflects the data landscape of the organization.

Expanding the definition of data assets to include various types of data, such as external data sources, helps in building a more comprehensive inventory that reflects the true breadth of the organization's data environment. It is important to consider not only the data itself, but also the context in which it is used, such as the associated metadata, the relationships between different data sets, and the potential for data reuse across different departments or projects. This broader perspective ensures that the inventory captures the full scope of data assets, enabling better decision-making and more effective data governance. Additionally, by clearly defining what constitutes a data asset, organizations can establish better data management practices, ensuring that all valuable data is properly cataloged, secured, and utilized.

Process for Collecting Metadata

Once you have defined what constitutes a data asset, the next step is to develop a well-defined process for collecting metadata. Metadata is the information that describes the data assets, such as the source of the data, its format, its owner, its usage history, and its sensitivity level. A robust process for collecting metadata ensures that your Data Asset Inventory is comprehensive, accurate, and up to date. This process should involve identifying data owners and stewards who are responsible for documenting the metadata for each asset. Additionally, automation tools can be deployed to regularly scan and update metadata, reducing the risk of outdated information. The collection process should be standardized across the organization to ensure consistency and completeness. Investing in a meticulous metadata collection process creates a reliable foundation for your Data Asset Inventory, which in turn supports better data management and utilization.

Establishing a consistent and automated process for metadata collection not only improves accuracy but also significantly reduces the manual effort required to maintain the inventory. Automation can be implemented through data governance tools that continuously monitor data assets and update their metadata in real time, ensuring that the inventory remains current and reflects the organization's data landscape. Moreover, involving data stewards in the metadata collection process fosters a sense of ownership and accountability, encouraging better data management practices across the organization. This approach also allows for capturing more detailed and relevant metadata, such as data quality metrics and usage patterns, which are essential for advanced data governance and analytics initiatives.

Key Metadata for the Inventory

To make your Data Asset Inventory truly valuable, it's important to consider the types of metadata to include. This metadata goes beyond just the name and location of the data asset. It should include:

- **Data Asset Name**: A unique identifier or title that clearly represents the specific data asset within the organization.

- **Data Asset Description**: A detailed explanation that outlines the content, purpose, and relevance of the data asset in the context of the organization's operations.

- **Location**: The physical or digital storage location where the data asset is housed, including details such as database, server, cloud storage, or specific application.

- **Source Information**: Where the data comes from, whether internally generated or externally sourced.

- **Data Owner**: Who is responsible for the data, including who has the authority to make decisions about it.

- **Data Sensitivity**: The level of confidentiality and security required for the data.

- **Data Format**: The structure of the data, such as whether it's structured, unstructured, or semi-structured.

- **Usage and Access Patterns**: Information on how frequently the data is accessed and by whom.

- **Data Quality**: Metrics and records of data quality assessments, including completeness, accuracy, and timeliness.

- **Compliance and Legal Constraints**: Any regulations or policies that govern the data's use.

- **Relationships to Other Data**: How the data is related to or interacts with other data assets.

Including this comprehensive metadata not only helps in managing the data more effectively but also provides valuable insights into how the data is used and how it should be governed.

Including detailed metadata in the Data Asset Inventory supports a wide range of data management activities, from ensuring compliance with regulatory requirements to optimizing data usage across the organization. For example, understanding the sensitivity of data can inform access control decisions, while data quality metrics help identify areas where improvements are needed. Additionally, metadata about data relationships and usage patterns can drive more effective data integration and analytics, enabling the organization to extract greater value from its data assets. By maintaining a rich set of metadata, organizations can ensure that their data assets are not only well-managed, but also leveraged to their full potential, driving innovation and competitive advantage.

Presenting the Inventory through a Data Catalog

The true power of a Data Asset Inventory is unlocked when it is presented through a formal data catalog. A data catalog serves as the interface between the inventory and the end users, providing an accessible and searchable platform for finding and understanding data assets. Through a data catalog, business users can easily discover relevant data without needing to understand the technical intricacies of where or how the data is stored. This democratization of data access leads to more informed decision-making and fosters a data-driven culture within the organization. Additionally, a data catalog can integrate with other tools, such as data quality monitors and data governance frameworks, providing a holistic view of the organization's data health and compliance status. However, even without a formal data catalog, a well-maintained Data Asset Inventory can provide significant business value by offering a centralized repository of metadata that supports data governance, compliance, and risk management efforts.

Data catalogs enhance the usability of the Data Asset Inventory by providing advanced search capabilities, visualization tools, and integration with other data management systems. This makes it easier for users to find the data they need quickly and to understand the context in which the data is used, which is particularly important in complex, data-rich environments. Furthermore, data catalogs can support self-service analytics, allowing users to explore and analyze data independently while ensuring that they work with high-quality, governed data. By making the Data Asset Inventory accessible and user-friendly, organizations can encourage broader adoption of data-driven practices, leading to more effective decision-making and improved business outcomes.

Use Cases and Business Value

Deploying a Data Asset Inventory is not just a technical exercise; it directly impacts business value and operational efficiency. Here are some specific use cases where a Data Asset Inventory proves its worth:

- **Enhanced Decision-Making**: By providing easy access to a comprehensive catalog of data assets, decision-makers can quickly find the information they need to make informed choices. This reduces the time spent searching for data and increases the accuracy of decisions.

- **Compliance and Risk Management**: A well-documented inventory helps ensure that all data assets are accounted for and comply with relevant regulations. This is especially important in industries with stringent data privacy laws, like healthcare and finance.

- **Data Quality Improvement**: With clear ownership and regular monitoring, data quality issues can be identified and addressed more efficiently. This leads to more reliable data and better outcomes in analytics and reporting.

- **Operational Efficiency**: By reducing data silos and improving data accessibility, organizations can streamline operations and reduce redundancies. This leads to cost savings and a more agile business environment.

- **Support for AI and Machine Learning Initiatives**: A comprehensive inventory of data assets, complete with metadata, is crucial for training AI models. Knowing what data you have and its quality can accelerate the development and deployment of AI-driven solutions.

Importance of the Inventory to NIDG Efforts

A well-maintained Data Asset Inventory is integral to successfully implementing Non-Invasive Data Governance (NIDG) efforts. In the NIDG framework, the inventory serves as the foundation for understanding and managing an organization's data landscape without disrupting existing workflows. By cataloging all data assets, including their origins, usage, and governance status, organizations can ensure that data governance is seamlessly integrated into everyday operations. This alignment with NIDG principles enables organizations to implement governance policies effectively, monitor compliance, and maintain data quality without imposing burdensome processes on employees.

A Data Asset Inventory supports the nature of being non-invasive by providing transparency and clarity across the organization. It helps identify key data assets that require governance, thereby allowing for targeted interventions rather than a one-size-fits-all approach. This focus on critical data elements ensures that governance efforts are both efficient and effective, aligning with the NIDG goal of embedding governance practices naturally into existing processes. As a result, organizations can maintain high data management and governance standards while minimizing resistance and fostering a culture of accountability and responsibility.

Importance of the Inventory to AI and AI Governance

The Data Asset Inventory also plays an important role in an organization's AI and AI governance efforts. As organizations increasingly rely on AI to drive innovation and efficiency, the quality and comprehensiveness of the data used to train AI models become paramount. A well-maintained Data Asset Inventory ensures that all relevant data assets are accounted for and readily accessible, providing a solid foundation for AI development. Organizations can ensure that AI models are trained on reliable, high-quality data by cataloging data assets, including their quality, provenance, and usage history. This not only improves the accuracy and effectiveness of AI outcomes but also reduces the risk of bias or errors in AI decision-making processes. Moreover, a comprehensive Data Asset Inventory helps AI teams quickly identify and access the data they need, accelerating the development and deployment of AI solutions.

In addition to supporting AI development, a Data Asset Inventory is essential for AI governance. As AI systems become more complex and integrated into critical business processes, organizations must ensure that these systems operate ethically and transparently. A Data Asset Inventory provides the necessary oversight by documenting the sources, usage, and governance status of the data used in AI models. This enables organizations to track and audit AI decisions, ensuring that they comply with regulatory requirements and ethical standards. Furthermore, by linking the inventory to AI governance frameworks, organizations can establish clear guidelines for data usage in AI, such as avoiding sensitive or biased data. This proactive approach to AI governance not only mitigates risks but also builds trust in AI systems, ensuring they deliver value in a responsible and controlled manner.

Conclusion

Asking the question, "What data do we have?" is the first step toward unlocking the full potential of your organization's data assets. Deploying a Data Asset Inventory, supported by a clear definition of data assets, a robust process for metadata collection, and a thoughtful presentation through a data catalog, lays the foundation for better data management, compliance, and business value. This approach not only addresses the immediate needs of data governance but also positions the organization to leverage data as a strategic asset, driving innovation and growth.

They Cannot All Be Critical: Governing CDEs

Organizations face the challenge of identifying and governing the data that is truly critical to their operations. While labeling everything (or a lot) as critical might seem tempting, this approach can lead to inefficiencies and confusion. Instead, adopting a structured method for identifying and managing Critical Data Elements (CDEs) is essential.

Understanding Critical Data Elements

A Critical Data Element (CDE) is a data element deemed essential for the organization's key operations. These elements serve as the "connective tissue" or "grout between the tiles," holding the business processes and systems together. They are pivotal for decision-making, compliance, and operational efficiency. However, not all data can be equally critical, and treating it as such can dilute focus and resources.

CDEs are identified through a rigorous assessment of their impact on critical business processes and outcomes. These elements are carefully evaluated for their role in operational workflows, regulatory compliance, and strategic decision-making. The identification process often involves collaboration across departments to ensure that the most relevant and impactful data is recognized. By doing so, organizations can prioritize their governance efforts, ensuring that the highest quality and security standards are applied to the most vital data elements, thus enhancing overall operational efficiency and reducing risks associated with data mismanagement.

The Challenge of Identifying CDEs

When asked to identify critical data, business stakeholders often respond with lengthy lists, asserting that all (or at least a large amount) of the data that they use is critical. This broad-brush approach can lead to a lack of clarity and prioritization, making it difficult to manage data effectively. To address this, some organizations categorize their CDEs into levels of criticality—high, medium, and low. However, this often raises concerns among data stewards about the implications of "low criticality" data still being labeled as critical.

Categorizing CDEs into levels of criticality helps to streamline data management by prioritizing resources and efforts.

High-criticality CDEs are absolutely vital to the core operations, regulatory compliance, and strategic initiatives of the organization. Medium-criticality CDEs, while important, may not require the same level of stringent controls but still play a significant role in supporting essential functions. Low-criticality CDEs, though still labeled as critical, typically involve data that is less frequently accessed or has less direct impact on high-level decision-making. This classification enables organizations to allocate resources efficiently, ensuring that the most critical data receives the highest level of governance while still maintaining appropriate oversight of all identified CDEs.

The CDE Class System: A Better Approach

A more effective way to manage CDEs is by using a Class System. This method categorizes data into three distinct classes, each with its own level of governance and monitoring:

Class 1: Most Highly Governed and Monitored—Class 1 CDEs are the most crucial. These data elements are subject to stringent governance and continuous monitoring due to their significant impact on business operations. They require the highest level of data quality, security, and compliance controls.

- Regular audits and assessments to ensure compliance and quality.
- Strict access controls to maintain data security.
- Continuous monitoring for any changes or anomalies.
- Frequent data quality checks and validation processes.
- Detailed metadata documentation to track data lineage and usage.

Class 2: Governed—Class 2 CDEs are important but do not require the same level of oversight as Class 1 elements. These data elements are governed to ensure they meet necessary standards, but the monitoring is less intensive. They are still essential for business processes but have a slightly lower impact than Class 1 CDEs.

- Periodic reviews to ensure data standards are met.
- Access controls appropriate to the data's sensitivity.
- Scheduled monitoring to identify any significant changes.
- Regular data quality checks, though less frequent than Class 1.
- Metadata maintenance to ensure data context and usage are recorded.

Class 3: Recognized Ownership and Metadata Collection—Class 3 CDEs are recognized for their importance, with designated ownership and stewardship. Metadata about these elements is collected and maintained, but they are not subject to the same rigorous governance as Class 1 or Class 2 CDEs. This classification helps in acknowledging their relevance without overburdening the governance framework.

- Recognizing ownership to ensure formal accountability.
- Collecting and maintaining metadata to provide context.
- Basic access controls to manage data usage.
- Occasional reviews to update and validate metadata.
- Awareness programs to ensure all stakeholders recognize the importance of these data elements.

Using this Class System, organizations can efficiently allocate resources, ensuring the most critical data elements receive the attention they need while still maintaining oversight of all CDEs. This approach provides a balanced framework that enhances data governance without overwhelming the organization.

Using the Class System to Focus Governance

Implementing the Class System brings clarity and precision to data governance efforts, enabling organizations to focus resources on the data elements that require the highest level of oversight. By categorizing data into Class 1, Class 2, and Class 3, stakeholders can clearly understand which data elements are the most critical and thus warrant stringent governance protocols. This method helps prevent the dilution of governance efforts by ensuring that not all data is treated equally, but rather according to its importance and impact on business operations.

Additionally, the CDE Class System aids in managing and limiting the scope of data governance by prioritizing high-impact data elements. Class 1 CDEs, which have the most significant impact on business functions and compliance, receive the most intensive governance measures. Class 2 CDEs, while still important, are governed with a slightly reduced level of oversight. Class 3 CDEs are recognized for their importance, with basic governance practices and metadata collection in place. This approach helps data stewards and stakeholders understand that not all critical data needs to be governed in the same way, allowing for more efficient allocation of governance resources and ensuring that the most crucial data elements are managed with the highest standards.

Benefits of the Class System

Adopting a Class System for managing Critical Data Elements (CDEs) offers numerous advantages, streamlining governance efforts and ensuring that resources are allocated effectively. This approach provides a structured way to prioritize data governance, enhance stewardship, and optimize resource utilization across the organization.

By classifying CDEs into different levels of criticality, organizations can tailor their governance practices to meet specific needs, ensuring that the most vital data elements receive the attention they deserve. Here are some key benefits of the Class System:

- **Clarity and Prioritization**: The Class System helps clearly define the importance of each data element, ensuring that resources are allocated effectively.

- **Focused Governance**: By differentiating the levels of governance required, organizations can ensure that the most critical data elements receive the attention they need.

- **Improved Stewardship**: Recognizing and documenting the ownership and metadata of all CDEs, even at the lowest level, enhances accountability and traceability.

- **Resource Optimization**: Allocating governance efforts according to the class of data helps optimize resources and avoid the pitfalls of treating all data as equally critical.

Implementing the Class System

To implement the Class System effectively, organizations should follow a structured approach. This process involves several critical steps to ensure that each data element is appropriately managed according to its level of importance. Organizations can enhance data quality, compliance, and operational efficiency by systematically identifying, classifying, and governing Critical Data Elements (CDEs). Here are the key steps for implementing the Class System:

- **Identify and Catalog CDEs**: Start by identifying all potential CDEs within the organization. Engage stakeholders from different departments to ensure a comprehensive list.

- **Classify CDEs**: Evaluate each CDE based on its impact on business operations, compliance requirements, and risk factors. Assign each data element to the appropriate class.

- **Define Governance Protocols**: Establish clear governance protocols for each class. Specify the monitoring, quality controls, and compliance measures required for Class 1, Class 2, and Class 3 CDEs.

- **Assign Ownership**: Designate data stewards for each CDE, ensuring accountability and proper management.

- **Monitor and Review**: Continuously monitor the CDEs according to their class-specific protocols. Regularly review and adjust classifications and governance measures as needed.

Conclusion

Governing data by identifying and classifying Critical Data Elements (CDEs) is essential for maintaining data quality, security, and compliance. The Class System offers a structured approach to managing CDEs, ensuring that the most critical data elements receive the necessary attention while optimizing resources. By implementing this system, organizations can enhance their data governance practices and ensure they are well-prepared to effectively leverage their data assets.

In conclusion, while everything might seem critical, adopting a structured approach like the Class System can bring clarity, efficiency, and effectiveness to data governance efforts. It ensures that truly critical data is managed with the rigor it deserves, paving the way for better decision-making and operational success.

Measuring the Effectiveness of Data Governance Roles

In every one of my data governance implementation projects, measuring the effectiveness of roles across various levels of the organization has been as intricate as the data landscapes these roles aim to manage. From the executive heights of the Steering Committee down to the operational depths where individual Data Stewards work, the Non-Invasive Data Governance (NIDG) approach provides a practical path for evaluating performance in a structured and minimally disruptive manner. This essay explores strategies for assessing the impact of the data governance operating model and the governance roles across different organizational tiers, using the principles of NIDG as a framework.

Executive Level

At the executive level, the Steering Committee plays a pivotal role in setting the direction and priorities for data governance initiatives. Measuring the effectiveness of this group involves evaluating how well its directives align with overall business objectives and the extent to which these directives are realized across the organization. Key performance indicators (KPIs) might include successfully implementing strategic data governance policies, achieving compliance targets, and improving enterprise-wide data quality metrics. The NIDG approach emphasizes the importance of leveraging existing leadership and decision-making structures, suggesting that the effectiveness of the Steering Committee can also be assessed by its ability to integrate data governance seamlessly into the broader business strategy without significant upheaval.

To further gauge the effectiveness of the executive level's engagement in data governance, organizations can look at the Steering Committee's influence on creating a culture of data awareness and literacy throughout the enterprise. Measure this by tracking the proliferation of data governance training programs, the engagement level of employees in data-related initiatives, and the degree to which data governance principles are embedded in daily operations.

The Steering Committee's ability to foster collaboration between different departments and ensure that data governance initiatives receive the necessary resources and support can serve as a crucial indicator of their effectiveness. The impact of their leadership on overcoming data silos and encouraging a unified approach to data management across the organization further reflects their role's success under the Non-Invasive Data Governance framework.

Strategic Level

Moving to the strategic level, the Data Governance Council is tasked with translating executive directives into actionable strategies. Measure the effectiveness of this council by its ability to foster cross-departmental collaboration and to develop governance frameworks that are both comprehensive and adaptable. Metrics here could include the number of strategic data governance initiatives launched, the degree of participation across departments, and the timeliness and relevance of the data governance policies and standards it develops. Under the NIDG approach, the council's success is also marked by its ability to engage with existing organizational structures and encourage a shared Data Stewardship culture.

The impact of the Data Governance Council on the organization's overall data maturity can provide deeper insights into its effectiveness. Assess this by observing improvements in data management practices, such as data quality, data integration, and data sharing capabilities, before and after implementing the council's strategies. The council's ability to identify and address emerging data governance challenges, adapt to regulatory changes, and incorporate feedback from data users and stewards into governance practices further exemplifies its effectiveness. The strategic level's success under the Non-Invasive Data Governance approach is not just in setting policies but in catalyzing real, measurable improvements in how data is valued, managed, and utilized across the organization.

Tactical Level

At the tactical level, cross-business function Data Domain Stewards are critical for bridging the gap between strategic plans and operational execution. Measure their effectiveness through specific domain-related outcomes, such as improvements in data quality within their domains, the successful resolution of data issues, and the advancement of domain-specific data governance goals. The NIDG framework places importance on recognizing and formalizing these roles within existing job functions, suggesting that effectiveness can also be gauged by the extent to which data governance responsibilities are integrated into regular workflows and by the level of domain-specific data governance expertise developed.

To further assess the effectiveness of Data Domain Stewards at the tactical level, organizations can examine the extent of collaboration and communication facilitated by these stewards among different departments. This includes their ability to act as liaisons, ensuring that data governance policies are understood and implemented consistently across the organization. Another critical metric for measuring their effectiveness is the speed and efficiency with which data-related queries and issues are addressed, demonstrating their role in maintaining the organization's data agility.

The contribution of domain stewards to fostering a data-informed culture within their domains—evidenced by increased use of data in decision-making and greater engagement in data governance activities—also serves as a testament to their effectiveness. Through these measures, the essential role of Data Domain Stewards in operationalizing data governance strategies and achieving tangible outcomes is further underscored.

Operational Level

On the ground, at the operational level, stewards of data within business functions are the front-line workers in the data governance framework. Their effectiveness can be directly measured by observing improvements in the day-to-day handling of data, such as enhanced data accuracy, accessibility, and compliance within their respective functions. Additionally, under the NIDG approach, integrating data governance tasks into daily activities without causing disruption is a key indicator of success, alongside the active participation in and contribution to wider data governance initiatives.

Expanding on these measures of effectiveness, another vital aspect to consider is the feedback from end-users and stakeholders regarding the quality and utility of data managed by these stewards. Customer satisfaction surveys, internal feedback mechanisms, and the reduction in data-related complaints can offer tangible evidence of the operational level's performance.

Assess the operational level's effectiveness through metrics such as the reduction in time spent on data-related issues, increased efficiency in data processing and reporting tasks, and the level of adherence to data standards and policies over time. These indicators not only reflect the stewards' competency in executing data governance tasks, but also their role in enhancing the overall data culture within their spheres of influence, showcasing the practical impact of their contributions to the organization's data governance objectives.

Support Level

Finally, at the support level, including program administration, program partners, and working teams, effectiveness is measured by the support infrastructure's ability to facilitate the work of Data Stewards at all levels, ensure adherence to data governance policies, and provide ongoing education and resources related to data governance. Here, metrics might encompass the efficiency of support processes, the level of engagement in data governance training programs, and the quality of support provided to data governance bodies. The NIDG principle of leveraging existing roles and resources suggests evaluating how well these support functions are integrated into the organizational fabric and their impact on promoting a non-invasive yet effective data governance culture.

To explore deeper into measuring the effectiveness of the support level, one can also look at the quantifiable outcomes of their efforts, such as the reduction in data incidents (breaches, leaks, or quality issues) due to improved governance practices, or the increased number of successful data projects and initiatives supported by these teams. Another significant measure is the speed and effectiveness with which data governance policies and procedures are updated and communicated across the organization, reflecting the support level's agility and responsiveness.

The extent to which these teams can foster a sense of ownership and accountability among all employees regarding data governance, turning passive participants into active Data Stewards, further underscores their effectiveness. Such outcomes not only highlight the critical role of support teams in sustaining and enhancing data governance frameworks, but also their ability to adapt and respond to the evolving data landscape within the organization.

Conclusion

The journey of measuring the effectiveness of data governance roles from the executive to the support level unveils the multifaceted nature of data governance within organizations. Through the lens of the Non-Invasive Data Governance (NIDG) framework, this exploration underscores the importance of aligning data governance initiatives with overarching business objectives, fostering cross-departmental collaboration, and embedding data governance into the fabric of daily operations. The effectiveness of data governance roles is not merely about adherence to policies or the implementation of technology; it's about creating a culture where data is recognized as a valuable asset and managed with the care and strategic foresight it deserves. Each level of the data governance hierarchy plays a pivotal role in achieving this aim, with measures of effectiveness evolving from strategic alignment at the executive level to operational excellence and support infrastructure efficiency.

As organizations strive to navigate the complex data landscapes of the modern business world, the insights gleaned from measuring the effectiveness of data governance roles offer a roadmap for continuous improvement. The NIDG approach, with its emphasis on leveraging existing structures and roles, provides a practical framework for embedding data governance into the organization's DNA. By doing so, businesses can unlock the full potential of their data, driving better decision-making, enhancing operational efficiency, and ensuring regulatory compliance. Ultimately, the success of data governance lies in its ability to transform data into a strategic asset that propels the organization forward, guided by the skilled hands of those who steward its journey from the executive level to the trenches of daily operation.

Make Data Governance Fun

Around the beginning of 2023, I wrote a series of essays with Alation, including one titled *What Does It Mean to Make Data Governance Fun?* The essays were well received. I continue to consider ways to make data governance attractive and interesting to people within the organization, including making data governance more memorable by using decorative analogies of stewards as gardeners and domains as grocery stores. But I keep coming back to trying to make data governance "engaging" (let's not say "fun" this time) for people throughout an organization.

The intersection of "fun" and "data governance" might seem like an unlikely pairing at first glance. After all, the latter conjures up images of strict rules, invasive processes, and the stern enforcement of data policies. However, in a world increasingly driven by data, the need for robust data governance cannot be overstated—and neither can the potential for making it an engaging, even enjoyable, part of organizational culture. Enter Non-Invasive Data Governance (NIDG), which promises not just to demystify, but also to democratize data governance, making it a less daunting and more user-friendly endeavor.

Embracing Non-Invasive Data Governance

NIDG operates on the principle of leveraging existing roles, responsibilities, and processes to govern data, rather than imposing new, rigid structures. This approach naturally aligns with how organizations already function, making adopting data governance practices feel less like an imposition and more like a natural extension of current operations. It's the difference between crafting a new language from scratch and adopting a few new phrases into your vocabulary—the latter is undoubtedly more accessible and fun.

Is Making Data Governance Fun a Real Possibility?

Making data governance fun is not only a real possibility, but also an effective strategy to enhance engagement and compliance across an organization. By infusing traditionally dry and technical data governance processes with elements of gamification, storytelling, interactive learning, and community building, organizations can transform how stakeholders perceive and participate in data governance. These methods not only make the concepts more accessible and enjoyable, but also encourage a culture of collaboration and innovation. Incorporating fun into data governance can lead to higher levels of participation, improved data quality, and a more cohesive approach to managing an organization's data assets.

Let's explore some innovative ways to inject fun into your data governance initiatives, making them more appealing and effective for everyone involved.

Gamification

Introducing game mechanics into data governance can transform mundane tasks into exciting challenges. Leaderboards, point systems, and achievement badges motivate and provide tangible recognition of contributions to data quality and integrity. By gamifying data stewardship tasks, organizations can foster a competitive yet collaborative environment that celebrates progress and mastery in data governance.

Implementing a gamification strategy requires thoughtful planning and alignment with organizational goals to ensure that it effectively engages participants and reinforces the desired outcomes of the data governance program. Consider customizing challenges and rewards to match the unique context of your organization and its data governance objectives. This could involve creating themed challenges that address specific governance issues or celebrating milestones related to data cleanup efforts. The key is to make these activities relevant and rewarding, encouraging ongoing participation and making data governance an integral, enjoyable part of the organizational culture.

Storytelling and Relatable Analogies

Complex data concepts become more digestible and memorable when told as stories or illustrated through familiar analogies. Drawing parallels between data governance and everyday experiences, like the organization of a library or the rules of a sport, can illuminate the value and necessity of well-governed data. These narratives make the abstract concrete, bridging the gap between esoteric data principles and the practical realities of organizational life.

Integrating storytelling and analogies into the Non-Invasive Data Governance Framework helps to demystify governance activities and responsibilities. For example, explaining data quality in terms of a communal garden where everyone plays a part in weeding, planting, and harvesting can vividly illustrate the collective effort required for data governance success. Such stories engage and empower employees by showing how their roles and actions contribute to the overall data ecosystem, fostering a deeper connection to the governance objectives and a more vibrant, participative culture around data governance initiatives.

Celebrating Successes

Recognizing achievements in data governance, both big and small, fuels a culture of appreciation and motivation. Celebratory events, shout-outs in company newsletters, or even simple thank-you notes can significantly boost morale and underscore the importance of everyone's role in maintaining data quality. When people see the impact of their contributions, their engagement and enthusiasm for data governance naturally increase.

Incorporating Non-Invasive Data Governance into these celebrations emphasizes the value of integrating data governance seamlessly into everyday work without adding extra layers of complexity. Highlighting stories where employees have successfully adopted NIDG principles to enhance data quality or efficiency demonstrates practical applications and benefits, making the concepts more tangible. For example, showcasing a department that streamlined data access while respecting privacy and security protocols under NIDG can inspire others. These acknowledgments not only celebrate the success but also reinforce the non-invasive approach as a viable and beneficial strategy for data governance, encouraging ongoing participation and innovation in the program.

Interactive Learning Experiences

Replace the traditional, didactic training sessions with interactive workshops, role-playing games, and simulation exercises. Such active learning experiences not only make the absorption of data governance principles more enjoyable, but also more effective. Participants can experiment with data governance scenarios in a low-risk setting, fostering a deeper understanding and appreciation for the practices and principles of NIDG.

Incorporating Non-Invasive Data Governance into interactive learning experiences allows for a practical exploration of how non-invasive principles apply in real organizational contexts. For example, a workshop might simulate a data quality improvement project where teams must navigate through the organization's existing roles and responsibilities to enhance data accuracy without disrupting daily operations. This hands-on approach encourages participants to think critically about applying NIDG principles to their work, promoting a proactive and engaged approach to data governance. These sessions not only educate but also build a sense of camaraderie and shared purpose among participants, further embedding the culture of data governance within the organization.

Fostering a Community of Practice

Creating a physical or digital space for data stewards and governance professionals to share insights, challenges, and successes builds a sense of camaraderie and collective purpose. This community becomes a source of support, inspiration, and innovation, driving home the idea that data governance is a shared responsibility and a shared benefit.

Integrating the principles of Non-Invasive Data Governance into this community of practice enhances its effectiveness by promoting the notion that data governance should work within the natural flow of the organization's operations. By sharing stories and strategies that align with NIDG's approach, such as how data stewards have successfully engaged with their peers without formal authority or how subtle changes in data handling processes have led to significant improvements, members can see practical examples of non-invasive principles in action. This bolsters the community's knowledge base and encourages members to think creatively about applying these principles in their areas, further solidifying the community's role as a cornerstone of the organization's data governance framework.

Conclusion

Integrating the core concepts of Non-Invasive Data Governance into an organization's data management strategies makes data governance not just more efficient but opens the door to making it a more engaging, rewarding, and fun part of organizational life. By adopting strategies that emphasize the human aspect of data governance, we can transform it from a dreaded task into an integral part of our corporate culture that people are not only willing to engage with but are excited to be a part of. In doing so, we not only enhance our data governance outcomes, but also foster a more informed, data-savvy, and collaborative workforce.

Communication's Crucial Role in Data Governance

The adoption of effective governance practices has become a strategic imperative for organizations seeking to harness the full potential of their data assets. This journey towards robust data governance is multifaceted and the communications that are necessary comprise three integral phases: Orientation Communications, Onboarding, and Ongoing Communications. Each phase plays a distinct role in shaping a comprehensive and Non-Invasive Data Governance (NIDG) program.

The initial phase, labeled **Orientation Communications** in the non-invasive approach, sets the tone, building awareness and fostering a cultural shift towards a data-centric mindset. It not only introduces stakeholders to the fundamental principles of data governance and the non-invasive approach but also lays the groundwork for a collaborative and informed journey towards effective data management.

The narrative advances to **Onboarding Communications**, a critical juncture where individuals transition from awareness to active participation in their designated data governance roles. Tailored communications become the compass guiding executives, strategic stakeholders, tactical and operational teams, as well as support functions into a nuanced understanding of their roles. Clarity in defining roles and responsibilities, bridging the gap between strategic objectives and day-to-day execution, and continuous support mechanisms are the hallmarks of this phase, ensuring a seamless integration into the evolving governance landscape.

As the data governance program gains momentum, **Ongoing Communications** emerge as the vital threads weaving a dynamic narrative throughout its lifecycle. Regular updates, acknowledgments of achievements, continuous training opportunities, and transparent discussions around challenges collectively contribute to a thriving governance culture. This ongoing dialogue sustains stakeholder engagement, fosters a sense of community, and showcases the tangible impact of the program. Together, these three phases form a symphony, harmonizing awareness, action, and continuous growth, ultimately positioning data governance as a strategic asset for organizational success.

The rest of this essay focuses on providing additional details about the three phases of Non-Invasive Data Governance communications.

Orientation Communications

Building a strong foundation for Non-Invasive Data Governance begins with orientation communications. This phase can be considered the initial notes of a symphony, setting the tone for what lies ahead. Awareness of data governance, its significance, and the inherent value it brings to the organization is critical. Orientation communications should not merely convey the existence of a data governance program; rather, they must articulate its relevance in driving informed decision-making, ensuring data quality, and navigating regulatory landscapes.

During this phase, stakeholders at all levels, from executives to support teams, should be introduced to the fundamental principles of data governance. Clear and compelling messaging is crucial to instill a sense of ownership and shared responsibility for data assets. This involves demystifying the technical jargon and illustrating how each individual's role contributes to the broader Non-Invasive Data Governance framework:

- **Setting the Stage:** Orientation communications serve as the inaugural act in the data governance master work, capturing the attention of stakeholders and providing a compelling introduction to the program. To effectively set the stage, organizations need to articulate the purpose, goals, and potential impact of the data governance initiative. This involves crafting a narrative that resonates with the broader organizational objectives and demonstrates how data governance is not merely a procedural addition but a strategic enabler.

- **Defining Data Governance:** The orientation phase is an opportune moment to demystify the concept of data governance. Communications should distill complex governance frameworks into accessible language, emphasizing that it is not an exclusive domain of IT but a collective responsibility spanning all departments. Illustrating real-world scenarios and success stories helps individuals grasp the tangible benefits of effective data governance in their daily workflows.

- **Showcasing Relevance:** Understanding the relevance of data governance to individual roles is crucial for fostering engagement. Orientation communications should explicitly address the 'What's In It

For Me' (WIIFM) question for each stakeholder group. Executives may see improved strategic decision-making, while operational teams may experience streamlined processes and enhanced data quality. The messaging should underscore that data governance is not an additional burden but a catalyst for efficiency and innovation.

- **Introducing Key Concepts:** This phase is an opportunity to introduce key concepts and terminology associated with data governance. Clear definitions of terms like data stewardship, metadata management, and data quality provide a common language for all stakeholders. Visual aids, infographics, and interactive sessions can enhance comprehension and retention, ensuring that everyone is on the same page as they embark on the governance journey.

- **Cultivating a Cultural Shift:** Orientation communications play a pivotal role in initiating a cultural shift towards a data-centric mindset. This involves challenging existing perceptions and instilling a sense of shared responsibility for the organization's data assets. Emphasizing that data is not just a byproduct but a strategic asset encourages a proactive rather than reactive approach to data management.

- **Establishing Communication Channels:** An effective orientation strategy includes establishing communication channels for ongoing engagement. Whether through town hall meetings, newsletters, or dedicated online platforms, these channels should serve as a two-way street, allowing stakeholders to seek clarification, share insights, and actively participate in the evolving data governance narrative.

- **Interactive Training:** Supplementing traditional communications with interactive training sessions can solidify understanding. Workshops, webinars, or e-learning modules tailored to different stakeholder groups provide a hands-on experience, allowing individuals to navigate through the practical aspects of data governance in a simulated environment.

- **Emphasizing Compliance and Regulatory Considerations:** For industries subject to regulatory frameworks, orientation communications should stress the role of data governance in ensuring compliance. Clearly articulating how governance practices align with industry regulations and safeguard against potential risks creates a sense of urgency and importance, particularly for executives and those in compliance-related roles.

- **Celebrating Early Wins:** Orientation communications should not solely focus on the future but acknowledge and celebrate any early wins or successes associated with data governance. Recognizing and showcasing quick wins helps build confidence and demonstrates the tangible impact of the program, reinforcing the value proposition outlined during the orientation phase.

- **Feedback Mechanisms:** Closing the orientation phase involves establishing feedback mechanisms. Encouraging stakeholders to share their thoughts, concerns, and expectations creates a sense of inclusivity. Feedback loops also provide insights into the effectiveness of orientation communications, allowing for iterative improvements as the data governance program unfolds.

Orientation Communications lays the groundwork for a successful NIDG program by introducing stakeholders to the strategic importance of data governance, cultivating a cultural shift, and providing the necessary tools for engagement and understanding. This phase is the overture, setting the tempo for a collaborative and informed journey toward effective data management.

Onboarding Communications

Onboarding communications mark the transition from awareness to action, as individuals step into their designated Non-Invasive Data Governance roles. Tailor the onboarding communications to different levels of the organization: Executive, Strategic, Tactical, Operational, and Support. Executives need to understand how data governance aligns with strategic objectives, while those at the operational level require guidance on specific data management practices within their functions.

Executive onboarding communications should emphasize the strategic advantages of data governance, linking it directly to business goals. Strategic onboarding should provide a deeper understanding of the governance framework and its implications for decision-making. Tactical onboarding should focus on cross-business function collaboration, and operational onboarding must delve into the specific data management procedures relevant to each department. Support onboarding partners, IT, working teams, and program administration to necessitate clear communication on their unique roles in sustaining the governance ecosystem.

The onboarding process is not a one-size-fits-all; hence, communications should be tailored, engaging, and interactive. This ensures that individuals comprehend not only the technical aspects, but also the cultural shift toward a data-centric mindset:

- **Tailored Messaging for Different Levels:** Onboarding communications mark the transition from awareness to action, guiding individuals into their designated roles within the NIDG framework. Tailoring messages to different organizational levels is essential. Executive onboarding should articulate how data governance aligns with strategic objectives and the overarching vision. Strategic onboarding should provide a deeper understanding of the governance framework and its implications for decision-making. Tactical onboarding should focus on cross-business function collaboration, and operational onboarding must delve into specific data management procedures relevant to each department.

- **Defining Roles and Responsibilities:** Clarity in roles and responsibilities is paramount during onboarding. Communications should provide a detailed overview of what each role entails, emphasizing how individual contributions fit into the broader data governance landscape. This involves clearly defining data stewardship responsibilities, outlining the role of data custodians, and explaining the collaborative nature of governance efforts.

- **Bridging the Gap Between Strategy and Execution:** Onboarding communications play a crucial role in bridging the gap between strategic objectives and day-to-day execution. Executives need to understand how their decisions impact the broader data governance ecosystem, while those at the operational level require guidance on translating high-level strategies into actionable tasks. Strategic onboarding should focus on linking strategic goals to tangible data governance practices, ensuring a seamless alignment between vision and execution.

- **Hands-On Training:** Supplementing theoretical knowledge with hands-on training enhances the onboarding process. Interactive workshops, simulated scenarios, and practical exercises provide individuals with the skills and confidence to execute their data governance responsibilities effectively. This approach is particularly beneficial for tactical and operational onboarding, where practical application is paramount.

- **Communication of Expectations:** Onboarding communications should clearly communicate expectations for each role. This involves outlining performance metrics, deliverables, and key milestones associated with data governance. Transparency in expectations helps individuals understand their responsibilities and establishes a benchmark for success, facilitating ongoing performance assessments.

- **Fostering a Collaborative Culture:** Emphasizing the collaborative nature of NIDG is crucial during onboarding. Communications should highlight how different roles intersect and rely on each other for successful data management. This collaborative culture should be embedded in the communication strategy, fostering a sense of shared responsibility and encouraging cross-functional teamwork.

- **Continuous Support Mechanisms:** Onboarding is not a one-time event but a phased process. Communications should emphasize the availability of continuous support mechanisms, such as mentorship programs, knowledge-sharing forums, and access to resources. This ensures that individuals feel supported as they navigate their roles within the evolving NIDG landscape.

- **Customized Communications for Support Teams:** Onboarding communications for support teams, including partners, IT, working teams, and program administration, should be customized to reflect the unique contributions of each group. Clear communication on how these support functions integrate with core data governance activities ensures a cohesive and well-coordinated governance ecosystem.

- **Celebrating Onboarding Milestones:** Recognizing and celebrating onboarding milestones is crucial for maintaining momentum. Whether it's acknowledging the successful completion of training modules or the successful execution of initial data governance tasks, these celebrations reinforce the value of each individual's contributions and motivate ongoing engagement.

- **Feedback Channels:** Establishing feedback channels during onboarding is vital for continuous improvement. Encouraging new participants to share their experiences, ask questions, and provide insights creates a culture of open communication. This feedback loop informs the refinement of onboarding processes for future participants.

Onboarding Communications are the compass that guides individuals into their roles within the NIDG program. Tailored messaging, hands-on training, clear expectations, and ongoing support mechanisms ensure a smooth transition from awareness to active participation, setting the stage for a collaborative and effective data governance journey.

Ongoing Communications

The Non-Invasive Data Governance journey is dynamic, marked by continuous growth, adaptations, and achievements. Ongoing communications are the threads that weave the fabric of a thriving data governance program. Regular updates on program status, milestones achieved, and upcoming objectives are vital to sustaining enthusiasm and commitment.

Executives benefit from high-level insights into the program's impact on strategic goals, while strategic stakeholders appreciate progress reports aligned with their specific objectives. Tactical and operational teams should receive communications that resonate with their daily data management challenges, showcasing how NIDG addresses these issues. Support teams require updates on the collaborative efforts and outcomes achieved through their contributions.

These communications should not be mere broadcasts but should encourage feedback and participation. Establishing open channels for dialogue and forums for sharing success stories, and addressing challenges fosters a sense of community within the NIDG framework:

- **Status Updates and Milestones:** Ongoing communications serve as the lifeblood of a successful data governance program, providing stakeholders with regular status updates and highlighting key milestones. These updates should be tailored to different audience segments, ensuring that executives receive strategic insights while operational teams are informed about specific achievements and challenges. Clear and concise reporting helps maintain visibility and reinforces the program's progress.

- **Program Updates and Evolution:** Regular communications should articulate the evolution of the data governance program. This involves outlining any adjustments to the governance framework, changes in processes, or the introduction of new tools and metrics. Keeping stakeholders informed about the program's dynamic nature fosters transparency and ensures that individuals are aligned with the latest strategies and methodologies.

- **Recognition and Acknowledgment:** Ongoing communications should include a mechanism for recognizing and acknowledging individual and team contributions. Whether through newsletters, announcements, or dedicated recognition events, celebrating successes fosters a positive culture and motivates continued engagement. Tie recognition to achieving specific data quality improvements, successful completion of projects, or innovative contributions to the governance framework.

- **Continuous Training Opportunities:** To keep stakeholders abreast of emerging trends, tools, and best practices, ongoing communications should highlight continuous training opportunities. This can include webinars, workshops, or access to educational resources. Continuous learning ensures that individuals remain equipped with the latest skills and knowledge, contributing to the overall efficacy of the data governance program.

- **Addressing Challenges and Providing Solutions:** Transparently addressing challenges and presenting viable solutions is crucial in ongoing communications. This includes addressing data quality issues, security concerns, or any obstacles encountered during the governance journey. Open communication about challenges fosters a culture of problem-solving and encourages stakeholders to collaborate on finding effective solutions.

- **Feedback Loops:** Establishing robust feedback loops is an ongoing commitment in a data governance program. Regularly seeking input from stakeholders regarding their experiences, challenges, and suggestions creates a two-way communication channel. This iterative feedback process helps refine governance strategies, ensuring that the program remains responsive to the evolving needs of the organization.

- **Community Building:** Ongoing communications should contribute to community building within the data governance ecosystem. This involves facilitating online and offline forums where stakeholders can exchange ideas, share insights, and collaborate on common challenges. Community building fosters a sense of belonging and collective ownership of the data governance program.

- **Regular Audits and Assessments:** Communications should inform stakeholders about upcoming data audits and assessments. This involves outlining the purpose, scope, and expected outcomes of such evaluations. Regular audits contribute to the continuous improvement of data quality, adherence to governance policies, and the program's overall effectiveness.

- **Flexible Communication Channels:** Ongoing communications should leverage a variety of flexible channels, considering the diverse preferences of stakeholders. This includes traditional methods such as newsletters and emails, as well as more interactive platforms like webinars, discussion forums, and collaborative workspaces. A multi-channel approach ensures that communications are accessible and engaging for all participants.

- **Demonstrating Return on Investment (ROI):** To reinforce the value of the data governance program, ongoing communications should provide tangible evidence of its impact on the organization's bottom line. This may involve showcasing improvements in data quality, cost savings due to streamlined processes, or enhanced decision-making capabilities. Demonstrating ROI helps sustain stakeholder support and justifies ongoing investments in the program.

Ongoing Communications are the vital thread that weaves the narrative of the Non-Invasive Data Governance program throughout its lifecycle. Regular updates, recognition, continuous learning opportunities, and a commitment to addressing challenges contribute to a thriving and dynamic governance culture, ensuring that the program remains a strategic asset for the organization.

Conclusion

A Non-Invasive Data Governance program's communications plan is essential, unfolding in three phases: Orientation, Onboarding, and Ongoing Communications:

- The **Orientation** phase introduces and builds awareness about data governance, tailoring messages across organizational levels to foster a data-centric culture and celebrate initial achievements.

- The **Onboarding** phase transitions individuals into their specific roles within data governance, emphasizing the strategic importance for executives, operational procedures for teams, and unique contributions of support roles, alongside hands-on training and collaboration to ensure a seamless integration.

- Lastly, **Ongoing Communications** maintains the program's vitality by delivering regular updates, recognizing contributions, offering training, and establishing feedback mechanisms to highlight the program's evolving impact, ensuring data governance continues to be a strategic asset across the organization.

Address all three of these phases of communication (often simultaneously) as you progress through your program's definition, delivery, expansion, and maintenance lifecycle.

How to Make Data Governance More Memorable

Making the principles and practices of your Data Governance program stick in the minds of people in your organization can be a daunting task. Yet, the importance of data governance in today's data-driven environment cannot be overstated. Data Governance ensures that data is accurate, accessible, and protected, leading to better decision-making and compliance with regulations. The theory and practice around Non-Invasive Data Governance (NIDG), my favorite topic, provides an effective and engaging framework while providing valuable opportunities to make your program memorable.

The challenge of making your program memorable lies not only in understanding the technicalities of data governance, but also in embedding its values and practices into the organizational culture. When effectively implemented, data governance transforms how data is perceived, managed, and utilized across departments and teams.

The Non-Invasive Data Governance approach, with its emphasis on enhancing existing processes and empowering current roles, offers a less disruptive and more intuitive path to achieving this integration. By focusing on practical, actionable strategies, this essay aims to demystify data governance and showcase how it can be made a natural and memorable part of daily operations, fostering a culture of data excellence and innovation. Here are six ways to make data governance memorable within your organization, with NIDG theory and practice playing a pivotal role in each method.

Simplify Concepts with Relatable Analogies and Stories

One of the most effective ways to make data governance memorable is to break down its complex concepts into simple, relatable analogies and stories. NIDG, with its emphasis on leveraging existing roles and responsibilities without introducing significant disruptions, offers a rich basis for storytelling. For instance, likening data governance to the rules of the road can help individuals understand the importance of standard procedures and roles in preventing chaos and ensuring smooth operations. By using analogies that relate to everyday experiences, the abstract concepts of data governance become tangible, making it easier for members of the organization to grasp and remember.

Consider the story of a library as an analogy for data governance. Just as a library organizes books to make them easily accessible and useful to its patrons, data governance organizes data to ensure its readily available, accurate, and secure for the organization's members. This analogy can illustrate how data governance helps navigate the vast information within a company, ensuring that every piece of data, like every book in a library, is correctly cataloged, maintained, and leveraged for maximum value. Through these stories, the principles of Non-Invasive Data Governance come alive, embedding the concepts deeply within the organizational culture and making the idea of data governance understood, appreciated, and remembered.

Craft a Memorable Slogan and Logo for Your Program

Do not underestimate the power of a memorable slogan and visually striking logo to represent a data governance program. These branding elements serve not only as a means of communication, but also as symbols of the program's goals, values, and aspirations. A well-crafted slogan and logo can summarize the essence of NIDG and its focus on integrating data governance seamlessly into existing organizational structures, making the program instantly recognizable and relatable to all members of the organization.

Creating a slogan that succinctly communicates the benefits and objectives of the NIDG program is crucial. It should be catchy yet meaningful, resonating with the organization's culture and the specific goals of the data governance initiative. For example, a slogan like "Empowering Data, Empowering Decisions" can highlight the program's aim to enhance decision-making through improved data management. Similarly, "Data Governance: Simplify, Clarify, Amplify" underscores the NIDG principles of simplifying processes, clarifying roles and responsibilities, and amplifying the value derived from data.

Complementing the slogan, a logo acts as the visual anchor for the data governance program, providing a constant reminder of its presence and purpose within the organization. The logo should reflect the themes of unity, clarity, and strategic oversight central to NIDG. It could incorporate imagery that suggests structure and connectivity, such as interconnected nodes or a lattice, symbolizing the interconnected nature of data across the organization. Choose colors and design elements to align with the organization's branding while standing out enough to draw attention to the data governance initiative.

Together, a memorable slogan and a compelling logo serve as the cornerstone for building awareness and fostering engagement with the data governance program. They function as tools for storytelling, making the abstract and often complex concepts of data governance more accessible and relatable. By embedding these branding elements in communications, presentations, and the digital and physical spaces where employees interact, the organization can continuously reinforce the importance and benefits of effective data management. This strategic use of branding not only aids in adopting and internalizing data governance principles but also cultivates a sense of pride and ownership among all stakeholders involved in the program.

Engage with Interactive Workshops and Training

Interactive workshops and training sessions are invaluable for embedding data governance principles into the organizational culture. When designed around the NIDG framework, these sessions encourage participation and hands-on learning. Role-playing exercises, where employees can simulate data governance scenarios, help reinforce the non-invasive approach by showing how it integrates with existing roles and workflows. This hands-on approach not only aids in retaining information but also builds a sense of ownership and familiarity with data governance practices among participants.

To further enhance the effectiveness of these workshops, incorporating real-world case studies and examples that reflect the organization's specific challenges and opportunities can be particularly impactful. For example, using actual data incidents from the organization's history or hypothetical scenarios that closely mimic potential data governance issues can make the lessons more relevant and compelling. Facilitators can guide participants through problem-solving exercises, demonstrating how the NIDG principles apply in each case.

Utilize Visual Aids and Infographics

Visual aids and infographics are powerful tools for making complex information understandable and memorable. Creating visual representations of the NIDG framework, including its core components and how it overlays with the organization's existing structure, can demystify data governance for all employees.

Infographics that outline the flow of data governance processes, roles, and responsibilities under the NIDG model can serve as quick-reference guides that reinforce learning and provide ongoing support as employees navigate data governance tasks.

In addition to static visuals, an interactive homepage for data governance and your data stewards, infographics, and digital dashboards that allow users to explore various aspects of the data governance framework can further enhance engagement and retention. For instance, clickable elements could reveal more detailed information about specific roles or processes, offering a deeper dive into how each element contributes to the overall data governance strategy. By integrating these visual tools into the company intranet or data governance portals, organizations can ensure that employees have easy access to essential information, making the principles of NIDG not just memorable but actively utilized in daily operations.

Celebrate Successes and Share Stories of Impact

Recognizing and celebrating successes in data governance is crucial for making its importance stick. Sharing stories of how your selected approach has led to improvements in data quality, decision-making, or regulatory compliance can serve as powerful testimonials. Highlighting specific examples where data governance has had a tangible impact on the organization not only validates the effort invested in it but also inspires and motivates the workforce. These stories can be shared through internal newsletters, meetings, or special recognition events, making the abstract concept of data governance concrete and valued across the organization.

Incorporating visual elements, such as before-and-after data quality dashboards or infographics detailing the journey towards compliance, can enhance these stories, making the successes even more vivid and understandable. Creating a dedicated space on the organization's intranet or a regular spot in corporate communications for these success stories can ensure that achievements in data governance are continuously highlighted. Additionally, involving those who contributed to these successes in telling their stories can foster a sense of ownership and pride, further embedding the value of data governance in the organizational culture.

Foster a Community of Data Governance Advocates

Creating a community of data governance advocates within the organization can provide a support network that reinforces the value and principles of data governance. This community, guided by the principles of NIDG, can serve as a forum for sharing best practices, discussing challenges, and exploring new ideas in data governance. Regular meetings, online forums, and collaborative projects can help maintain engagement and momentum. By empowering members from various departments to take active roles in this community, data governance becomes a shared responsibility that is woven into the fabric of the organization's culture. Implementing mentorship programs within the community can be highly beneficial. Experienced data governance practitioners can mentor newcomers, sharing insights and guiding them through the complexities of implementing NIDG principles in their daily work. This accelerates the learning curve for new members and strengthens the community's collective knowledge base. Additionally, celebrating the achievements of community members, such as successful project completions or innovative solutions to governance challenges, can boost morale and encourage active participation. Such recognition highlights the tangible benefits of data governance and the critical role of the community in fostering an environment of continuous improvement and excellence in data management.

Conclusion

Implementing these methods, with the theory and practice of Non-Invasive Data Governance at their core, can transform data governance from a set of guidelines and procedures into a central, memorable part of an organization's identity. By making data governance relatable, engaging, visually understandable, celebrated, and supported by a community, organizations can ensure that it is not just remembered, but integrated into everyday operations. The NIDG approach, with its emphasis on working within existing organizational structures and cultures, provides a flexible and effective framework for achieving this, making data governance not just a necessity but a memorable aspect of organizational excellence.

Non-Invasive Data Governance

Chapter 7, titled *Non-Invasive Data Governance*, serves as the cornerstone of this book, aligning directly with its subtitle, *Empowering People to Govern Data and AI*. This chapter explores the defining concepts, methodologies, and practical strategies of Non-Invasive Data Governance (NIDG), emphasizing how this approach seamlessly integrates governance into everyday processes. By highlighting the empowerment of individuals across all organizational levels, this chapter positions NIDG as the most effective and sustainable model for governing AI and data.

The chapter begins with *Non-Invasive Data Governance - The Most Practical and Pragmatic Approach*, which introduces the core philosophy behind NIDG. This essay details how this approach minimizes disruption and resistance by embedding governance naturally into existing workflows. It highlights why this pragmatic and people-first methodology sets the foundation for sustainable governance success, particularly in data-driven and AI-intensive environments.

Next, *Non-Invasive Data Governance By Design* delves into the intentional planning and alignment required to ensure NIDG fits seamlessly into an organization's culture and operations. This essay emphasizes how proactive design, rather than reactive fixes, leads to governance frameworks that are both efficient and resilient.

In *Essential Roles of Non-Invasive Data Governance™*, the focus shifts to the human element, detailing the critical roles that make NIDG work. By defining the responsibilities of data stewards, owners, and other stakeholders, this essay underscores how role clarity fosters accountability and collaboration, enabling governance to thrive across all levels of the organization.

Changing the Narrative with Non-Invasive Data Governance invites readers to rethink their perceptions of governance. It argues that traditional governance models often focus on control and enforcement, whereas NIDG repositions governance as a supportive and enabling force. This shift in narrative not only improves adoption but also transforms governance into a valued component of organizational strategy.

The structural aspects of NIDG are further explored in *The Non-Invasive Data Governance Framework: Summarized Across Organizational Levels*. This essay provides a comprehensive overview of how NIDG operates at executive, strategic, tactical, operational, and support levels, ensuring alignment and consistency across the entire organization.

You Are Already Governing Your Data—Non-Invasive Data Governance as a Solution builds on a powerful realization: organizations are already governing their data, albeit informally. This essay explains how NIDG formalizes these efforts without adding unnecessary complexity, turning informal practices into efficient, structured processes that drive measurable outcomes.

The chapter concludes with *Where Data Governance Should Live*, an exploration of where governance responsibilities fit within an organization's structure. By addressing questions of ownership, oversight, and accountability, this essay provides actionable insights for embedding NIDG into the fabric of organizational operations.

Through these essays, Chapter 7 not only makes a compelling case for Non-Invasive Data Governance but also provides a detailed roadmap for its implementation. By empowering people to govern data and AI effectively, this chapter demonstrates how NIDG transforms governance from a daunting task into a practical, achievable, and impactful organizational practice.

Non-Invasive Data Governance - The Most Practical and Pragmatic Approach

Effective data governance is essential for organizations looking to harness the full potential of their data assets. Among the various approaches, Non-Invasive Data Governance emerges as the most pragmatic and practical choice. This approach prioritizes seamless integration within existing workflows, minimizing disruptions and resistance from stakeholders. Thus, the reason the subtitle to my first book was *The Path of Least Resistance and Greatest Success*.

By leveraging current processes and existing accountability, non-invasive governance accelerates implementation, leading to a faster return on acceptance and subsequent return on investment. Furthermore, it fosters a culture of collaboration and open communication, ensuring that all relevant stakeholders are actively involved in shaping governance policies.

One of the key strengths of Non-Invasive Data Governance lies in its adaptability to changing business needs. Unlike more rigid methods, it allows organizations to respond flexibly to evolving organizational structures, data sources, technologies, and compliance requirements. This adaptability also translates to cost-effectiveness and resource efficiency.

Non-Invasive Data Governance optimizes existing resources, avoiding the need for expensive specialized expertise. It provides cost predictability and a strong return on investment from where money is being spent, making it a practical choice for organizations seeking to enhance their data management practices. In the following sections, I dig a bit deeper into these advantages, providing detailed insights into why Non-Invasive Data Governance is a highly effective approach in today's dynamic business landscape.

Minimizes Disruption and Resistance

Non-Invasive Data Governance operates within the existing organizational design, making it more practical to implement. It doesn't require a major overhaul of established processes or systems, reducing stakeholder resistance. Instead, it builds on current practices, gradually integrating and applying governance measures. This approach ensures that employees can adapt to changes at their own pace, resulting in smoother transitions and higher compliance rates:

- **Preserves Established Workflows**: Non-Invasive Data Governance is designed to work alongside and complement existing business processes and workflows. It integrates seamlessly with the current operations of the organization, ensuring that employees can continue their tasks without major interruptions. This minimizes the learning curve and resistance typically associated with large-scale changes.

- **Avoids Disruption of Critical Operations**: Invasive data governance methods often require significant restructuring of data processes. Non-invasive approaches, on the other hand, do not necessitate these disruptive events. Critical operations, such as real-time processes or customer interactions, can continue without interruption.

- **Reduces Pushback from Stakeholders**: Employees often resist changes that disrupt their routines. Non-Invasive Data Governance recognizes this and aims to minimize pushback by introducing governance practices gradually. This allows staff to adjust at their own pace, reducing resistance and creating a more positive reception towards the governance program.

- **Lowers Implementation Costs**: Since Non-Invasive Data Governance builds on existing infrastructure and processes, it requires fewer financial resources than more invasive methods. There's no need for extensive investments in new technology or costly data migration projects. This cost-effectiveness makes it an attractive option for organizations with budget constraints.

- **Preserves Data Integrity**: Intrusive data governance approaches can sometimes pose risks to data integrity, especially during large-scale migrations or system overhauls. Non-invasive methods, by contrast, are less likely to introduce errors or data corruption since they rely on established structures and metadata. This helps maintain the accuracy and reliability of critical business information.

Faster Implementation and ROI

Non-Invasive Data Governance allows for quicker deployment compared to more interfering methods. It focuses on leveraging existing data and process documentation, which means there is less of a need for time-process migration or reconfiguration. This expedites the realization of return on investment (ROI) as governance practices can be applied swiftly, leading to immediate improvements in data quality, accessibility, and compliance:

- **Utilizes Existing Metadata and Structures**: Non-Invasive Data Governance leverages the existing metadata and structures within an organization's systems. This means there's no need for time-consuming efforts to define new data models or migrate data to a completely different platform. Instead, governance practices can be applied directly to the existing data environment.

- **Avoids Lengthy Data Migration Processes**: Invasive data governance methods often require extensive data migration processes, which can be time-consuming and resource intensive. Non-invasive approaches dodge this requirement, allowing organizations to implement governance measures immediately, resulting in faster time-to-value.

- **Reduces Overhead Costs**: The absence of extensive process migration and reconfiguration efforts reduces overhead costs. This is because Non-Invasive Data Governance potentially minimizes the need for additional hardware, software, and professional services typically associated with major business or system overhauls.

- **Accelerates Compliance and Quality Improvements**: Since Non-Invasive Data Governance can be implemented more swiftly, organizations can rapidly enforce data quality standards and compliance measures. This leads to immediate improvements in data accuracy, completeness, and reliability. Consequently, the organization can see a quicker return on investment through improved decision-making and reduced risks associated with poor data quality.

- **Enhances Agility in Responding to Business Needs**: Non-Invasive Data Governance enables organizations to quickly adapt to changing business needs by avoiding lengthy implementation processes. This agility is crucial in dynamic environments where the ability to respond promptly to new data sources, regulations, or market conditions is a competitive advantage.

- **Facilitates Iterative Improvement**: Non-invasive approaches allow for incremental improvements over time. Organizations can start with foundational governance practices and then iterate and refine them as they gain experience and understanding of their specific data challenges. This iterative approach promotes the continuous enhancement of data management practices.

Enhanced Collaboration and Communication

By involving all relevant stakeholders from the outset, Non-Invasive Data Governance promotes a culture of collaboration. It encourages business units and IT teams to work together to define and maintain data standards and policies. This approach fosters open communication channels and a shared understanding of data, breaking down silos and promoting a unified approach to data management:

- **Encourages Inclusive Stakeholder Involvement**: Non-Invasive Data Governance encourages the active participation of subject matter experts and stakeholders from various business units and IT teams. This inclusive approach ensures that diverse perspectives and expertise are always brought to the table. It fosters a sense of stewardship and shared formal accountability for data quality and compliance.

- **Establishes Common Language and Understanding**: Effective data governance requires a common language and understanding of data across different departments. Non-invasive methods facilitate this by promoting regular communication and collaboration. It encourages discussions about data definitions, business rules, and usage, which helps bridge the gap between technical and non-technical stakeholders.

- **Breaks Down Silos and Fosters Cross-Functional Teams**: Traditional, top-down or command-and-control governance models can create silos between business units and IT teams. Non-invasive approaches aim to break down these silos by emphasizing cross-functional working teams. This collaborative structure ensures that governance decisions are made collectively, with input from all appropriate parties.

- **Facilitates Knowledge Transfer and Skill Development**: Through collaboration, team members have the opportunity to learn from each other. IT teams can share technical expertise, while business units can contribute their domain and business knowledge. This knowledge transfer strengthens the effectiveness of data governance and helps team members develop new skills and capabilities.

- **Promotes a Culture of Formal Accountability**: When stakeholders are actively involved in data governance decisions, they feel a greater sense of accountability for data quality and compliance. This sense of ownership (rather stewardship) encourages individuals to take responsibility for the accuracy and reliability of the data they work with, leading to higher overall data quality.

- **Fosters Continuous Feedback and Improvement**: Regular communication and collaboration foster an environment where feedback is valued. This enables organizations to continuously refine their data governance practices based on real-world experiences and evolving business requirements.

Adaptability to Changing Business Needs

Non-Invasive Data Governance is inherently flexible, allowing for adjustments as business needs evolve. Since it doesn't impose rigid structures, it can adapt to new data sources, technologies, and compliance requirements without causing major disruptions. This adaptability is crucial in today's rapidly changing business environment, ensuring that governance practices remain relevant and effective over time:

- **Designs Flexible Data Management Practices**: Non-Invasive Data Governance is designed to be adaptable to evolving business needs. It doesn't impose rigid structures or processes, allowing organizations to adjust their data governance practices in response to changing requirements, new technologies, or emerging data sources.

- **Accommodates New Data Sources and Technologies**: As organizations adopt new technologies and incorporate additional data sources, Non-Invasive Data Governance can seamlessly incorporate these elements into the Non-Invasive Data Governance Framework. This adaptability ensures that governance practices remain relevant and effective in the face of technological advancements.

- **Responds to Regulatory Changes and Compliance Requirements**: Regulatory landscapes constantly change, requiring organizations to adapt their data management practices to remain compliant. Non-Invasive Data Governance allows for the efficient and effective application of new compliance measures without disrupting existing operations. This ensures that the organization can stay in compliance with relevant regulations without major disruptions.

- **Supports Scalability and Growth**: Non-Invasive Data Governance practices are scalable and can grow with the organization. As the volume and complexity of data increase, the governance program can expand its formal processes to accommodate these changes. This scalability is particularly important for rapidly growing businesses or those operating in industries with high data velocity.

- **Minimizes Risk of Obsolescence**: In rapidly evolving industries, data management practices that are too rigid or inflexible can quickly become obsolete. Non-Invasive Data Governance mitigates this risk by providing a framework that can adapt to emerging trends, technologies, and business models. This ensures that the organization's data governance practices remain relevant and effective over time.

- **Facilitates Continuous Innovation**: By providing a flexible and adaptable governance framework, Non-Invasive Data Governance encourages a culture of innovation. Teams are empowered to explore new data sources, technologies, and analytical approaches, knowing that the governance framework can accommodate these innovations without causing disruptions.

Cost-Effectiveness and Resource Efficiency

Non-Invasive Data Governance typically requires fewer resources compared to more invasive methods. It leverages existing people, tools, and technologies, minimizing the need for expensive investments in new infrastructure or software. Additionally, it relies on the expertise of existing stewards, staff, and subject matter experts, reducing the need for specialized training or hiring additional personnel. This makes it a cost-effective approach that aligns with the organization's budget constraints while delivering substantial improvements in data management practices:

- **Optimizes Existing Resources**: Non-Invasive Data Governance maximizes utilizing existing resources, including technology infrastructure, personnel, and tools. It typically does not require substantial investments in new hardware, software, or specialized training. This efficient use of resources helps organizations achieve their data governance goals without incurring significant additional costs.

- **Reduces Dependency on Specialized Expertise**: More intrusive data governance approaches often require specialized expertise and data subject matter knowledge, which can be costly to acquire and maintain. Non-invasive methods rely on the existing knowledge and skills of the organization's staff, reducing the need for expensive consultants or dedicated governance teams. This cost-saving aspect makes non-invasive governance a practical choice for organizations with budget constraints.

- **Avoids Costly Data Process Overhauls**: Invasive data governance methods often necessitate extensive data process overhauls, which can be expensive and complicated. The non-invasive approach sidesteps these costs by applying formal accountability and executing and enforcing formal authority within the current data process and personnel environment. This avoids the need for costly and confusing upgrades to existing data processes.

- **Minimizes Disruption-Related Costs**: Major disruptions to business operations, such as system downtimes or data migrations, can lead to significant financial losses. Non-Invasive Data Governance, by its very nature of complementing and not interfering with major events, reduces the risk of such disruptions. This translates to cost savings by ensuring that critical operations can continue uninterrupted.

- **Provides Cost Predictability**: Non-Invasive Data Governance typically involves fewer unpredictable costs. Since it builds on existing infrastructure, accountability, and processes, organizations have a clearer understanding of the financial implications. This predictability is valuable for budget planning and ensures that the organization can allocate resources efficiently.

- **Delivers Strong ROI Through Appropriate Channels**: Due to its cost-effective nature, Non-Invasive Data Governance often leads to a higher return on investment (ROI) from the substantial organizational initiatives that benefit from highly governed data. The benefits of improved data quality, compliance, and decision-making outweigh the relatively low implementation and maintenance costs. This strong ROI through the application of governance to the data from critical information investments (data mesh and fabric, artificial intelligence, improved analytical capabilities ... to name a few) reinforces the practicality and pragmatism of non-invasive governance.

Conclusion

In summary, Non-Invasive Data Governance offers a pragmatic and effective approach to enhancing data management practices within organizations. By seamlessly integrating with existing workflows, this method minimizes disruptions and reduces stakeholder resistance. Leveraging current processes and metadata structures, non-invasive governance accelerates implementation, leading to a swift return on investment.

NIDG fosters a culture of collaboration, ensuring that all relevant stakeholders actively participate in shaping governance policies. This inclusive approach not only strengthens data quality and compliance but also establishes a common understanding of data across departments.

One of the standout strengths of Non-Invasive Data Governance is its adaptability to evolving business needs. This flexibility allows organizations to stay responsive to changes in personnel, data sources, technologies, and compliance requirements without incurring significant costs or disruptions.

By optimizing existing resources and minimizing dependency on specialized expertise, non-invasive governance is cost-effective and resource-efficient. It provides a level of predictability in budgeting and delivers a strong return on investment, making it an attractive choice for organizations seeking to elevate their data management practices. Overall, Non-Invasive Data Governance stands as a practical and forward-thinking approach for organizations navigating the complexities of modern data governance.

Non-Invasive Data Governance By Design

Organizations are navigating the complex waters of governance to ensure the responsible use and stewardship of their most valuable asset—data. Among the three approaches to data governance, Non-Invasive Data Governance stands out as a strategic model that champions efficiency, collaboration, and adaptability. This essay explores the implementation of Non-Invasive Data Governance by design, unraveling the intricacies of its adoption, its transformative impact, and the strategic considerations that underpin this paradigm shift.

Foundations of Non-Invasive Data Governance

At its core, Non-Invasive Data Governance changes the narrative from the authoritarian models of data governance. Instead of imposing rigid structures and stringent policies, it embraces a more holistic and inclusive approach. By design, Non-Invasive Data Governance recognizes that governance is already happening within the organization, often informally. It seeks to harness and enhance these existing governance practices rather than overhaul them.

The implementation journey begins with a fundamental shift in mindset. It involves acknowledging that everyone within the organization, regardless of their formal title, plays a role in data governance. This inclusive philosophy becomes the cornerstone of Non-Invasive Data Governance, laying the groundwork for a collaborative and adaptive framework.

Cultural Transformation

Implementing Non-Invasive Data Governance is not merely a procedural change; it necessitates cultural movement. Organizations embracing this approach understand that governance is not solely the responsibility of a select few; it's a shared commitment woven into the fabric of daily operations. By design, Non-Invasive Data Governance fosters a culture of accountability, transparency, and shared responsibility.

This cultural shift starts with leadership buy-in and commitment. Leaders must champion the values of Non-Invasive Data Governance, emphasizing the importance of collaboration and recognizing the potential in every individual to contribute to the governance landscape. The strategic implementation plan includes targeted training sessions, workshops, and communication initiatives to embed these values into the organizational DNA.

The beauty of Non-Invasive Data Governance lies in its adaptability to different organizational cultures. Whether a startup fostering innovation or a well-established enterprise valuing tradition, this governance method molds itself to fit seamlessly within the existing cultural framework. This adaptability is a deliberate choice made during the implementation phase, ensuring that Non-Invasive Data Governance is not a disruptive force but an enabler of positive change.

Collaboration Across Silos

Traditional governance models often result in limited adoption and organizational silos, where data is hoarded within departments, hindering its free flow and optimal utilization. Non-Invasive Data Governance, by design, seeks to break down these barriers. It promotes collaboration across departments, encouraging the sharing of insights, data, and expertise.

Implementation involves identifying cross-functional teams responsible for different aspects of data governance. These teams include representatives from various departments, ensuring a diversity of perspectives and experiences. These teams work together through collaborative workshops and ongoing communication channels to align governance practices with organizational objectives.

The breaking down of silos is not a one-time effort but an ongoing process. Non-Invasive Data Governance encourages continuous collaboration, ensuring that data-related decisions are well-informed, holistic, and considerate of the multifaceted nature of organizational challenges.

Strategic Considerations

Implementing Non-Invasive Data Governance by design requires a strategic roadmap that considers the unique needs, goals, and challenges of the organization. Here are key strategic considerations integral to the successful adoption of this governance paradigm:

- **Assessment and Understanding:** Before embarking on the implementation journey, organizations conduct a comprehensive assessment of their existing governance landscape. This involves understanding current practices, identifying informal governance structures, and recognizing potential areas for improvement.

- **Leadership Alignment:** Successful implementation requires the unmistakable support and alignment of leadership. Leaders play a pivotal role in shaping the organization's culture and priorities, making their commitment to Non-Invasive Data Governance crucial. Leadership training and engagement sessions are integral components of the strategic plan.

- **Training and Skill Development:** Non-Invasive Data Governance introduces a shift in roles and responsibilities. Therefore, a strategic implementation plan includes training programs to equip employees with the necessary skills and knowledge. This extends beyond formal data roles, reaching every individual who interacts with data in their daily responsibilities.

- **Technology Integration:** The implementation plan considers integrating technology solutions that support Non-Invasive Data Governance. This may include data cataloging tools, collaboration platforms, and other technologies that enhance the visibility, accessibility, and management of data across the organization.

- **Communication Strategy:** Transparency and effective communication are paramount in Non-Invasive Data Governance. A well-defined communication strategy ensures that all stakeholders are informed about the changes, understand their role in the governance framework, and feel empowered to contribute.

- **Pilot Programs and Iterative Implementation:** Organizations often opt for pilot programs to test the waters instead of a one-size-fits-all approach. These pilots allow for iterative implementation, enabling organizations to learn from successes and challenges, refine their approach, and scale gradually.

- **Continuous Monitoring and Improvement:** Non-Invasive Data Governance is not a static model; it evolves with the organization. Therefore, a strategic plan includes mechanisms for continuous monitoring, feedback collection, and improvement. Regular assessments ensure that the governance framework aligns with organizational goals and adapts to changing dynamics.

Transformative Impact

As Non-Invasive Data Governance takes root within the organization, its transformative impact becomes increasingly apparent. One of the key outcomes is the democratization of data. By breaking down silos and fostering collaboration, data becomes more accessible across departments, empowering individuals at all levels to make informed decisions.

Non-Invasive Data Governance enhances data quality and reliability. The inclusive approach to governance means that more eyes are on the data, leading to quicker identification and resolution of issues. Treat data as a shared asset, and its accuracy becomes a collective responsibility.

This governance paradigm also contributes to a more agile and responsive organization. The collaborative nature of Non-Invasive Data Governance allows for faster adaptation to changing business environments. Base decisions on a comprehensive understanding of data, and the organization becomes more adept at leveraging data for strategic advantage.

Challenges and Mitigations in Implementation

While the benefits of Non-Invasive Data Governance are substantial, organizations may encounter challenges during implementation. These challenges include resistance to cultural change, potential disruptions to existing workflows, and the need for additional resources for training and technology integration.

To address these challenges, the strategic plan includes change management initiatives. This involves targeted communication campaigns to address concerns and highlight the positive aspects of the new governance model. Additionally, phased implementation helps mitigate disruptions, allowing individuals and teams to adapt gradually.

Design training programs to be inclusive and accessible to ensure everyone can participate and contribute regardless of their familiarity with data concepts. Leadership plays a crucial role in setting the tone for cultural change, and their visible commitment is a powerful mitigating factor.

Conclusion

In the ever-accelerating digital age, where data is the lifeblood of organizational success, Non-Invasive Data Governance emerges as a signal of innovation and adaptability. Implementing this governance paradigm by design is not just a strategic choice; it's a commitment to fostering a culture where data is a shared asset, decisions are informed by collective intelligence, and the organization thrives in the face of evolving challenges.

The journey towards Non-Invasive Data Governance is an odyssey that transforms not only the way an organization manages its data, but also the way it collaborates, innovates, and navigates the complexities of the modern business landscape. As organizations embark on this strategic odyssey, they chart a course toward intelligent data governance that ensures they not only survive but thrive in the data-driven future.

Essential Roles of Non-Invasive Data Governance

Data Governance, the ability to execute and enforce authority over the management of data definition, production, and usage of data at all levels of the organization, has become an indispensable cornerstone of assuring enterprise success. Formalizing accountability for data and guaranteeing the accuracy, integrity, and accessibility of data is not only essential for informed decision-making but also critical for regulatory compliance. This necessitates a comprehensive framework and operating model that transcends traditional data governance models, empowering every facet of an organization to be held formally accountable for its data actions.

Each level within the Non-Invasive Data Governance Framework and role within the Non-Invasive Data Governance Operating Model plays a unique and vital part, collectively contributing to establishing a robust and sustainable data governance program. This essay quickly unravels the intricacies of these levels, specifically the roles, shedding light on their collective impact in driving a Non-Invasive Data Governance program.

The Executive Level

The Executive level, represented by the *Data Governance Steering Committee,* holds a pivotal role in implementing a sustainable Non-Invasive Data Governance program. They set the strategic direction and provide the necessary resources and support for the program's success. Their endorsement and commitment signal to the entire organization that data governance is a top priority. Executives also play a critical role in resolving any conflicts or issues that may arise, leveraging their authority to ensure that the program aligns with overarching business goals. Their leadership and decision-making at this level are essential for establishing a strong foundation that will enable the data governance program to thrive in the long term.

Identifying individuals for Executive roles in a Non-Invasive Data Governance program requires looking within the organization's existing leadership team. The Steering Committee should consist of high-level executives, such as the CEO, CFO, CIO, and other key decision-makers with a strong understanding of the organization's strategic goals. These individuals should already hold positions of authority and have a vested interest in the success and growth of the company. They can be selected based on their track record of making strategic decisions and their commitment to aligning data governance with broader business objectives.

Responsibilities:
- Setting high-level data governance strategies and objectives.
- Providing oversight and guidance for data governance initiatives.
- Allocating resources and support for data governance efforts.
- Approving major data-related policies and decisions.
- Handling significant data-related incidents or breaches.

Members:
- C-Level Executives (CEO, CFO, CIO, etc.).
- Chief Data Officer (CDO) or equivalent.
- Business Leaders representing key functional areas.

The Strategic Level

At the Strategic level, typically labeled as the *Data Governance Council* (or similarly named body), the emphasis shifts towards translating high-level strategies into actionable data governance policies and frameworks. This level is crucial for establishing the guidelines that will guide data management practices across the organization. The Data Governance Council promotes data ownership, stewardship, and accountability, setting the stage for sustainable data quality and integrity. By identifying critical data assets and their strategic value, they prioritize efforts and resources toward managing the most valuable information. The Council's role in monitoring and evaluating the program's effectiveness ensures that adjustments can be made over time, contributing to its long-term sustainability.

Source the individuals on the Data Governance Council from various business functions within the organization. It is essential to seek out leaders with a deep understanding of their respective domains and a passion for data governance. Look for individuals with a proven track record of effectively translating strategic objectives into actionable policies and frameworks. These individuals could include senior managers, department heads, or subject matter experts with a demonstrated expertise in data-related matters. They should be able to think strategically and have a broad understanding of how data impacts the organization's overall strategy.

Responsibilities:
- Defining overarching data policies and priorities aligned with business strategy.
- Establishing data governance frameworks and standards.
- Assigning data ownership and stewardship responsibilities.
- Identifying critical data assets and their strategic value.
- Monitoring and evaluating the effectiveness of data governance initiatives.

Members:
- Representatives from key business functions (e.g., Sales, Marketing, Finance, Operations).
- Data Governance Manager or Leader.
- Compliance Officer.

The Tactical Level

The Tactical level, represented by *Data Subject Matter Experts* (SMEs) or Data Domain (subject area) Stewards, is instrumental in the day-to-day coordination and execution of data subject area-related activities. Their expertise and deep knowledge of specific business functions enable them to implement data governance practices in a practical and effective manner. They work closely with operational teams to ensure that data processes are carried out consistently and in compliance with established standards. This level's contribution is crucial for sustaining the momentum of the data governance program on a practical, functional level, ensuring that it becomes an integral part of everyday operations.

When filling roles of Data SMEs, it's crucial to recognize individuals who have a strong grasp of the specific business functions and domains they represent. Look for experts within the organization who deeply understand their functional areas, such as Sales, Marketing, Finance, or Operations. These individuals should have a proven track record of executing data-related activities effectively within their domains. They could include business analysts, process owners, or experienced professionals with a solid understanding of data operations. These experts will play a critical role in coordinating data-related activities for their domain across different business functions.

Responsibilities:
- Coordinating and facilitating data-related activities across different business functions.
- Conducting data profiling, cleansing, and integration.
- Ensuring consistency and quality of data within their respective domains.
- Collaborating with data stewards and IT teams for seamless information flow.

Members:
- Functional experts from various business units.
- Business Analysts.
- Data Analysts.

The Operational Level

The Operational level, represented by the *Data Stewards*, is where the rubber meets the road in terms of data governance implementation. They are responsible for executing the detailed tasks involved in data management within specific business functions. Data Stewards ensure that data is captured accurately, validated, and reported on a day-to-day basis. Their efforts in maintaining data quality and integrity directly impact the sustainability of the program. Without effective operational-level governance, even the most well-defined strategic and tactical efforts would falter, underscoring the critical importance of this level in a sustainable Non-Invasive Data Governance program.

Recognizing people for Data Steward roles requires looking for ways people at the operational level interact with the data through their specific business functions. People who define data as part of their function and who are held accountable for this action are Data Definition Stewards. People that are accountable for producing data are Data Production Stewards. The same can be said for people who are held formally accountable for how they use data. Look for individuals already responsible for data-related tasks within their respective areas. These could be individuals currently handling data entry, validation, and reporting. They must have a strong attention to detail and a track record of ensuring data accuracy and integrity. These individuals may already be familiar with the specific data sets and processes within their business functions, making them ideal candidates for operational-level data stewardship.

Responsibilities:
- Executing day-to-day data management tasks within specific business functions.
- Ensuring accurate data entry, validation, and reporting.
- Managing data access and permissions and enforcing security measures.
- Overseeing the quality and integrity of specific data sets.
- Providing subject matter expertise on data-related matters.

Members:
- Individuals are recognized as being formally accountable for the actions they take with data within their respective functional areas.

The Support Level

The Support level, consisting of *governing partners, Information Technology (IT), working teams, and program administration*, provides the essential infrastructure, tools, and expertise necessary for the sustainable operation of the data governance program. They ensure that the technology platforms and systems supporting data processing and analysis are robust and well-maintained. Their coordination with external partners and vendors, as well as program administration efforts, contribute to the program's efficiency and longevity. Without a solid support structure, sustaining the Non-Invasive Data Governance program would be challenging, making this level integral to its long-term success.

For roles at the Support level, recognize individuals from various departments within the organization. IT professionals can be drawn from the existing IT department, ensuring that they have the technical expertise to support data management systems. Governing partners and the program administrator can be identified from relevant departments responsible for vendor management and program administration. Assemble working teams from tactical and operational individuals with expertise in areas like training, communication, and documentation. By drawing from existing departments and teams, the organization can leverage internal expertise to build a strong support structure for the data governance program.

Responsibilities:
- Providing the necessary infrastructure, tools, and expertise to enable effective data governance and management.
- Overseeing IT systems, data platforms, and applications supporting data processing and analysis.
- Managing partnerships with external vendors and ensuring compliance with data governance policies.
- Coordinating training, communication, and documentation efforts related to data governance.

Members:
- IT Professionals.
- External Partners and Vendors.
- Program Administrators.
- Cross-Functional Working Teams.

Conclusion

The successful implementation of a Non-Invasive Data Governance program hinges on the collaboration and commitment of every facet of an organization. It is a collective endeavor where each individual becomes a steward of data integrity and quality regardless of their specific role. By fostering a culture of data consciousness and accountability, organizations can fortify their foundations, ensuring that data remains a reliable asset in pursuing their objectives.

As the digital landscape continues to evolve, this adaptive approach to data governance will prove invaluable, enabling organizations to navigate the complexities of an ever-changing data ecosystem with confidence and agility. In this dynamic era, where data reigns supreme, a holistic and inclusive approach to governance is not only a strategic imperative, but a fundamental driver of sustained success.

Changing the Narrative with Non-Invasive Data Governance

The traditional narrative surrounding data governance often depicts it as a disruptive force, requiring invasive measures and extensive overhauls. However, the paradigm shift of Non-Invasive Data Governance is reshaping this narrative. Far from the misconception that effective governance necessitates upheaval, this approach seeks to seamlessly integrate into existing workflows, challenging the notion that data governance must be invasive and over-and-above existing work efforts.

Breaking free from the shackles of the past, Non-Invasive Data Governance positions itself as a facilitator rather than a hindrance. It envisions a future where governance becomes an organic part of everyday operations, working in tandem with existing processes rather than imposing a burdensome structure. This introduction sets the stage for a deeper exploration into the principles, benefits, and implementation strategies of Non-Invasive Data Governance, introducing a path that organizations can tread to harness the power of governance without the past constraints of invasiveness.

Dispelling the Myths: Rethinking Data Governance

Non-Invasive Data Governance challenges the rooted belief that governance must be intrusive to be effective. Instead, it embraces an agile and collaborative model that aligns with existing structures. The essence lies in positioning data governance as an enabler rather than a disruptor, fostering a culture where data is seen as a strategic asset that enhances organizational processes rather than hinders them. It redefines the narrative around governance efforts, dispelling the myth that governance is a separate, isolated function. It advocates for an approach that effortlessly aligns with the natural flow of work.

This mindset shift acknowledges that effective governance doesn't necessitate a complete overhaul. Non-Invasive Data Governance seeks to work within the fabric of the organization, leveraging existing processes and structures. It dismantles the myth that governance has to be an external force imposing rigid rules, opting instead for a model where governance is an integral and harmonious component of the organizational ecosystem, not an over-and-above effort.

Unlocking Tangible Benefits: Non-Invasive Data Governance in Action

Non-Invasive Data Governance delivers tangible benefits without causing organizational friction. By leveraging existing workflows, it streamlines processes related to data quality, integrity, and accessibility. Contrary to the misconception that effective governance requires significant disruptions, organizations embracing the non-invasive approach witness practical advantages seamlessly integrated into their everyday operations.

Non-Invasive Data Governance recognizes and amplifies the existing strengths of an organization's data management practices. Instead of imposing rigid structures, it identifies areas of improvement and introduces enhancements that complement and extend the current workflows. This approach ensures that governance efforts are not perceived as an additional burden but as catalysts for efficiency.

Instead of imposing rigid structures, NIDG identifies areas of improvement and introduces enhancements that complement and extend the current workflows.

The non-invasive model emphasizes the seamless integration of governance into existing processes, eliminating the need for extensive overhauls. This not only minimizes disruption, but also reduces the learning curve for staff, ensuring that governance practices are embraced with minimal resistance. The approach demonstrates that governance can be an enabler of innovation rather than a hindrance, fueling organizational growth and resilience.

Implementation Strategies: Collaborative and Seamless Integration

Implementing Non-Invasive Data Governance involves a strategic shift in mindset and practices. It begins by fostering a collaborative culture where stakeholders at all levels actively participate in governance initiatives. Rather than imposing new structures, the approach is to identify and work within the existing structures, aligning governance practices with the organization's objectives. This collaborative integration ensures that governance becomes a shared responsibility, woven into the fabric of everyday operations.

Continuous training and support, both technical and cultural, empower staff, while clear communication channels ensure stakeholders are informed and engaged. Regular communication, including newsletters and town hall meetings, builds trust and transparency. Fostering a culture of continuous improvement encourages feedback, celebrates successes, and ensures governance practices remain responsive and relevant. This collaborative strategy creates a unified, adaptive approach to data governance.

Success Stories: Organizations Leading the Non-Invasive Charge

Numerous organizations have successfully embraced Non-Invasive Data Governance, debunking the myth that governance initiatives have to be disruptive. Case studies reveal how these entities have seamlessly integrated governance practices into their existing workflows, achieving improved data quality, streamlined processes, and enhanced decision-making capabilities.

A large financial institution seamlessly integrated governance practices into its existing data and information management processes. By engaging employees at all levels, clarifying roles, and providing comprehensive training, the institution experienced a significant reduction in data errors and a marked improvement in decision-making capabilities.

A prominent provider implemented non-invasive governance in the healthcare sector by aligning it with strategic care goals. By incorporating governance principles into routine processes, they achieved better data quality, improved regulatory compliance, and streamlined reporting. These success stories serve as compelling evidence that Non-Invasive Data Governance is not only feasible, but also capable of delivering measurable and meaningful results.

Overcoming Resistance: Communicating the Value Proposition

Resistance to change is natural, especially when it comes to reshaping established practices like data governance. Communicating the value proposition of Non-Invasive Data Governance becomes crucial in overcoming this resistance. Emphasizing how this approach adds value without overhauling existing work efforts, and highlighting the positive impact on efficiency, innovation, and compliance, is key to garnering support from stakeholders across the organization.

Successful organizations have navigated this resistance by fostering a culture of collaboration and emphasizing the collective benefits of governance. Open communication channels, town hall meetings, and regular feedback sessions allow employees to express concerns and voice their opinions. Involving resistant stakeholders in the governance process, making them active participants rather than passive recipients, is another key strategy.

Continuous education on the value of non-invasive governance, through workshops, webinars, and accessible resources, helps demystify the process and dispel misconceptions. By showcasing success stories and tangible benefits, organizations can gradually change perceptions and build a groundswell of support for the non-invasive approach. Over time, this proactive communication strategy becomes a cornerstone in dismantling resistance and creating a positive mindset towards governance initiatives.

As organizations grapple with the evolving data landscape, the non-invasive revolution in data governance offers a promising path forward. By dispelling the myths surrounding invasive governance practices, this approach paves the way for a future where data governance is collaborative, inclusive, and seamlessly integrated into the fabric of organizational operations.

Looking Ahead: A Collaborative and Inclusive Future for Data Governance

Looking ahead, successful entities recognize the importance of staying aware of technological advancements and industry trends. This forward-looking approach ensures that their governance frameworks remain agile and responsive to the changing data landscape.

One aspect of future-proofing Non-Invasive Data Governance involves integrating emerging technologies such as artificial intelligence and machine learning. These technologies can enhance the efficiency of data governance processes, automating routine tasks and providing valuable insights for decision-making. Moreover, the evolution of non-invasive governance extends beyond technology to encompass regulatory landscapes.

Organizations anticipate and prepare for shifts in data protection and privacy regulations, aligning their governance practices with evolving legal requirements. This proactive stance not only ensures compliance, but also reinforces the resilience and adaptability of their governance programs in the face of regulatory changes.

Looking ahead involves a commitment to continuous learning, flexibility, and a proactive mindset. By staying ahead of the curve, organizations can navigate the complexities of the data-driven future, leveraging non-invasive governance as a strategic asset for sustainable growth and resilience in an ever-evolving digital landscape.

Conclusion

The essay investigated the concept of Non-Invasive Data Governance, challenging the traditional notion that governance initiatives must be invasive and disruptive. It explores the myths surrounding data governance, dispelling the misconception that it hinders existing work efforts. The piece highlights the tangible benefits of adopting a non-invasive approach, emphasizing efficiency, collaboration, and improved decision-making.

In the section on implementation strategies, the essay shares how organizations can seamlessly integrate non-invasive governance into existing workflows. It underscores the importance of collaboration and offers insights into fostering a culture of data ownership. Success stories showcase real-world examples of entities thriving with non-invasive governance, demonstrating its practical impact. Overcoming resistance is addressed by emphasizing communication, education, and showcasing the positive outcomes of the approach.

Leaving you with thoughts about the future, the essay looks ahead, emphasizing the importance of continuous evolution. It anticipates integrating emerging technologies like AI and ML, suggesting that these innovations can enhance governance processes. In summary, the narrative highlights the proactive stance organizations should take in adapting to evolving regulatory landscapes.

The Non-Invasive Data Governance Framework: Summarized Across Organizational Levels

Central to the Non-Invasive Data Governance approach and framework are six core components: data, roles, processes, communications, metrics, and tools. Each serves as a pillar essential to the success of a data governance program. This essay navigates through the complex web of organizational levels: Executive, Strategic, Tactical, Operational, and Support. There are challenges at each level, and the framework provides strategic guidance on overcoming these challenges. An image of an empty framework is shared below.

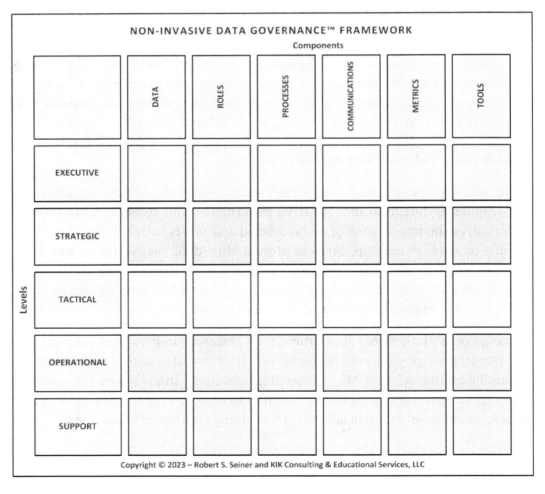

The Non-Invasive Data Governance Framework

The information that completes the framework (fills in the boxes) is multi-faceted and multi-dimensional beyond the two obvious dimensions of the core components and the organizational levels. The art of completing the boxes requires analysis and a detailed definition of why each box is important, the critical considerations that address the component at that level, as well as organizational dimensions such as industry, organization size, and overall governing approach that heavily influence how the program must be structured.

Why Addressing Data Governance is Crucial

The significance of data governance surpasses the borders of a routine organizational checklist; it is the cornerstone that underpins the strategic utilization, safeguarding, and optimization of an organization's invaluable data assets. A comprehensive approach to data governance that utilizes a thorough framework is the key to unlocking a multitude of benefits that extend far beyond mere compliance. From heightened decision-making capabilities and elevated data quality to uniform adherence to regulatory requirements and bolstered stakeholder trust, the impacts are transformative.

The Non-Invasive Data Governance Framework can be used as a guiding beacon in this journey. It offers organizations a well-defined roadmap to harness their data as a true strategic asset, shifting the paradigm from considering data as a byproduct of operations to recognizing it as a potent force for strategic advantage.

Data is not just a passive repository of information but a dynamic and influential object that shapes critical decision-making processes. A robust data governance strategy ensures that this influential force is exercised strategically, fostering innovation, mitigating risks, and contributing directly to achieving organizational goals.

Data is not just a passive repository of information but a dynamic and influential object that shapes critical decision-making processes.

As organizations recognize data as a cornerstone of their operations, the Non-Invasive Data Governance Framework can take center stage, not merely as a set of guidelines but as a transformative tool that empowers organizations to navigate the complexities of data management with agility and foresight. Within this context, the roadmap provided by the framework becomes not just a route to compliance but a transformative journey toward unleashing the full potential of data within an organization's data ecosystem.

The Executive Level: Nurturing Data as a Strategic Asset

The Executive level of the framework spotlights the imperative of viewing data as a dynamic and strategic asset capable of steering the organization's overarching course. The pivotal challenge at this level involves translating lofty strategic goals into tangible and executable data initiatives. Organizations can overcome this challenge by dedicating resources to comprehensive executive education programs, emphasizing an acute awareness of the strategic value inherent in data assets. To navigate this stage successfully, executives must not only recognize the importance of safeguarding data, but also become reliable advocates for fostering a culture where data is actively harnessed to fulfill strategic objectives.

In this context, executive leaders play a crucial role in shaping the narrative around data within the organization. Beyond the traditional roles of overseeing operations, executives become torchbearers of a data-centric philosophy, infusing every facet of the organizational culture. The strategic deployment of data at the Executive level extends beyond protective measures to proactive utilization, where data becomes a driving force for innovation and a catalyst for achieving long-term strategic goals.

By championing a data-centric culture, executives pave the way for an organizational mindset that views data not merely as a passive resource but as a dynamic and influential asset that propels the organization toward sustained success.

The Strategic Level: Aligning Core Components for Effective Execution

Within the Strategic level, the merging of executive strategies into actionable operational plans takes center stage. The value lies in aligning the six core components to facilitate effective execution: data, roles, processes, communications, metrics, and tools. A vital challenge at this juncture is sustaining unity among these components while ensuring their alignment with the overarching strategic goals of the organization. Organizations must prioritize investments in robust communication strategies to defeat these challenges, continuously define and refine processes, and conduct regular evaluations to guarantee aligning these critical components with strategic objectives.

The alignment of core components is pivotal in bridging the gap between high-level strategic intent and practical, day-to-day operations. Organizations must strategically position roles, fortify communication channels, streamline processes, institute metrics for performance evaluation, and deploy tools that not only support these functions individually, but also synergize as an integrated system. This concerted effort ensures that the strategic vision set by executives is not lost in translation but is methodically translated into operational realities.

Effective execution at the Strategic level hinges on calibrating these core components, transforming them from abstract concepts into tangible mechanisms that drive the organization toward its strategic aspirations.

The Tactical Level: Navigating Cross-Business Function Governance

The Tactical Level is responsible for coordinating governance efforts across diverse business functions, a delicate activity that requires alignment with strategic objectives while accommodating the unique needs of each functional domain. Challenges emerge as organizations grapple with the dual mandate of maintaining standardization across the governance landscape while flexibly addressing the distinct requirements of individual functions.

To effectively navigate these challenges, organizations must actively promote and foster cross-functional collaboration, institute specialized governance working teams, and underscore the substantial benefits of embracing standardized data practices. This approach encourages widespread adoption and ensures that the governance framework remains agile enough to address the nuanced demands of diverse business functions.

Addressing the Tactical Level of the framework reveals a complex interplay between standardized governance practices and the inherent variability across business functions. It requires a delicate balance between imposing overarching standards for consistency and allowing flexibility to accommodate the unique characteristics of each functional and data domain. Organizations must establish governance working teams with a deep understanding of the overarching governance strategy and the specific requirements of their functions.

This targeted approach facilitates tailoring governance mechanisms to suit the nuances of diverse business functions while maintaining a cohesive and standardized framework that aligns with strategic objectives. Successful governance at the Tactical Level hinges on finding this balance, ensuring that the governance approach remains adaptable and responsive to the multifaceted landscape of cross-business function requirements.

The Operational Level: Streamlining Governance within Business Functions

The Operational Level drills down to the heart of governance within individual business functions, where the emphasis shifts to the efficient and effective execution of data governance processes. Challenges arise in striking a delicate balance—ensuring consistency across functions while being adaptive to the unique requirements inherent to each operational domain. To navigate this terrain successfully, organizations must employ tailored strategies, including customizing governance processes to suit the distinct characteristics of specific functions, providing targeted training programs, and establishing feedback capabilities.

These process components are instrumental in guaranteeing that operational governance not only meets the granular needs of individual business functions, but also seamlessly aligns with the broader organizational objectives.

The Operational Level is activated to follow standardized governance procedures while addressing habits present within different business functions. It necessitates a nuanced approach that combines the overarching governance principles with the specific demands of each operational domain. Organizations should invest in tailoring governance processes to suit the unique characteristics of each business function, ensuring that the execution of governance initiatives remains closely aligned with the operational intricacies of individual departments.

Additionally, targeted training programs become invaluable tools in empowering operational teams to adhere to standardized governance practices while accommodating the distinctive requirements of their respective functions. Establishing feedback loops further reinforces the iterative nature of operational governance, fostering continuous improvement and alignment with broader organizational goals.

The Support Level: Orchestrating Governance for Partners, IT, and Teams

The Support Level orchestrates governance by harmonizing existing control efforts across partners, IT, and working teams, ensuring the sustained vitality of the data governance program. Challenges at this level entail aligning support functions with overarching governance goals and ensuring that IT systems robustly support governance processes. To overcome these challenges, organizations must invest in strategies that foster clear communication channels, implement specialized training programs tailored for IT teams, and cultivate a collaborative environment that encourages active participation from all support functions.

Navigating the Support Level involves recognizing the involved dance between governance and the diverse entities that reinforce its success. The alignment of support functions with governance goals requires a strategic approach involving clear communication channels that facilitate a shared understanding of objectives. Specialized training programs tailored for IT teams are essential to equip them with the skills and knowledge necessary to seamlessly integrate governance processes into the technical fabric of the organization. Fostering a collaborative environment ensures that working teams actively engage with governance initiatives, contributing their insights and expertise to the continual refinement of the data governance program.

This collaborative attitude ensures that the Support Level serves not only as a pillar of strength for the governance structure, but also as a dynamic force that propels the program forward.

Conclusion

The Non-Invasive Data Governance Framework emerges as a versatile and transformative tool for organizations navigating the complexities of data management. By addressing the six core components of data, roles, processes, communications, metrics, and tools at every organizational level, this framework provides a comprehensive roadmap for fostering a culture of continuous improvement. The journey through this framework is not a one-size-fits-all solution but a dynamic blueprint that adapts to the unique contours of each tier within an organization.

As we've explored, the Executive level sets the stage by nurturing data as a strategic asset, where leaders champion a data-centric culture, propelling the organization toward sustained success. The Strategic level refines this vision, aligning the core components to execute strategic plans effectively. The Tactical level orchestrates governance across diverse business functions, balancing standardization and unique requirements. The Operational level focuses on streamlining governance within specific business functions, ensuring efficient execution while catering to individual needs.

At the Support level, the orchestration of governance efforts involves harmonizing support functions, IT, and working teams. Meet challenges with strategies such as clear communication, specialized training, and fostering a collaborative environment. The Non-Invasive Data Governance Framework is not a static guideline but a dynamic force that propels organizations toward a future where data is not just managed but harnessed for strategic advantage.

In essence, this journey through the Non-Invasive Data Governance Framework summarizes the evolution of organizations in their approach to data. It signifies a transformative shift from viewing data as a passive resource to recognizing it as a dynamic and influential asset that shapes critical decision-making processes. By actively engaging with the framework at each organizational level, organizations can cultivate a data-driven culture that propels them toward success in the ever-evolving landscape of data management.

You Are Already Governing Your Data – Non-Invasive Data Governance as a Solution

Organizations are increasingly acknowledging the critical need for effective data governance. However, a prevalent topic persists: many organizations are beginning to recognize that they are already informally governing their data, leading to inefficient and ineffective data practices. This essay addresses the transformative potential of Non-Invasive Data Governance by highlighting how organizations, albeit informally, are already managing their data. It also explores the drawbacks of these informal approaches.

Current State of Informal Data Governance

Many organizations engage in informal data governance, where data management practices are decentralized and lack a cohesive, structured framework. In these scenarios, decision-makers often rely on ad-hoc processes, leading to inconsistent data quality, security vulnerabilities, and regulatory compliance risks. While there might be an inherent understanding of the importance of data, the absence of formalized structures hampers organizations from fully realizing the value of their data assets.

The decentralized nature of data management practices often stems from a historical evolution rather than a deliberate strategy. As organizations grow and adapt to evolving business landscapes, data management approaches can organically develop in silos. This decentralization manifests as disparate data practices across departments, each with its own data storage, processing, and analysis methods. While this flexibility can initially accommodate the specific needs of individual teams, it eventually gives rise to challenges in maintaining a unified, standardized view of the organization's data landscape.

The reliance on ad-hoc processes within informal data governance further exacerbates these challenges. Decision-makers often resort to reactive measures, addressing issues on a case-by-case basis rather than implementing proactive, preventive strategies. This reactive stance not only contributes to inconsistent data quality, but also exposes the organization to potential security vulnerabilities and regulatory compliance risks. Organizations find it difficult to enforce standardized security measures and regulatory controls uniformly across their data ecosystem without a cohesive, structured framework. The consequence is a fragmented approach to data governance that hinders the organization's ability to holistically understand, manage, and derive value from its data assets.

Inefficiencies in Current Approaches

In the landscape of informal data governance, organizations often find themselves navigating a complex web of disjointed decision-making processes. The absence of formal collaboration mechanisms results in disparate teams working in isolation, with limited communication channels hindering the cohesive development of data-related strategies. This lack of alignment often leads to redundant efforts, as different departments may unknowingly pursue similar data objectives without the benefit of shared insights.

Informal governance models tend to perpetuate an environment where data is viewed through departmental lenses rather than as a collective organizational asset. Consequently, the untapped potential of cross-functional collaboration remains elusive, hindering the organization's ability to harness the full value of its data.

The issue of unclear ownership and accountability in informal governance structures exacerbates data-related challenges. Without recognized stewards and clearly defined responsibilities, organizations grapple with persistent data quality issues and an increased risk of errors. The absence of a formalized accountability framework often results in a reactive rather than a proactive approach to data management.

In this scenario, addressing data-related issues becomes a fragmented and challenging process, further perpetuating inefficiencies. As organizations recognize the limitations of these informal approaches, the appeal of Non-Invasive Data Governance becomes increasingly evident as a solution to bridge the existing gaps and streamline the collective effort toward more effective and efficient data management.

Several of the causes of these inefficiencies include:

- **Lack of Collaboration and Alignment:** Informal data governance often results in siloed decision-making, with different departments or teams operating in isolation. This lack of collaboration and alignment impedes the organization's ability to derive meaningful insights from data and hinders the development of a unified data strategy.

- **Unclear Ownership and Accountability:** Informal governance models struggle to establish clear lines of data ownership and accountability. Without designated stewards and defined responsibilities, data-related issues may persist with no clear path for resolution. This lack of clarity can lead to confusion and an increased likelihood of data errors.

- **Rigidity in Decision-Making:** The absence of a flexible governance framework limits an organization's ability to adapt to changes in technology, regulations, or business priorities. Informal approaches often result in rigid decision-making processes that struggle to keep pace with the rapidly evolving data landscape.

Non-Invasive Data Governance as a Solution

Recognizing the shortcomings of informal data governance, organizations are increasingly turning towards non-invasive approaches. This methodology offers a structured yet adaptable framework that aligns with the current informal practices while addressing their inherent inefficiencies. Non-invasive governance seeks to formalize and optimize existing processes without imposing a burdensome structure.

Recognizing the limitations and inefficiencies inherent in informal data governance practices, organizations are increasingly turning their attention towards a transformative solution: Non-Invasive Data Governance. This approach doesn't seek to disrupt existing informal practices but rather to elevate and structure them into a more coherent and purposeful framework.

Non-Invasive Data Governance acknowledges that organizations already engage in data-related activities but need a guiding structure to ensure these efforts align with broader strategic objectives. This evolution is akin to transitioning from a collection of solo performances to orchestrating a harmonious symphony where each department contributes its unique expertise, enhancing the overall organizational data strategy.

At its core, Non-Invasive Data Governance empowers organizations to capitalize on the strengths of informal data management while mitigating its shortcomings. The emphasis is on providing a structured yet flexible framework that accommodates existing practices and encourages collaboration, fostering a collective sense of responsibility for data quality, security, and compliance.

Non-Invasive Data Governance empowers organizations to capitalize on the strengths of informal data management while mitigating its shortcomings.

By recognizing the informal governance already in place and formalizing it into a unified strategy, organizations can bridge the gap between departmental autonomy and organizational alignment, ensuring that their data assets become a cohesive force for informed decision-making and strategic advancement. Now, let's delve into the key benefits that Non-Invasive Data Governance brings to the forefront of organizational data management.

Key Benefits of Non-Invasive Data Governance

Embracing Non-Invasive Data Governance signifies a departure from the limitations of rigid, top-down governance models that often encounter end-user resistance. Instead, it cultivates an environment where data governance becomes integral to day-to-day operations, seamlessly embedded within the organization's culture. This paradigm shift empowers business units to take ownership of their data, providing them with the autonomy to define data requirements and quality standards that align with their unique needs. In doing so, Non-Invasive Data Governance not only addresses the challenge of data ownership, but transforms it into a shared responsibility, fostering a sense of pride and commitment to maintaining high-quality data.

One of the fundamental advantages of Non-Invasive Data Governance lies in its ability to cultivate a flexible and agile environment. Traditional governance models often struggle to keep pace with the dynamic nature of data and the evolving needs of the organization. Non-invasive governance, on the other hand, operates on the premise that change is constant. By incorporating flexibility into the governance framework, organizations can adapt seamlessly to technological advancements, shifts in regulatory landscapes, and changes in business strategies. This agility ensures that the governance structure remains relevant and responsive, safeguarding the organization against the pitfalls of rigidity and enabling it to navigate the complexities of the ever-evolving data ecosystem. Now, let's delve into the benefits organizations can derive from adopting Non-Invasive Data Governance.

Key benefits of following the Non-Invasive Data Governance approach include:

- **Enhanced Collaboration:** By formalizing collaboration channels, non-invasive governance encourages departments to work together cohesively. This approach allows organizations to leverage collective expertise, fostering a more holistic understanding of data requirements and objectives.

- **Business-Led Agility:** Non-invasive governance empowers business units to take the lead in defining data requirements and quality standards. This business-led agility ensures that data practices align with organizational goals, driving faster, more informed decision-making.

- **Decentralized Stewardship with Structure:** Rather than disrupting existing informal data stewardship, non-invasive governance integrates decentralized stewardship into a structured framework. This ensures that individuals closest to the data actively engage in governance efforts while operating within a clear and organized structure.

Conclusion

The shift towards Non-Invasive Data Governance is not a rejection of existing practices but an evolution towards a more efficient and effective data management paradigm. Organizations can unlock the full potential of their data assets by recognizing the informal governance already in place and addressing its inefficiencies through structured yet adaptable frameworks. As the data landscape evolves, embracing non-invasive governance is a strategic move toward creating a more resilient, collaborative, and value-driven data governance model.

In conclusion, this essay has shed light on the pervasive yet often overlooked reality: many organizations are already informally governing their data, leading to inefficiencies and missed opportunities. The decentralized nature of data management, driven by historical evolution rather than deliberate strategy, results in siloed decision-making, unclear ownership, and a reactive approach to data challenges. As organizations navigate this complex web of disjointed processes, the limitations of informal governance become increasingly apparent, hindering their ability to harness the full value of data assets.

Recognizing these challenges, the essay has introduced the concept of Non-Invasive Data Governance as a transformative solution. This approach doesn't seek to overhaul existing practices but aims to elevate and structure informal governance into a cohesive and purposeful framework. By empowering business units, promoting collaboration, and integrating flexible structures, Non-Invasive Data Governance bridges the gap between decentralized autonomy and organizational alignment. The key benefits of enhanced collaboration, business-led agility, and decentralized stewardship with structure underscore the potential for organizations to thrive in the ever-evolving data landscape. Embracing Non-Invasive Data Governance is not just a strategic move, but a paradigm shift toward a more resilient, collaborative, and value-driven approach to data management.

Where Data Governance Should Live

Determining the optimal administrative placement for a data governance program, and specifically a Non-Invasive Data Governance program, is a pivotal decision that can significantly influence its success. This critical choice often boils down to three primary areas within an organization: a specific business area, information technology (IT), or a shared services part of the organization. Each option comes with its own merits and considerations, compelling a thoughtful evaluation of the organization's structure, goals, and existing workflows. Striking the right balance between technical expertise and alignment with business objectives is crucial in establishing an effective Non-Invasive Data Governance framework.

In exploring the administrative landscape for Non-Invasive Data Governance, I will share the advantages and potential challenges of each placement option. Whether housed within a specific business area, under the purview of IT, or administered through a shared services model, the decision-making process requires a comprehensive understanding of the organization's unique dynamics. By examining the implications of each choice, organizations can make informed decisions tailored to their specific needs, fostering a governance approach that seamlessly integrates with their overarching strategy.

In a Business Area

Embedding the Non-Invasive Data Governance program within a specific business area brings a business-centric focus. Many people will tell you that if your data governance program does not reside in a business area, your program will fail. I am not one of those people.

Placing governance responsibility in a business unit ensures that governance initiatives are closely aligned with the goals and operations of that specific area. This approach acknowledges that data governance is not solely a technical endeavor, but a strategic initiative that impacts business processes and decision-making.

Selecting the right business area involves evaluating which department or unit is most data-intensive or needs high-quality, reliable data. Common choices include finance, marketing, or operations. For instance, if customer data is a key asset, the marketing department might be a suitable home for data governance.

While this approach fosters a deeper understanding of business requirements, it may present challenges in terms of consistency across the organization. Ensuring a standardized approach to governance practices and data quality metrics becomes crucial to avoid silos and fragmentation.

When a Business Area May Not Be Appropriate

While embedding a Non-Invasive Data Governance program within a business area has its advantages, there are circumstances where this approach might not be the most appropriate. One significant concern arises when the governance responsibilities are concentrated solely within a business unit, leading to potential fragmentation and inconsistency in governance practices across the organization. Each department may develop its own interpretation of governance, resulting in a lack of standardized processes and data quality metrics. This fragmentation can hinder the organization's ability to maintain a cohesive and unified approach to data governance.

Business areas might prioritize immediate operational needs over the broader organizational data strategy. This can lead to a myopic view of data governance, focusing on the specific requirements of the business unit rather than considering the holistic needs of the entire organization. The risk here is that governance initiatives may lack the necessary coordination to address overarching goals and might inadvertently create data silos, impeding the free flow of information across departments.

Business areas may not possess the technical expertise required for certain aspects of data governance, such as implementing and maintaining data infrastructure, ensuring security protocols, and managing complex technical aspects of data management. Without a strong technical foundation, governance practices might fall short in ensuring the consistent application of standards and policies throughout the organization. In such cases, a more centralized approach, potentially led by the information technology (IT) department, could be more suitable to guarantee comprehensive and standardized governance across the entire organizational landscape.

In Information Technology (IT)

Placing the Non-Invasive Data Governance program under the umbrella of IT may have its merits as well. IT departments are typically well-versed in managing data infrastructure, tools, and technologies. Having governance oversight within IT ensures a close alignment with data architecture, security protocols, and technical aspects of data management. This can be advantageous in implementing and enforcing data standards consistently across the organization.

IT teams often possess a comprehensive understanding of the organization's overall data landscape, making them well-equipped to ensure that data governance aligns with broader IT strategies. The centralized nature of IT can facilitate a streamlined approach to governance, where policies, standards, and procedures are implemented uniformly.

However, potential drawbacks include the risk of data governance being perceived as a purely technical initiative, potentially neglecting the business context and specific needs of individual departments. There's also a risk of the IT department becoming overwhelmed with governance responsibilities, stretching their resources thin.

When IT May Not Be Appropriate

While placing the administration of a Non-Invasive Data Governance program within the information technology (IT) department can be beneficial in many respects, there are situations where this approach might not be the most suitable. One concern lies in the potential detachment from business objectives. IT departments often have a technical focus, and if they solely administer data governance, there might be a risk of prioritizing technical aspects over aligning governance initiatives with broader organizational goals. This misalignment can result in governance practices that don't adequately address the specific needs and strategic objectives of different business units.

IT departments might encounter challenges in understanding the nuanced requirements of various business areas. Data governance is not solely a technical endeavor; it involves understanding the unique data needs, challenges, and priorities of different departments within the organization. If the administration is too IT-centric, there's a risk of overlooking crucial business context, which can lead to governance strategies that are not fully aligned with the intricacies of the organization's operations.

Another consideration is that IT departments may face resistance from business units if they are perceived as imposing governance measures without a deep understanding of specific business processes. Effective data governance requires collaboration and buy-in from various stakeholders, and an IT-centric approach might encounter resistance from business areas that feel their unique requirements are not adequately considered. In such cases, a more business-oriented approach to administration, possibly within specific business areas, might be more effective in fostering collaboration and tailoring governance practices to meet the diverse needs of the organization.

In Shared Services

Administering Non-Invasive Data Governance through a shared services model within an organization can offer several advantages. Shared services often act as centralized units that provide common support services to different business units, creating a cohesive and standardized approach to data governance. By centralizing the administration, shared services can ensure consistency in governance practices, making it easier to establish and maintain standardized data policies, procedures, and quality standards across the organization.

One key benefit is the potential for increased efficiency. Shared services teams are equipped to streamline processes, reducing duplication of efforts across various business areas. They can leverage economies of scale, centralizing expertise, and resources, which can be particularly advantageous in implementing consistent governance practices and ensuring compliance with standards and regulations. This efficiency can contribute to a more cohesive and effective data governance strategy.

A shared services model facilitates cross-functional collaboration. The central administration unit can serve as a hub for collaboration, bringing together representatives from different business areas to actively participate in the data governance process. This collaborative environment fosters the sharing of best practices, insights, and challenges, leading to a more holistic and well-rounded governance approach that considers the diverse needs of various business units.

When Shared Services May Not Be Appropriate

However, challenges may arise if the Shared Services model is not well-aligned with the unique requirements of individual business units. The shared services team must have a deep understanding of the specific data needs, priorities, and challenges of different departments. If the administration is too detached or generic, it might struggle to address the nuanced governance requirements of diverse business areas, potentially leading to a lack of engagement and alignment with the organization's strategic goals. Therefore, carefully considering the balance between centralization and customization is essential when implementing Non-Invasive Data Governance through a shared services approach.

Conclusion

The decision on where to administer Non-Invasive Data Governance should be driven by a holistic understanding of the organization's structure, culture, and objectives. Establishing a collaborative model where IT and business units work together might be beneficial, leveraging each other's strengths.

A thorough assessment of data needs, existing workflows, and organizational goals will guide this decision. Regular communication and collaboration between IT and business areas are essential to bridge potential gaps and ensure that the Non-Invasive Data Governance program aligns seamlessly with the organization's overall strategy. Regardless of the chosen path, the key is to strike a balance that harmonizes technical capabilities with business requirements, creating an effective and non-invasive governance framework.

CHAPTER 8

Future of Data Governance

Chapter 8, *Future of Data Governance*, serves as both a visionary outlook and a practical guide to advancing governance strategies in a rapidly evolving data landscape. Grounded in the ideals of *Empowering People to Govern Data and AI*, this chapter emphasizes the intersection of cultural shifts, technological innovation, and strategic foresight required to ensure governance continues to thrive in the age of AI and advanced analytics.

The chapter opens with *A Home for Data Stewards*, an exploration of creating a structured yet adaptable space for the critical roles of data stewards. This essay highlights the importance of aligning stewardship with organizational objectives while fostering an environment where these roles can flourish. By empowering stewards with clarity and support, organizations can unlock the full potential of their governance frameworks.

The Impact of Culture on Data Governance Success examines the reciprocal relationship between governance and culture. This essay provides actionable insights into how an organization's existing values and behaviors can either propel or hinder governance initiatives. By aligning governance efforts with cultural strengths, leaders can create a symbiotic relationship that benefits both.

Conversely, in *The Impact of Data Governance on Data Culture Success*, the focus shifts to the transformative power of governance in shaping organizational culture. This essay demonstrates how formal governance practices drive collaboration, trust, and accountability—fostering a culture where data is seen not just as a resource but as a strategic asset.

Mastering Metadata Governance delves into the critical role of metadata in governance success. It highlights how effective metadata management serves as the backbone for AI, analytics, and decision-making processes. By demystifying metadata governance, this essay offers practical strategies for leveraging metadata as a driver of efficiency and innovation.

In *Weave Data Literacy into Data Governance*, the conversation expands to the human side of governance, emphasizing the role of education and engagement. This essay argues that data literacy is not just a complementary skill but a cornerstone of successful governance. By embedding literacy initiatives into governance programs, organizations can empower their teams to make data-driven decisions with confidence.

The chapter concludes with *Data Modernization as a Pivotal Strategy*, which positions modernization as a critical component of future-ready governance. This essay outlines how updating legacy systems, processes, and mindsets is essential for organizations looking to stay competitive in an AI-driven world. By aligning governance efforts with modernization strategies, organizations can ensure their data practices remain agile and impactful.

Chapter 8 offers a forward-thinking perspective on governance, weaving together cultural, technological, and strategic elements to chart a path for long-term success. By addressing the challenges and opportunities of the future, this chapter reinforces the necessity of empowering people to govern data and AI effectively. It is a call to action for leaders to embrace governance as a dynamic, evolving practice that holds the key to unlocking the full potential of their organizations.

A Home for Data Stewards

Creating an internal organizational website or homepage for a Data Governance or Data Stewardship Community of Excellence (CoE) should be considered a critical step toward empowering those recognized and tasked with formalized accountability for data within an organization. Data stewards are provided with a vital resource hub by establishing a centralized web-based location. With the appropriate types of information, the hub will feel like home.

Communications, specifically directed at tactical and operational level stewards, is one of the six core components of the Non-Invasive Data Governance (NIDG) framework. The others include data, roles, processes, metrics, and tools. Effective communication ensures that stewards are well-informed about their roles, responsibilities, and the impact of their work on the organization's data governance goals, fostering a culture of data stewardship that aligns with strategic objectives.

The site can facilitate not only the exchange of knowledge and best practices, but also support the cultivation of a strong, collaborative community. Having a dedicated place for data stewards to go is paramount; it ensures they have access to the tools, information, and support necessary to effectively govern data. This enhances their ability to make informed decisions, align data governance initiatives with organizational goals, and navigate the complexities of data management with greater confidence and efficiency.

This essay outlines the potential components and content sections of such a website, emphasizing its role in fostering a culture of effective data management and governance within an organization.

Introduction to Data Governance

The opening section of the website should introduce the discipline of Data Governance and specifically the NIDG approach, explaining its principles and benefits. It highlights how NIDG leverages existing roles, responsibilities, and structures within an organization to manage data as an asset without significant disruption or overhaul. This foundational understanding sets the stage for the rest of the content on the website.

It's crucial to emphasize that NIDG is designed to fit seamlessly into the organization's existing culture and operational model. By focusing on enhancing what is already working in data management and governance, NIDG encourages a smoother transition and greater acceptance among team members. This section should underscore the adaptability of NIDG to various organizational sizes and types, showcasing its flexibility and efficiency in fostering a data-centric culture.

Community of Excellence Overview

This part of the site outlines the purpose, objectives, and expected outcomes of the Data Governance or Stewardship CoE. It describes the community's role in facilitating best practices, sharing knowledge, and developing data governance competencies across the organization.

The website should highlight the collaborative nature of the Community of Excellence (CoE), showcasing how it serves as a hub for innovation and continuous improvement in data governance. It should illustrate how the CoE brings together diverse stakeholders, including data stewards, IT professionals, business users, and executives, to foster a unified approach to data governance. By emphasizing the community's role in bridging gaps between different organizational silos, the overview can inspire members to actively contribute and benefit from the collective expertise within the CoE.

Resources and Tools

A comprehensive resources section provides members with access to data governance frameworks, policies, procedures, and best practices documentation. It also includes tools and templates to assist in data quality management, metadata management, data lineage documentation, and more. This section could be enriched with case studies and examples to illustrate successful data governance initiatives.

The resources and tools section should offer a carefully curated selection of materials catering to beginners and advanced data governance practitioners. Including interactive resources such as video tutorials, infographics, and dynamic templates can enhance user engagement and learning. Highlighting tools that facilitate collaboration and data sharing within the organization can further underscore the practical applications of these resources, making data governance more accessible and actionable for all community members.

Training and Development

This crucial component focuses on building data governance skills and knowledge within the organization. It might include a calendar of training sessions, workshops, webinars, and other educational opportunities. Online courses and self-paced learning modules can be featured here, along with access to external resources and certifications.

The section should stress the importance of continuous learning and professional development in the field of data governance. Offering a variety of learning paths tailored to different roles within the organization can help ensure that all community members find relevant and engaging educational opportunities. Highlighting success stories of individuals or teams who have leveraged these training resources to achieve significant improvements in data governance can serve as powerful motivation for others to participate and grow their skills.

Forums and Discussion Boards

Interactive forums and discussion boards encourage active participation and collaboration among community members. These platforms enable users to ask questions, share experiences, seek advice, and discuss challenges and opportunities related to data governance.

In addition to facilitating dialogue, these forums should be structured to promote easy navigation and efficient knowledge exchange. Implementing features such as topic tagging, expert Q&A sessions, and real-time notifications can enhance the user experience. Encouraging participation from data governance leaders and external experts can enrich discussions with diverse perspectives and insights, making these forums a vital resource for problem-solving and innovation in data governance practices.

Data Governance News and Updates

A news section informs the community about the latest developments, trends, and innovations in data governance. This might include summaries of recent essays, links to external publications, updates on data regulations and compliance requirements, and announcements of new tools or technologies.

This section should contextualize and analyze how these developments impact the organization and its data governance practices. Curating content that aligns with the interests and needs of the community can help members stay ahead of industry trends and regulatory changes. Providing expert commentary or hosting webinars to discuss the implications of significant news items can further engage the community and foster a culture of proactive adaptation and learning.

Success Stories and Case Studies

Highlighting success stories and case studies from within the organization serves as a powerful tool for demonstrating the value of data governance. This section can showcase projects that have led to significant business improvements, sharing insights into the strategies, processes, and outcomes.

To enrich this section, detailed narratives covering the challenges faced, strategies employed, and lessons learned can provide a more comprehensive understanding of the success factors in data governance initiatives. Encouraging community members to submit their own stories can foster a sense of ownership and pride in the organization's data governance achievements. This celebrates successes and serves as a practical learning resource for others looking to replicate similar results.

FAQs and How-To Guides

A well-organized Frequently Asked Questions (FAQ) section addresses common questions about data governance, providing clear, concise answers. How-to guides offer step-by-step instructions for common data governance tasks and processes, helping to demystify complex concepts and activities.

Each FAQ and How-To guide should be crafted to address the specific concerns and operational challenges the community members encounter. Incorporating interactive elements like video tutorials or infographics within these guides can enhance understanding and retention. Regularly updating this section based on feedback and emerging questions will ensure it remains a valuable resource for immediate and practical data governance solutions.

Community Engagement and Events

Details of upcoming events, meetings, and networking opportunities encourage active engagement within the CoE. This section could include information about data governance conferences, internal workshops, and special interest groups.

Incorporating a user-friendly calendar interface that allows members to easily view and RSVP to events can increase participation. Offering a mix of in-person and virtual events caters to a wider audience, facilitating engagement regardless of geographical location. Highlighting past event recordings and key takeaways can also serve those unable to attend, ensuring the entire community benefits from these learning and networking opportunities.

Feedback and Improvement

A mechanism for community members to provide feedback on the CoE's activities, resources, and overall direction ensures the community remains relevant and responsive to its members' needs. This could take the form of surveys, suggestion boxes, or interactive feedback sessions.

Enhancing this section involves actively demonstrating how feedback leads to tangible improvements within the community. Sharing summaries of feedback received and actions taken validates member input and encourages continuous dialogue. Implementing a transparent tracking system for suggestions and their outcomes can further promote a culture of openness and continuous improvement.

Leadership and Contact Information

Finally, providing clear information on the CoE's leadership and how to get in touch with data governance experts within the organization encourages open communication and support. This section can include profiles of community leaders and subject matter experts, along with their contact details.

Featuring interviews or essays from CoE leaders can provide insights into their visions and strategies for data governance, fostering a personal connection with the community. Offering an easy-to-navigate contact directory that includes areas of expertise can streamline the process for members seeking advice or collaboration, enhancing the sense of community and support within the CoE.

Conclusion

In crafting this website, it's essential to ensure that the content is accessible, engaging, and regularly updated to reflect the evolving nature of data governance. The website should serve as a central hub for all things related to data governance within the organization, promoting a culture of continuous improvement and strategic data management.

Such a platform is particularly vital for data stewards, providing them with a go-to resource for guidance, tools, and community support. It empowers stewards to effectively manage data assets by offering a wealth of information and resources tailored to their unique needs, thereby enhancing their ability to contribute to the organization's data governance objectives.

The Impact of Culture on Data Governance Success

Organizational culture plays a significant role in the success of Data Governance, specifically a Non-Invasive Data Governance (NIDG) program. The NIDG approach emphasizes leveraging and formalizing existing roles, responsibilities, and data-related practices rather than imposing new ones. This means that the existing data culture—how employees perceive, manage, and use data—forms the foundation for implementing the NIDG framework.

In an organization with a strong data culture, where data is valued as an asset and there's a general awareness of the importance of data quality and governance, the NIDG program is likely to be more readily accepted and integrated into daily operations. Conversely, in organizations where the data culture is weak or data is undervalued, there may be more resistance to governance initiatives, even non-invasive ones.

Assessing and understanding the organization's current data culture and its impact on Data Governance is a crucial first step in the NIDG approach. It helps to recognize the natural data stewards and tailor the governance program to fit the cultural context of the organization, thereby enhancing its chances of success.

Assessing and understanding the organization's current data culture and its impact on Data Governance is a crucial first step in the NIDG approach.

Cultural Impact on Data Governance

The complexity of an organization's culture fundamentally shapes the path of its Non-Invasive Data Governance program. As a reflection of collective values, behaviors, and attitudes toward data, the cultural environment within an organization can either accelerate the adoption of NIDG principles or present barriers that require strategic navigation. The following aspects outline the cultural dimensions that are pivotal in determining the effectiveness of implementing a NIDG program, each acting as either a catalyst for success or a potential hurdle to overcome:

- **Value Placed on Data**: Organizations that recognize data as a critical asset are more likely to prioritize governance and understand its role in achieving business objectives.

- **Leadership Support, Sponsorship, and Understanding**: Strong support from senior management is essential. Leadership must endorse and actively promote the importance of data governance.

- **Employee Engagement and Ownership**: Cultures that encourage employee involvement and recognize contributions towards data management efforts help foster a sense of responsibility and ownership.

- **Openness to Change and Innovation**: Organizations that are adaptable and open to refining their processes and workflows according to governance principles are more likely to integrate NIDG successfully.

- **Collaboration and Silo-Breaking**: A culture that promotes cross-departmental collaboration and communication can effectively break down data silos, which is crucial for effective data governance.

- **Data Literacy**: The general level of data literacy across the organization impacts how well employees can contribute to and benefit from data governance initiatives.

- **Transparency and Trust**: Cultures with high levels of trust and transparency are more conducive to sharing information and upholding the data governance framework.

- **Accountability Structures**: The presence of clear accountability structures, where individuals understand their roles in data management, supports the NIDG approach's goal of formalizing existing roles and responsibilities.

- **Learning and Development**: A culture that values ongoing learning and skill development will likely embrace the training and educational aspects necessary for a robust data governance program.

- **Risk Tolerance**: An organization's tolerance for risk affects how data governance is perceived, whether as a necessary safeguard or a hindrance to innovation and agility.

Each cultural aspect plays into how well a Non-Invasive Data Governance program can be assimilated into the organization's way of working, influencing its overall success or failure.

Strategic Integration of NIDG in Culture

The seamless incorporation of a Data Governance program into an organization's existing data culture is a strategic initiative that requires a thorough understanding of both the current cultural landscape and the objectives of the DG framework. The NIDG approach offers a blueprint for this integration, leveraging existing roles and responsibilities within the data ecosystem. The rest of this essay outlines a structured approach to aligning the NIDG framework with the prevailing data culture to optimize data management practices.

Understanding the Existing Data Culture

The first phase involves an in-depth analysis of the current data culture, identifying how data is perceived, used, and managed. An organization must assess its data culture's maturity, encompassing data quality, literacy, and stewardship. This phase should yield a comprehensive overview of the informal data roles that have organically developed and the gaps in data handling that need to be addressed.

Further delving into the existing data culture entails evaluating the everyday data-related interactions and decision-making processes. This deep dive clarifies the implicit norms and practices influencing data management, shining a light on the behavioral nuances that shape data transactions. Such insights enable the creation of targeted interventions that resonate with the workforce, fostering a more data-centric ethos.

Strategic Implementation of NIDG

With a firm grasp of the existing data culture, the NIDG framework can be introduced strategically. The framework's non-invasive nature allows it to reinforce and formalize the data-related activities already being performed, rather than introducing radical changes that could meet resistance. The emphasis here is on the recognition and formalization of roles, ensuring that data governance becomes an integral, almost invisible, part of the organizational routine.

Implementing the NIDG strategically also involves mapping the framework's principles to the organization's specific data processes and roles. It requires careful planning to seamlessly integrate governance activities with existing workflows, thus minimizing disruption and enhancing the natural adoption of new governance practices.

Change Management and Communication

Critical to the NIDG approach is a change management strategy that acknowledges the existing organizational ethos. Design communication plans to articulate the strategic importance of data governance and how it dovetails with the organization's broader goals. The message should highlight how the NIDG framework can enhance data quality and compliance without disrupting daily operations.

Effective change management also includes regular, transparent communication that keeps all stakeholders informed of the governance initiatives, progress, and individual contributions to the collective goal. It necessitates dialogues that facilitate mutual understanding between the data governance team and the wider organization, ensuring a unified approach to data management.

Cultivating Data Stewardship and Literacy

The next step is to cultivate a robust data stewardship model. This involves identifying and officially recognizing existing data stewards and providing them with the necessary tools and training. Concurrently, initiatives to enhance data literacy across the organization will ensure that all employees understand their role in the data lifecycle and the importance of data quality.

Augmenting data stewardship and literacy includes ongoing education and support mechanisms that empower employees to take proactive roles in data governance. This encompasses creating a supportive environment where data stewards are valued for their expertise and contributions, fostering a community of practice around data management.

Monitoring, Metrics, and Feedback Loops

Accompany the implementation with monitoring mechanisms and key performance indicators to track the effectiveness of the DG program. Feedback loops are crucial for continuous improvement, allowing the organization to respond dynamically to challenges and adapt the DG practices as needed.

This ongoing evaluation is not just about oversight but about creating a culture of accountability and recognition. It involves not just quantitative measurement but also qualitative assessment of how data governance is maturing within the organization, acknowledging achievements, and addressing shortcomings constructively.

Integrating NIDG with Organizational Goals

Align the NIDG framework with the organization's vision and mission. By tying data governance objectives with business outcomes, the organization can ensure that the DG program is not just a compliance exercise, but a key driver of business value. This requires the DG initiatives to be closely linked with business strategy, ensuring that they contribute to achieving business objectives.

This alignment ensures that data governance initiatives are not siloed IT projects but integrated business enablers. By linking governance activities directly to strategic objectives, organizations can translate data-related efforts into measurable business performance and competitive advantage.

Overcoming Challenges

Anticipating resistance and barriers is a key part of the strategy. By identifying potential pitfalls, the organization can proactively develop interventions to mitigate these risks. This could involve leadership endorsement, incentive structures, and showcasing success stories to demonstrate the tangible benefits of the NIDG framework.

Addressing challenges also involves listening and responding to feedback from across the organization. Proactive management of resistance includes engagement initiatives that help individuals understand the 'why' behind data governance, thereby transforming potential adversaries into advocates for change.

Conclusion

The relationship between an organization's data culture and the successful implementation of my NIDG framework is multifaceted and requires a measured, strategic approach. By respecting and building upon the existing data culture and by positioning data governance as a means to enhance business performance, organizations can create a data governance program that is both effective and culturally compatible. This essay provides a roadmap for organizations to realize their data governance ambitions in a non-disruptive manner and closely aligned with their strategic business goals.

The Impact of Data Governance on Data Culture Success

The previous essay in this chapter is titled *The Impact of Culture on Data Governance Success.* That essay was never meant to stand alone. Not only does culture have an impact on data governance, but the same holds true in reverse. In this essay, I address how data governance can foster a data-centric culture within an organization by promoting data accountability, transparency, and trust among employees, leading to more informed decision-making and improved data utilization.

The nurturing of a robust data culture has become important for organizations aiming to thrive in an increasingly data-driven world. Implementing data governance is not merely a strategic choice but necessary to ensure that data becomes a cornerstone of an organization's culture, driving innovation and strategic decision-making. At the heart of this movement towards a data-centric organizational culture is Non-Invasive Data Governance (NIDG), a framework that plays a pivotal role in steering the success of a data culture.

Non-Invasive Data Governance: A Gentle Approach to Culture Change

Non-Invasive Data Governance is an approach designed to integrate data governance into an organization's natural workflow without causing significant disruption. Instead of the traditional top-down enforcement of policies and procedures, NIDG acknowledges and formalizes the informal governance activities already happening within an organization. This method respects and leverages existing roles and responsibilities, fostering a sense of ownership and empowerment among all stakeholders. By recognizing every organizational member as a data steward, NIDG cultivates fertile ground for data culture to grow and thrive.

NIDG operates on the understanding that data governance should complement, not complicate, the daily activities of its members. It moves away from the notion of governance as a series of mandates and towards a more integrated approach, where data governance principles are interwoven with the fabric of everyday business operations. This integration encourages a more natural and consistent adherence to data practices, as employees begin to see data governance as part of their standard operational procedures rather than an additional set of rules to follow. The NIDG framework thereby becomes a subtle yet powerful tool in the evolution of an organization's data culture, weaving governance into the tapestry of routine practices and long-term strategies.

Empowerment Through Ownership

One of the most profound impacts of Non-Invasive Data Governance on data culture is the empowerment it provides to individuals across the organization. By recognizing and formalizing roles related to data governance within the existing structure of an organization, NIDG enables individuals to recognize their part in the data lifecycle. Such empowerment leads to a more engaged workforce that values data as an asset and appreciates the role it plays in their daily activities, decision-making, and overall business success.

NIDG cultivates a sense of personal investment and responsibility in data quality and accuracy. Once aware of their roles in data governance, employees are more likely to take the initiative to correct discrepancies, suggest improvements, and promote best practices. This shift in mindset from passive data consumers to active data custodians can have a ripple effect throughout an organization, leading to enhanced data integrity, increased efficiency, and a more profound respect for the power of data. It's a transformative process that not only improves the quality of data management, but also bolsters the overall confidence in organizational data assets.

Improved Data Quality and Trust

A successful data culture builds on a foundation of data quality and trust. NIDG enhances data quality by encouraging a shared responsibility model. As every employee becomes an active participant in maintaining the integrity of data, the collective effort results in a higher quality of data. Trust in data is also reinforced, as stakeholders can rely on the processes and systems in place to deliver accurate and consistent information.

The shared responsibility model championed by NIDG creates a culture where data errors and inconsistencies are not just recorded but addressed and mitigated at the source. This proactive stance on data quality control turns each team member into a guardian of data, ensuring errors are not merely corrected but analyzed for underlying causes. Such diligence elevates the overall trustworthiness of data across the organization, as stakeholders are not just passive recipients of information but are actively assured of its veracity through transparent and reliable governance practices.

Agility and Responsiveness

Data culture thrives in an environment that is agile and responsive to change. NIDG's flexibility allows organizations to adapt governance practices as business needs evolve without the constraints of rigid governance structures. This agility ensures that the organization's data culture remains dynamic and can rapidly respond to new challenges and opportunities.

The agility facilitated by NIDG allows for a seamless integration of new technologies and methodologies into the existing data governance framework. As market trends shift and technological advancements emerge, organizations can swiftly recalibrate their data strategies, ensuring that their data governance framework is resilient and cutting-edge. This nimble response to the changing landscape not only proves an organization's data assets but also fosters a culture of innovation, where employees continuously learn and evolve with the industry.

Democratization of Data

NIDG promotes the democratization of data by breaking down silos and making data accessible to a broader range of stakeholders within the organization. This accessibility allows for a more inclusive data culture where diverse perspectives contribute to insights and decision-making. Democratization under NIDG also ensures that governance is not the sole province of IT or a specific data team but a shared enterprise-wide commitment.

The democratization of data under the NIDG framework empowers various functional areas of the organization to make informed decisions without unnecessary gatekeeping. Enabling access to data across different levels fosters a sense of collective intelligence where insights are pooled and shared, leading to richer, more nuanced analyses and strategies. It encourages a collaborative environment where the input from various departments is not only welcomed but actively sought, thereby enriching the decision-making process with a multiplicity of viewpoints and expertise.

Regulatory Compliance and Ethical Use of Data

A data culture is not only about leveraging data for business success, but also about ensuring compliance with regulatory requirements and ethical standards. NIDG provides a framework for organizations to manage their data in a way that is compliant with laws and regulations, which is increasingly important in a world with growing concerns over data privacy and security. The ethical use of data is also championed, as NIDG encourages transparency and accountability in data practices.

NIDG underlines an organization's need to establish a proactive stance towards data governance, anticipating changes in the legal landscape and adapting accordingly. By instilling a culture that prioritizes ethical data use and regulatory compliance, organizations can avoid the pitfalls of non-compliance, including financial penalties and reputational damage. This proactive approach is crucial in sectors such as finance and healthcare, where regulations are constantly evolving. In fostering a forward-thinking mindset, NIDG helps embed a deep-rooted ethical consciousness within the organizational ethos, ensuring that data is used wisely and with integrity.

Continuous Improvement and Innovation

A robust data culture is one that continuously seeks to improve and innovate. NIDG supports this by promoting a culture of continuous learning and adaptation. The framework encourages feedback loops, allowing for governance practices to be regularly assessed and refined. This ongoing process of improvement ensures that data governance practices and the data culture of an organization remain current and effective.

NIDG also stimulates innovation by endorsing a trial-and-error approach in data handling and governance. This methodology allows organizations to experiment with new ideas in data utilization without the fear of immediate, large-scale consequences. It creates a safe space for creativity, where novel ideas can be tested and valuable lessons can be learned, thereby driving innovation. In an age where data is a key driver of competitive advantage, this aspect of NIDG can be a significant enabler for organizations to stay ahead of the curve.

Conclusion

The impact of data governance on data culture cannot be overstated, and adopting the Non-Invasive Data Governance framework can serve as a catalyst for cultural transformation. NIDG fosters an inclusive, quality-focused, agile, and compliant data culture, setting the stage for an environment where data is not just an asset but a core facet of the organizational identity. As data becomes ever more critical to the success of businesses, the NIDG framework provides a sustainable path for organizations to harness the full potential of their data, ensuring a thriving and resilient data culture.

Mastering Metadata Governance

Metadata, data stored in IT tools that improve the business and technical understanding of data and data-related assets, plays a crucial role in modern organizations, acting as the backbone of informed decision-making and strategic planning. As businesses explore deeper and deeper into data-driven practices, the significance of effectively governing metadata becomes paramount.

This short essay explores how to embed metadata governance within a Data Governance program, specifically utilizing the principles of Non-Invasive Data Governance (NIDG). The NIDG's core components of data, roles, processes, communications, metrics, and tools serve as guiding beacons in this journey.

Recognizing the Value of Metadata Governance

The first step is to understand the immense value of metadata and its governance. Metadata helps in understanding data lineage, improving data quality, and ensuring compliance. It's the contextual layer that transforms raw data into meaningful information. Without proper governance, metadata can become a chaotic and underutilized asset. Integrating metadata governance into a Data Governance program means creating a structured approach to handle, classify, and use metadata so that it aligns with organizational objectives.

Leveraging NIDG's Core Components

- **Data**: The cornerstone of NIDG, data in this context refers to metadata itself. Recognize that metadata is as valuable as the primary data it describes. The first step is cataloging existing metadata across systems. This catalog serves as a foundation for further governance actions.

- **Roles**: Identifying and defining roles is crucial in NIDG. This includes recognizing existing informal metadata stewards—individuals who, by the nature of their roles, manage metadata (like database administrators or data analysts). Formalizing these roles within the governance structure ensures clarity and accountability.

- **Processes**: Develop processes for metadata management that align with existing workflows. This might include processes for metadata creation, updating, quality checks, and usage. The goal is to embed these processes seamlessly into daily operations without disrupting the existing data culture.

- **Communications**: Effective communication strategies are essential in promoting the importance of metadata and its governance. Educate stakeholders about the benefits of well-governed metadata—such as enhanced data quality, easier compliance, and improved data understanding. Regularly communicate the progress and successes of metadata governance initiatives.

- **Metrics**: Establish metrics to measure the effectiveness of metadata governance. These could include the accuracy of metadata, the completeness of the metadata catalog, and user satisfaction with metadata-related processes.

- **Tools**: Utilize appropriate tools for metadata management that integrate well with existing technologies. Tools for metadata cataloging, lineage tracing, and quality control are fundamental. The choice of tools should consider user-friendliness to encourage widespread adoption.

Practical Steps for Integrating Metadata Governance

- **Assessment and Planning**: Begin by assessing the current state of metadata within the organization. Identify gaps in metadata management and areas where governance can bring immediate benefits. Develop a strategic plan that outlines goals, timelines, and required resources for metadata governance.

- **Stakeholder Engagement**: Engage with key stakeholders to gain support and input. This includes IT leaders, data stewards, and business users. Their involvement ensures that the governance strategy aligns with both technical and business needs.

- **Training and Empowerment**: Invest in training programs to enhance metadata literacy among employees. Encourage a culture where every team member feels empowered to contribute to metadata governance. Training should cover the importance of metadata, best practices in metadata management, and the use of metadata tools.

- **Pilot Projects**: Implement pilot projects to demonstrate the benefits of metadata governance. Choose areas where improvements in metadata can lead to visible gains, such as in compliance reporting or data analytics. Use the success of these pilots to build momentum and expand governance efforts.

- **Continuous Improvement and Adaptation**: Metadata governance is not a one-time project but an ongoing endeavor. Continuously monitor, review, and adapt governance practices to meet evolving organizational needs and technological advancements.

- **Feedback and Iteration**: Establish feedback loops where users can report issues, suggest improvements, and share successes. Use this feedback to iterate and refine governance strategies.

Conclusion

Integrating metadata governance into a Data Governance program, especially following NIDG principles, is a journey of strategic planning, stakeholder engagement, and continuous adaptation. By acknowledging the value of metadata, leveraging NIDG's core components, and following a structured approach, organizations can unlock the full potential of their metadata, turning it into a strategic asset that drives informed decision-making and operational efficiency. This journey is not just about managing metadata; it's about harnessing its power to gain a competitive edge in the data-driven business landscape.

Weave Data Literacy into Data Governance

Data Literacy is as crucial as financial literacy once was during the rise of the modern economy. Data Literacy is a skill that allows businesses to interpret, analyze, and leverage data, transforming it into actionable insights. Integrating data literacy within an organization is not a mere addition to the employee skillset; it's a transformation of the organizational mindset, a crucial evolution for the data-driven future.

Non-Invasive Data Governance (NIDG) offers a gentle yet effective pathway for embedding data literacy into the heart of a company's culture. It does so without disrupting existing processes or imposing daunting new systems, making the engagement of data competencies a natural progression.

The heart of NIDG lies in its ability to integrate with the current organizational character. This principle is also the keystone for introducing data literacy. The initiative begins by identifying the existing, albeit informal, data stewards within the company. These are the individuals who, by the nature of their day-to-day responsibilities, have developed an intuitive understanding of data's relevance and utility. They are the pioneers who will lead their peers into the data age, not through top-down mandates but through bottom-up, experience-based learning. They can share their expertise, derived from tangible interaction with data, in a manner that resonates with their colleagues' professional experiences.

As the recognized data stewards start sharing their knowledge, a crucial component of fostering data literacy is developing a common language of data within the organization. This involves defining key terms, data metrics, and concepts essential for data literacy and ensuring they are communicated consistently across all levels of the company. This shared vocabulary is the bedrock upon which data conversations can be built, allowing for clear and effective communication. Through these interactions, the mystery of data is dispelled, and a transparent, accessible framework for understanding data is constructed.

In the non-invasive approach, it is essential that the adoption of this common language and the subsequent data literacy efforts are directly correlated with business strategies and outcomes. Employees must see how their increased understanding of data can affect their roles and the organization's success.

Educational endeavors should be closely linked to strategic business initiatives to achieve this.

Educational endeavors should be closely linked to strategic business initiatives to achieve data literacy.

For instance, a marketing team can be shown how data literacy can help them understand customer behavior better, leading to more effective campaigns. Similarly, a customer service team can use data literacy to improve response times and customer satisfaction rates. This strategic alignment ensures that data literacy is not viewed as an abstract concept but as a practical tool for enhancing performance and achieving business goals.

A central tenet of NIDG is to promote the stewardship of data without bothering with burdensome controls. This principle extends to how the organization teaches and fosters data literacy. Rather than mandatory training programs that might meet with resistance, NIDG encourages voluntary, self-paced learning opportunities that employees can opt into. This could take the form of online courses, in-person workshops, or even informal learning groups. The aim is to create an environment where learning about data is as accessible and engaging as possible, encouraging natural curiosity and self-motivation among employees.

A non-invasive introduction of data literacy also leverages existing communication channels within the organization. From intranet pages dedicated to data insights to regular newsletters highlighting data success stories, these channels serve as instruments for spreading data knowledge. They can be used to spotlight how different departments use data, share tips and best practices, and celebrate data wins, no matter how small. This does not just educate but also inspires people, showcasing the tangible benefits of data literacy across the organization.

The gradual and comprehensive nature of NIDG means that data literacy can be scaled up as the organization matures in its data journey. What might start as basic training on data concepts can evolve into more advanced analytical skills as employees become more comfortable and skilled in working with data. This scalability is crucial, allowing the organization to keep pace with the ever-increasing complexity and volume of data without overwhelming its employees.

The success of introducing data literacy within a NIDG framework relies heavily on feedback and adaptation. As employees engage with data literacy initiatives, their input should be actively sought and valued. This feedback loop helps refine the data literacy program, ensuring it remains relevant, practical, and aligned with employee needs. It also serves as a reminder that data literacy, much like data governance, is a continuous process of learning, improving, and evolving.

Introducing data literacy as part of a Non-Invasive Data Governance program is a delicate balancing act. It requires respecting and utilizing the existing organizational knowledge base, developing a common data language, aligning literacy with business strategy, fostering a voluntary learning culture, leveraging communication channels for education and inspiration, ensuring scalability, and remaining open to feedback.

Conclusion

By adhering to these principles, an organization can instill its workforce with the power of data literacy, crafting a future where every decision is informed, every strategy is data-driven, and every employee is empowered by the knowledge they hold. Through these steps, data literacy becomes more than a skill—it becomes a cornerstone of the organizational identity.

Data Modernization as a Pivotal Strategy

Data Modernization, a fairly new term in the data jargon landscape, must be considered a pivotal strategy for organizations aiming to enhance their operational efficiency and decision-making capabilities. At its core, Data Modernization involves updating, consolidating, and optimizing the collection, storage, management, and analysis of data. This transformation enables organizations to leverage advanced technologies and methodologies, ensuring that data becomes a valuable asset in driving strategic goals and innovation. Integrating Non-Invasive Data Governance (NIDG) into Data Modernization efforts ensures that this transition respects existing organizational roles and workflows, thereby minimizing disruption and maximizing adoption.

The Benefits

The benefits of Data Modernization are diverse and impactful. First, it dramatically improves the quality and accessibility of data, enabling stakeholders to derive actionable insights more readily. Modernization efforts also enhance data security and compliance, which is crucial in today's landscape of stringent data protection regulations. By adopting advanced analytics and AI, organizations can unlock new opportunities for innovation and competitive advantage. Efficiency gains are realized through streamlined processes and reduced reliance on legacy systems, leading to cost savings and more agile operational capabilities.

A further look reveals a targeted impact on the organizational ecosystem. Enhanced data quality and accessibility empower employees at all levels, fostering a data-driven culture that accelerates decision-making and innovation. The implementation of cutting-edge technologies not only places organizations at the forefront of their industries but also attracts top talent eager to work with the latest tools and methodologies. The shift from legacy to modern, scalable platforms facilitates a more responsive and adaptable IT infrastructure that meets the demands of rapidly changing market conditions and customer expectations. This holistic improvement in operational efficiency and strategic agility underscores the profound advantages of embracing Data Modernization.

The Journey

The journey toward Data Modernization involves several detailed steps, each critical to ensuring a successful evolution. Initially, organizations must conduct a comprehensive assessment of their current data architecture, identifying areas of redundancy, inefficiency, or obsolescence. This assessment informs the development of a strategic modernization roadmap, prioritizing initiatives based on their potential impact and feasibility. Critical to this process is the engagement of stakeholders across the organization to ensure alignment with business objectives and user needs.

Incorporating Non-Invasive Data Governance into this journey further enhances the effectiveness of Data Modernization efforts. NIDG's emphasis on leveraging existing organizational roles and responsibilities ensures that data governance seamlessly integrates with the modernization process, avoiding disruption and resistance. This integration advances a culture of data stewardship across the organization, where stakeholders become active participants in improving data quality, governance, and utilization. As a result, the modernization process not only transforms the technical landscape but also builds the institutional knowledge and capacity necessary for sustaining long-term data excellence.

Technical Execution

The technical execution of modernization initiatives involves migrating data to more scalable, secure platforms such as cloud-based services, implementing advanced data management and analytics tools, and adopting practices that ensure data quality and integrity. Throughout this technical evolution, the principles of NIDG play a crucial role. By leveraging existing roles and processes, NIDG facilitates a smoother transition, ensuring that data governance evolves in tandem with modernization efforts without imposing undue burdens on the organization.

A key component of the technical execution phase is ensuring that data remains accessible and useful to end-users. This means that as data is transitioned to new platforms, it is also restructured and cleaned to enhance its usability. Integrating Non-Invasive Data Governance during this phase helps maintain focus on the organization's existing data culture and practices, encouraging adherence to data standards and protocols that have been proven effective. This approach minimizes disruptions to daily operations, allowing for a seamless integration of new technologies and methodologies that underpin a successful data modernization strategy.

Neglecting Data Modernization

Organizations that neglect Data Modernization face numerous challenges that can significantly impede their ability to operate effectively and efficiently. With their high maintenance costs and inflexibility, legacy systems become barriers to innovation and agility. Data silos emerge, obstructing a unified view of information and hindering comprehensive analysis and insights. Perhaps most critically, the failure to modernize data management practices can result in increased security risks and non-compliance with data protection regulations, leading to potential financial and reputational damage.

This neglect can also lead to a significant competitive disadvantage. As peers in the industry adopt modern data practices, they gain the ability to respond more swiftly to market changes, understand customer needs better, and streamline their operations. In contrast, organizations stuck with outdated systems may struggle with slower decision-making processes and a lack of actionable insights, ultimately impacting their bottom line and market position. Incorporating Non-Invasive Data Governance as part of a proactive approach to Data Modernization can mitigate these risks by fostering a data-centric culture that embraces continuous improvement and adaptability.

NIDG as Part of Data Modernization

Incorporating Non-Invasive Data Governance as part of Data Modernization efforts is not merely a strategic choice but essential. NIDG ensures that as data assets become more integrated, accessible, and powerful, they are also governed with a clear understanding of ownership, accountability, and compliance. The NIDG framework supports the modernization process by providing a structured yet flexible approach to managing data across its lifecycle, ensuring that data practices not only contribute to organizational efficiency and effectiveness but also adhere to the highest standards of quality and integrity.

Integrating NIDG within Data Modernization initiatives brings an additional layer of strategic foresight to the revolutionary journey. It ensures that the advancements in data management and technology are underpinned by a governance model that scales with organizational growth and adapts to evolving regulatory landscapes. This preemptive alignment of governance with modernization efforts prevents potential pitfalls related to data privacy, security, and usability, ultimately facilitating a seamless transition to new platforms and technologies. With NIDG, organizations can confidently navigate the complexities of modernizing their data ecosystem while securing stakeholder trust and fostering a culture of informed data usage.

Conclusion

Data Modernization, when executed with the strategic foresight of incorporating Non-Invasive Data Governance (NIDG), indicates a transformative era for organizations. This holistic approach ensures not only the technical upgrading of data systems but also a cultural shift towards improved data stewardship, enhancing the overall efficiency, effectiveness, and agility of organizations. The journey towards modernization, underpinned by NIDG, transcends mere technical upgrades; it fosters a dynamic environment where data governance and modernization efforts are synergistically aligned. This alignment empowers organizations to leverage their data assets fully, ensuring that data management practices evolve to meet current and future challenges. By prioritizing data modernization, organizations can anticipate and mitigate the risks associated with outdated systems, embrace opportunities for innovation, and sustain a competitive edge in the rapidly evolving digital landscape.

The critical role of NIDG in supporting Data Modernization efforts cannot be overstated. As organizations navigate the complexities of modifying their data ecosystems, NIDG offers a blueprint for governance that is both structured and adaptable. This approach not only safeguards the integrity and compliance of data but also enhances its strategic value, ensuring that data serves as a cornerstone of decision-making and innovation. The successful integration of NIDG into Data Modernization initiatives represents a forward-thinking strategy that positions organizations for long-term success. It underscores the imperative for a comprehensive, forward-looking approach to data management—a strategy that recognizes the indispensable value of data as a strategic asset and embraces the principles of Non-Invasive Data Governance to unlock its full potential.

Leadership and Governance

Chapter 9, *Leadership and Governance*, explores the pivotal role that organizational leadership plays in creating a robust and sustainable data governance framework. Aligned with the ideals of *Empowering People to Govern Data and AI*, this chapter examines how leadership must guide, support, and sustain governance efforts to unlock the full potential of an organization's data. Through insightful essays, this chapter equips leaders with strategies to embrace governance as a critical business function, balancing influence, politics, and realistic expectations.

The chapter begins with *Data Governance Leadership and the Triad of Support, Sponsorship, Understanding (SSU)*, an essay that delves into the foundational elements of effective leadership in governance. It emphasizes that success in governance requires more than just directives from the top—it demands active sponsorship, informed support, and a clear understanding of governance's strategic importance. Leaders will discover how to leverage these three pillars to build momentum and maintain alignment across the organization.

In *Let's Not Kid Ourselves: Realistic Data Governance Goal Setting*, the focus shifts to setting achievable and meaningful objectives for governance initiatives. This essay challenges leaders to be pragmatic in their ambitions, recognizing the organization's readiness and capacity while setting the stage for long-term success. It underscores the importance of balancing vision with practicality to create governance goals that resonate with both leadership and operational teams.

Incorporating Politics Into Data Governance takes a candid look at the often-overlooked role of organizational politics in governance success. This essay acknowledges that politics are an inherent part of any leadership dynamic and provides actionable advice for navigating these complexities. Leaders will learn how to turn political challenges into opportunities for collaboration, building stronger coalitions to support governance efforts.

Finally, *SEE Your Data Governance Council* rounds out the chapter by offering a practical guide to creating and empowering governance councils. Through the lens of SEE—Support, Empower, and Engage—this essay shows how leadership can establish councils that not only oversee governance but also drive its adoption and integration throughout the organization. By fostering collaboration and shared accountability, this essay highlights how councils can become powerful advocates for governance.

Chapter 9 reinforces that leadership is not just a supporting role in governance—it is the driving force that ensures its success. By focusing on realistic goal setting, navigating politics, and empowering governance councils, this chapter empowers leaders to embrace their critical responsibilities in governing AI and data. It is a call to action for leadership to step into the spotlight, champion governance, and inspire their organizations to reach new heights in a data-driven world.

Data Governance Leadership and the
Triad of Support, Sponsorship, Understanding (SSU)

There is a keystone that holds the arch of Data Governance together. This arch is the resolute support, sponsorship, and understanding of your organization's Senior Leadership when it comes to your Data Governance program. This is particularly true for the Non-Invasive Data Governance (NIDG) approach, where the subtlety and effectiveness of the program hinge on top-level endorsement. As the person responsible for the NIDG approach, I firmly believe that the involvement of Senior Leadership isn't just beneficial; it's a fundamental prerequisite for success.

When conducting a data governance assessment for my clients, my company typically begins the endeavor with the definition of best practices customized to their needs and interests. These best practices must pass two criteria. The best practices must be practical and doable, given the organization's present and future data environment. And second, if the best practice is not achieved, the program's success will be at risk. One hundred percent of the time, our clients select "Senior Leadership support, sponsor, and understand data governance" (or something close to that) as their first best practice. I kid you not. One hundred percent. It is that important.

In another essay titled "SEE Your Data Governance Council," I emphasized the importance of Standing up, Empowering, and Engaging your Data Governance Council at the Strategic Level. Now, let's extend this acronym concept to the Senior Leadership and Executive level with a new acronym. In the world of data governance fulfillment, Senior Leadership's support, sponsorship, and understanding (SSU) are the golden triad of a successful Data Governance program. In this essay, I dive into why SSU is so important when it comes to steering your Data Governance ship.

The Imperative of Support (The First "S")

Support from Senior Leadership is the foundation upon which the NIDG approach is built. It's not merely about approving budgets or signing off on policies; it's about being actively involved in and committed to the data governance journey. Senior Leadership's support is the beacon that guides the organization through the often-murky waters of data governance. It sends a clear message across the organization: data governance is not a side project; it's a program and a core aspect of our business strategy. Without this support, even the most well-designed NIDG program risks becoming a ship without a sail, directionless and vulnerable to the changing tides of organizational priorities.

In the context of the NIDG approach, this support translates into a leadership style that fosters a culture of data responsibility at every level. Senior Leadership's involvement is crucial in validating and reinforcing the idea that data governance is a collective responsibility, not just the purview of a single department or individual. By advocating for a non-invasive approach, they encourage the organic growth of data governance practices, rooting them in the existing organizational culture and workflow. This support is not just about providing resources; it's about leading by example, demonstrating a commitment to data excellence and a willingness to adapt and evolve. It's about creating an environment where data governance is integrated into the daily decision-making process, ensuring its relevance and effectiveness in achieving the organization's strategic goals.

The Power of Sponsorship (The Second "S")

Sponsorship goes a step further. It's about championing the cause. Senior Leaders, as sponsors, don't just passively approve; they actively advocate for the NIDG program. They understand that data governance is not a one-off task but a strategic initiative that requires ongoing commitment. Their role as sponsors is crucial in breaking down barriers, be they cultural, structural, or financial, ensuring that the NIDG program has the necessary resources and authority to make impactful changes. Sponsorship from the top echelons elevates the program from a tactical initiative to a strategic imperative.

In leveraging the NIDG approach, sponsorship by Senior Leadership translates into a proactive advocacy and visible commitment to the principles of non-invasive data governance. This entails not just endorsing the program, but actively promoting a culture of data stewardship and accountability throughout the organization. Senior leaders who sponsor NIDG effectively utilize their influence to communicate the value of data governance, aligning it with the organization's overall vision and objectives. They play a pivotal role in fostering cross-departmental collaboration, ensuring that data governance is not siloed but integrated across various business functions.

Through their sponsorship, they also facilitate developing and adopting governance policies and practices that resonate with the existing organizational culture and workflows, thereby enhancing buy-in and reducing resistance. In essence, their sponsorship is the catalyst that transforms data governance from a concept into a living, breathing aspect of the organization's ethos, driving meaningful and sustainable change.

The Necessity of Understanding (The "U")

Understanding is perhaps the most nuanced yet critical aspect of leadership involvement. Senior Leaders must grasp the "why" and "how" of the NIDG approach. This understanding isn't just about acknowledging the importance of data governance; it's about appreciating the specific nuances of the Non-Invasive approach—its focus on leveraging existing roles, its emphasis on enhancing accountability, and its strategy of integrating governance into the fabric of the organization's operations. When leaders understand these nuances, their support and sponsorship are not just perfunctory but informed, intentional, and impactful.

The necessity of understanding by Senior Leadership extends beyond mere recognition of data governance as a strategic need. It involves a deep appreciation of the subtleties that make NIDG unique: recognizing that effective governance is not about imposing new rules or roles, but about recognizing and formalizing the existing data-related activities and responsibilities. This level of understanding enables leaders to see data governance as a natural extension of the organization's existing processes, thereby ensuring smoother implementation and greater acceptance. It empowers them to champion a governance model that is collaborative, empowering the existing workforce rather than disrupting it.

By understanding the intricacies of NIDG, Senior Leaders can effectively articulate the value of data governance to the organization, leading to a cohesive, organization-wide approach that aligns with and enhances the organization's overall mission and strategic goals.

The Risk of Non-Compliance with This Best Practice

Failure to secure this triad of support, sponsorship, and understanding from Senior Leadership is not just a minor setback; it's a fundamental flaw that can jeopardize the entire Data Governance initiative. In the absence of strong leadership backing, Data Governance programs often struggle to gain traction, facing resistance at various organizational levels. This lack of endorsement can lead to a disconnect between the governance team's efforts and the broader organizational goals, rendering the program ineffective or, worse, irrelevant.

Without the guiding hand of Senior Leadership, the NIDG approach risks becoming another checkbox exercise, lacking the depth and breadth required to truly transform an organization's data culture. Data governance, especially in its non-invasive form, demands a cultural shift that can only be catalyzed and sustained by those at the organization's helm.

Nurturing a Culture of Data Governance

Senior Leadership's active involvement in the NIDG program does more than just provide resources and remove obstacles; it nurtures a culture where data is valued, understood, and governed effectively. Their understanding and advocacy of the program's principles and objectives help infuse the importance of data governance throughout the organization, embedding it into the very DNA of the company's operations.

This cultural shift is critical for the sustainability of the Data Governance program. It ensures that governance becomes integral to every data-related activity, from compliance and reporting to decision-making and innovation. Senior Leadership's role in fostering this culture cannot be overstated. They are the custodians of the organization's data vision, and their endorsement is pivotal to making data governance an ingrained practice rather than a mandated directive.

Conclusion

To summarize, the success and sustainability of a Non-Invasive Data Governance program hinge significantly on the involvement of Senior Leadership. Their support, sponsorship, and understanding are not just beneficial but essential.

These elements act as the driving force that propels the program forward, ensuring its alignment with organizational goals and embedding it into the corporate culture. As such, securing Senior Leadership's backing is not just a best practice; it's the cornerstone of any successful and sustainable Data Governance initiative.

The Non-Invasive Data Governance (NIDG) approach fundamentally relies on a culture of data responsibility that pervades every level of an organization. The actions and attitudes of Senior Leadership significantly influence this culture. Their active involvement and advocacy establish a tone of data stewardship that resonates throughout the organization. By embracing the NIDG philosophy, Senior Leaders demonstrate a commitment to recognizing and reinforcing existing data management behaviors rather than imposing new, potentially disruptive methods.

This approach fosters a more receptive environment for data governance and aligns seamlessly with the organization's existing operational rhythms. It's about enhancing, not overhauling, which ensures smoother adoption and integration of data governance principles. In essence, Senior Leadership's understanding and endorsement of NIDG are pivotal in creating a data governance ecosystem that is both effective and holistically integrated into the organization's fabric.

Let's Not Kid Ourselves:
Realistic Data Governance Goal Setting

In this quick essay, I address factors for setting realistic goals for data governance, specifically through the lens of Non-Invasive Data Governance (NIDG). Setting goals is about recognizing the real-world challenges we face in organizations, including limited resources, varying levels of leadership support, and the hurdles in achieving broad organizational adoption. At the heart of NIDG is the principle of leveraging existing roles and responsibilities to manage data as an asset. This approach is pragmatic and acknowledges that not every organization can afford a heavy-handed, resource-intensive governance program.

Setting realistic goals begins with understanding your organization's current data governance maturity. It's crucial to assess where you are today to set achievable milestones for tomorrow. This involves identifying the data governance activities already happening within your organization and formalizing them without introducing disruptive new processes.

---

*Setting realistic goals begins with understanding
your organization's current data governance maturity.*

Active Leadership

Leadership plays a pivotal role in the success of any data governance initiative. The strength of your program's leadership will significantly impact its ability to secure resources, gain organizational buy-in, and drive cultural change toward data-driven decision-making. Effective leadership is not just about having authority; it's about influencing change, demonstrating the value of data governance, and inspiring participation across the organization.

Strong leadership in data governance involves more than just **setting goals and expectations**. It requires leaders to actively engage with all levels of the organization, from executive stakeholders to frontline data users, ensuring that data governance principles are integrated into daily workflows and decision-making processes. Leaders must also be adept at navigating organizational politics and leveraging their influence to overcome resistance, fostering an environment where data is recognized as a valuable asset that supports the organization's strategic objectives. This proactive approach helps in embedding data governance into the organizational culture, making it a natural part of operations rather than an imposed mandate.

Resource Consideration

Resource availability is a constant challenge. It's essential to be creative and resourceful, focusing on high-impact activities that require minimal investment. This might mean **prioritizing efforts** that clean up critical data sets, implementing simple data quality metrics, or leveraging free or low-cost tools to support your governance activities.

It is important to acknowledge that the path to effective data governance doesn't always require significant financial outlays. Small, strategic actions can lead to meaningful improvements in data management. For instance, engaging with internal stakeholders to identify and share best practices can foster a collaborative environment that enhances governance with minimal costs. This approach leverages existing organizational knowledge and resources, demonstrating that successful governance is achievable even in resource-constrained settings.

Adoption is Key

Organizational adoption of data governance is another critical factor. Achieving widespread adoption requires a cultural shift that values data as a strategic asset. This shift doesn't happen overnight and requires ongoing education, communication, and reinforcement of the value that data governance brings to the organization. Setting realistic goals means starting small, demonstrating quick wins, and gradually expanding the scope of governance as the organization sees value and becomes more comfortable with the concept.

Fostering an environment where data governance is integrated into daily workflows can accelerate this cultural shift. Encouraging teams to share their success stories and challenges in data governance meetings can create a sense of community and shared purpose. This approach not only reinforces the concept of data as a valuable asset, but also highlights the tangible benefits of data governance, making the cultural shift more palpable and relatable across the organization.

Non-Invasive Data Governance focuses on enhancing what you're doing well, not reinventing the wheel. It means aligning your data governance goals with the organization's strategic objectives, ensuring that governance efforts directly support business outcomes. This alignment helps to secure executive support and ensures that data governance is seen as a critical component of the organization's success, not just an IT project.

Conclusion

In this essay, I explored setting achievable data governance objectives within the Non-Invasive Data Governance (NIDG) framework. Recognizing constraints like organizational adoption, resource availability, and leadership strength is crucial. NIDG emphasizes leveraging existing roles to manage data as an asset, a practical approach for organizations facing limitations.

Key to success are realistic goal setting based on the organization's current data governance maturity, influential leadership capable of securing resources and fostering a data-driven culture, innovative resource utilization to maximize impact with minimal investment, and fostering organizational adoption through small wins and gradual expansion. Aligning data governance with strategic objectives ensures it's viewed as essential for success. This approach advocates for realistic, attainable goals that enhance existing processes and encourage a culture that values data as a strategic asset.

Incorporating Politics Into Data Governance

You can either run from it or learn from it. I was motivated to write this essay to share considerations for incorporating organizational politics into your data governance solution rather than using it as an excuse for limited program success. The inspiration came from a friend, Tiankai Feng, who posted images and quotes from the Disney movie The Lion King and related them to data governance. I found this Lion King quote to be particularly relevant to this essay (https://www.goalcoast.com/the-lion-king-quotes):

Oh yes, the past can hurt.
But from the way I see it, you can either run from it, or learn from it.

Rafiki

Incorporating politics into your data governance framework is routinely viewed as navigating a minefield—an endeavor fraught with potential missteps and opposition. Yet, in reality, politics, when understood and leveraged properly, can significantly bolster the implementation and effectiveness of data governance initiatives. This essay explores proven techniques for turning organizational politics from a stumbling block into a stepping stone, emphasizing the role of Non-Invasive Data Governance (NIDG) in weaving political dynamics into the fabric of successful data governance.

Leveraging Politics

The first step in leveraging politics to the advantage of your data governance program is recognizing that politics are not inherently negative. Politics, in the context of an organization, simply refers to the dynamics of power, influence, and interests that exist within any group of people working together. Acknowledging these dynamics is crucial; it allows you to understand the key players, what motivates them, and how decisions are made. By identifying and engaging with influential stakeholders early on, you can align your data governance initiatives with their interests and goals, thereby securing their support and reducing resistance.

Organizational politics requires a strategic approach to stakeholder management. This involves mapping the political landscape of your organization to identify not only the most visible influencers but also the hidden champions who can sway opinion and foster consensus. Utilizing tools like stakeholder analysis matrices can be instrumental in this process, enabling a structured assessment of each individual's level of influence, interest, and potential to impact the data governance program. Through this level of analysis, you can tailor your engagement strategies to address specific concerns and aspirations, ensuring that every interaction contributes positively to the momentum of your data governance efforts.

Cultivate Champions

One effective technique is to cultivate champions among these key stakeholders. Champions are individuals who have both influence within the organization and a genuine interest in the success of data governance. They can be invaluable in advocating for the program, articulating its value to their peers, and navigating the political landscape. The Non-Invasive Data Governance model facilitates this by leveraging existing roles and responsibilities. It identifies and empowers individuals who already have a vested interest in the quality, management, and utilization of data, thus naturally aligning with the political structures and power dynamics within the organization.

To harness the power of these champions, it's critical to equip them with the tools, information, and authority they need to be effective advocates. This includes providing them with clear, compelling narratives about the benefits and achievements of the data governance initiatives, as well as the challenges they address. Additionally, offering training and resources to help them communicate effectively about data governance can amplify their impact. When champions are well-supported, they can create a ripple effect, fostering a broader organizational culture that values data as a strategic asset. This strategic advocacy builds a groundswell of support, making the path smoother for data governance policies and practices to be adopted and embraced across the organization.

Ensure Transparency

Another critical technique is to ensure transparency in the governance process. Transparency builds trust and demystifies governance initiatives, making it harder for opposition to form based on misinformation or fear of change. This involves clear communication about the goals, processes, and benefits of the data governance program, as well as regular updates on its progress. The NIDG approach supports transparency by promoting open communication channels and collaborative decision-making processes. By involving stakeholders in these processes and providing them with a clear understanding of how data governance will impact their work positively, you mitigate the risk of political pushback.

Consider establishing a governance dashboard that provides real-time insights into the status of data governance activities, achievements, and areas requiring attention. This dashboard should be accessible to all stakeholders and updated regularly to reflect the most current state of the data governance program. Additionally, hosting open forums or Q&A sessions where stakeholders can voice their concerns, ask questions, and offer suggestions can reinforce a culture of openness and inclusivity. Such proactive measures not only bolster the transparency of the data governance program but also encourage a more engaged and cooperative organizational environment, further diminishing the space for political resistance and fostering a united approach to achieving data governance goals.

Frame Business Outcomes

Framing data governance initiatives in terms of tangible business outcomes is a powerful strategy. Stakeholders are more likely to support and become actively involved in initiatives that they can see will directly impact their work and the organization's success. This means tying data governance efforts to strategic business objectives such as improving operational efficiency, enhancing customer satisfaction, or driving innovation. The NIDG model excels in this area by focusing on enhancing and formalizing the existing roles and processes that directly contribute to these outcomes. By demonstrating how data governance supports key business goals, you align the interests of various stakeholders, turning potential political obstacles into opportunities for collaboration and support.

Quantifying the expected outcomes of data governance initiatives wherever possible is essential. Establish key performance indicators (KPIs) and set clear, measurable targets that reflect the business value of improved data management and governance. Regularly sharing achievements against these KPIs reinforces the value of the data governance program and showcases the direct contribution to the organization's strategic objectives. Such evidence-based reporting highlights the real-world impact of data governance, making it easier for stakeholders to understand its importance and fostering a collective effort towards its success. By presenting data governance as a strategic enabler rather than a compliance requirement, you can effectively transform internal politics into a driving force for positive change.

Adapt With Patience

Finally, adaptability and patience are vital. The political landscape within any organization is subject to change, influenced by shifts in leadership, strategy, and external factors. A successful data governance program, particularly one based on the NIDG model, is flexible and capable of evolving with these changes. This means being prepared to adjust your strategies, engage with new stakeholders, and continuously demonstrate the value of data governance in the context of the organization's shifting priorities.

In practicing adaptability and patience, it's crucial to maintain an ongoing dialogue with all levels of the organization to understand the evolving needs and perspectives that may affect data governance. This approach ensures that the data governance framework remains relevant and aligned with organizational goals, even as they evolve. Regularly revisiting and revising the governance framework to reflect new insights and feedback can help sustain its effectiveness over time. Through this process, the organization cultivates a resilient data governance culture that can withstand and adapt to internal and external pressures, ensuring the longevity and success of the NIDG program amidst the complexities of organizational politics.

Conclusion

Incorporating politics into the implementation of effective data governance requires a nuanced understanding of the organization's internal dynamics, strategic alignment of governance initiatives with business goals, and leveraging the NIDG model to naturally integrate governance into the fabric of the organization. By viewing politics not as a barrier but as a conduit for engagement and support, you can establish a data governance program that is not only effective, but also resilient and aligned with the organization's direction and success.

Embracing the political landscape within an organization as an integral part of implementing data governance ensures that the program gains the traction and acceptance it needs to thrive. The Non-Invasive Data Governance model offers a pragmatic and effective framework for navigating these waters, turning potential obstacles into opportunities for advocacy, collaboration, and progress. With a strategic approach that includes recognizing the role of politics, cultivating champions, ensuring transparency, framing outcomes positively, and adapting with patience, organizations can unlock the full potential of their data governance initiatives, securing their place as data-driven leaders in their respective fields.

SEE Your Data Governance Council

Establishing a formal Data Governance Council at the strategic level is pivotal for organizations implementing Data Governance programs. This council serves as the linchpin for cultivating a collaborative culture, delineating clear responsibilities, and steering the triumph of governance initiatives.

The Data Governance Council, operating at the strategic level in a Non-Invasive Data Governance program, plays a pivotal role in shaping and steering the organization's data governance initiatives. This council oversees the governance framework and establishes a diverse and representative membership to ensure a comprehensive understanding of the organization's data landscape.

The Data Governance Council plays a pivotal role
in shaping and steering the organization's data governance initiatives.

In the early phase of a Non-Invasive Data Governance program implementation, the council sets the foundation, formalizing its structure and objectives with leadership involvement, signaling a commitment to prioritizing data governance. The council is granted decision-making authority, resources, and tools necessary to propel governance initiatives forward. The council actively participates in governance activities, fostering an open communication culture, aligning its efforts with organizational objectives, and becoming a dynamic force driving the success of Non-Invasive Data Governance.

The SEE Acronym

The S.E.E. ("SEE") acronym serves as a valuable guiding path for establishing and nurturing a Data Governance Council in the context of a Non-Invasive Data Governance program. The initial step, S (Stand Up), underscores the importance of strategically positioning the council, setting the stage for its pivotal role. E (Empower) reinforces the need to grant the council decision-making authority and resources, empowering it to lead governance initiatives effectively. Finally, E (Engage) emphasizes the ongoing participation and collaboration of the council in governance activities, aligning its efforts with organizational goals and fostering a culture of open communication.

By following the SEE approach, organizations can systematically establish, empower, and engage their Data Governance Council to drive the success of Non-Invasive Data Governance.

Standing Up the Data Governance Council

Standing Up the Data Governance Council marks the foundational phase where the organization lays the groundwork for an effective and representative governing body. During this crucial step, the focus is on creating and formalizing the Data Governance Council. This involves a meticulous process of defining the council's structure, composition, and overarching objectives. To ensure the council's efficacy, it is imperative to curate a diverse representation of stakeholders from various departments and functions. This diversity ensures a comprehensive insight into the organization's intricate data landscape, capturing perspectives that reflect the entire spectrum of data needs and challenges.

Establishing the Data Governance Council is not merely a procedural task; it is a strategic initiative that requires active leadership involvement. Leadership commitment at this stage clearly signals to the entire organization that data governance is a priority and a strategic imperative. The leadership's engagement in this initial phase sets the tone for the importance of data governance in driving organizational success. By standing up the council with a well-defined structure and diverse representation, the organization paves the way for an inclusive and collaborative approach to governance, essential for the success of a Non-Invasive Data Governance program.

Further ensuring the effectiveness of the Data Governance Council involves defining the roles and responsibilities of its members. Clear delineation of duties ensures that each council member understands their contribution to the governance framework, fostering a sense of ownership and accountability. Additionally, establishing communication channels and frameworks for interaction within the council and with other organizational stakeholders is vital. This encourages transparency, open dialogue, and the free flow of information, creating an environment conducive to collaborative decision-making. As the organization stands up the Data Governance Council, these detailed considerations lay the groundwork for a council that is not only representative but also strategically aligned with the goals of Non-Invasive Data Governance.

Empowering the Data Governance Council

Empowering the Data Governance Council is a critical phase that involves endowing the council with the authority, resources, and decision-making capabilities essential for driving effective governance initiatives. This empowerment process is multi-faceted, beginning with a clear delineation of the council's roles and responsibilities. This delineation ensures that each council member understands the scope of their contribution, fostering a sense of ownership and accountability within the governance framework. Moreover, providing the council with access to requisite tools and technologies is imperative. This includes investing in data management platforms, analytics tools, and other resources that enable the council to perform its functions efficiently.

In parallel, establishing robust communication channels between the Data Governance Council and executive leadership is crucial for alignment and support. Regular and transparent communication ensures that the council is aware of organizational priorities, while leadership remains informed about the progress and challenges the council faces. This bidirectional flow of information is foundational for a cohesive and synergistic approach to governance. The empowerment process goes beyond these structural aspects to confer decision-making authority upon the council. The council should be vested with the capacity to make informed decisions regarding data policies, quality standards, and overall governance strategies. This not only positions the council as a strategic decision-making body but also ensures its active participation in shaping the organization's data governance trajectory.

As the organization empowers the Data Governance Council, ongoing support and training become essential components. Continuous education and training programs ensure that council members stay abreast of evolving best practices, technologies, and industry standards. This dynamic empowerment approach transforms the council from mere advisory bodies to a dynamic force propelling governance efforts forward. It positions the council as a strategic partner in steering the organization towards data excellence within the framework of Non-Invasive Data Governance.

Engaging the Data Governance Council

In the critical phase of "Engaging," the focus shifts toward fostering active participation and collaboration within the strategic-level Data Governance Council. Regular and well-structured meetings serve as forums for in-depth discussions on emerging data governance trends, challenges, and best practices. Workshops provide opportunities for hands-on learning, enabling council members to delve into specific governance initiatives and gain practical insights. Tailored training sessions, customized to the evolving landscape of data governance, not only enhance the council's expertise but also ensure they remain well-informed about the latest advancements in the field.

Open communication is a linchpin in the engagement process. It is paramount to establish a culture that encourages council members to voice their perspectives, address challenges, and share valuable insights. This includes creating feedback loops where members can contribute their observations and recommendations, fostering a sense of ownership and collaboration. By integrating the council's activities seamlessly with broader organizational objectives, strategic engagement ensures that the council becomes an indispensable part of the decision-making fabric, contributing actively to the overarching goals and strategies of the organization.

Strategic engagement doesn't stop at formal meetings and workshops; it extends to the organization's day-to-day operations. Encouraging council members to actively participate in relevant projects, initiatives, and cross-functional teams embeds the principles of non-invasive data governance into the organizational culture. This participatory approach ensures that the council's expertise is leveraged in real-time decision-making, making them catalysts for driving governance practices throughout the organization. Strategic engagement thus becomes a dynamic force, seamlessly integrating the council's contributions into the broader spectrum of the organization's data governance framework.

Conclusion

Standing up, empowering, and engaging a formal Data Governance Council at the strategic level symbolizes a comprehensive approach to ensure the success of Non-Invasive Data Governance. This journey requires a dedicated commitment from leadership, a crystalline understanding of the council's purpose, and continuous efforts to sustain member engagement and empowerment. By investing in the establishment and effectiveness of the Data Governance Council, organizations can lay a solid foundation for the seamless integration of governance into existing workflows, thereby dispelling the unfounded myth that governance efforts must be inherently disruptive.

Metaphors, Analogies, and Stories in Data Governance

Chapter 10, *Metaphors, Analogies, and Stories in Data Governance*, taps into the power of storytelling to communicate the often complex and technical ideas surrounding data governance in a way that is relatable, engaging, and memorable. In keeping with the book's subtitle, *Empowering People to Govern Data and AI*, this chapter shows how creative approaches can demystify governance concepts and inspire action at all levels of the organization. By linking abstract principles to everyday experiences, the essays in this chapter bring data governance to life in a uniquely accessible and impactful way.

The chapter begins with *A Data Domain Analogy: The Grocery Store*. This essay cleverly compares the organization of data domains to the layout of a grocery store, making the concept of data domains intuitive and easy to grasp. Through this analogy, readers learn how to categorize and manage data effectively, much like organizing the aisles of a store to improve access and usability. It's a fresh and practical take that simplifies a critical component of governance.

Next, *Stop Complaining About Your Data—And Do Something About It* tackles the frustrations many organizations face when dealing with data quality and accessibility. This essay offers an empowering message: while it's easy to blame the data for organizational shortcomings, the real solution lies in taking proactive steps to govern it properly. Through relatable anecdotes and actionable advice, this piece inspires readers to move from grumbling to governing, driving meaningful change.

In *Data Governance Doesn't Have to Be Scary*, the essay dispels the myth that governance is an intimidating or overly complex discipline. By using light-hearted comparisons and relatable examples, it highlights how governance can be seamlessly integrated into existing workflows without creating fear or resistance. This essay emphasizes that governance, when approached thoughtfully, can be a natural and non-threatening part of organizational culture.

The penultimate essay, *Ask Not What Your Data Governance Program Can Do for You ...*, flips the script by challenging readers to consider their role in making governance successful. Borrowing from a well-known phrase, this essay underscores the importance of individual accountability and collective effort in achieving governance goals. It's an inspiring call to action that reframes governance as a shared responsibility, driven by purpose and collaboration.

Finally, *Data Governance is a Team Sport* rounds out the chapter with a compelling reminder that governance is not a solo endeavor. Using the metaphor of a sports team, this essay illustrates the importance of coordination, communication, and trust among team members to achieve governance success. It celebrates the collective effort required to govern data effectively, leaving readers with a sense of camaraderie and a shared mission.

By weaving together metaphors, analogies, and relatable narratives, Chapter 10 provides a fresh and engaging perspective on data governance. It reminds readers that understanding and implementing governance doesn't have to be a dry or daunting task—it can be insightful, empowering, and even fun. With this chapter, organizations can find new ways to communicate the value of governance, bridging gaps in understanding and fostering a culture of collaboration and accountability.

A Data Domain Analogy:
The Grocery Store

The concept of data domains and sub-domains comes up almost every day while working alongside world-class organizations implementing effective data governance programs. The topic came up in a meeting today which prompted me to recall one way a client of mine addressed how domains play a pivotal role in organizing and optimizing the way they handle their data. The client conversation was worthy of this essay.

Just as a well-organized grocery store facilitates a smooth shopping experience, a well-structured data governance approach using domains and sub-domains ensures efficient data management and governance. This analogy serves as the foundation for this exploration of incorporating data domains into Non-Invasive Data Governance (NIDG) implementations, a strategy critical for augmenting organizational data governance.

A Grocery Store Analogy for Data Domains

Imagine a grocery store, a place familiar to most of us. This store is divided into various sections or departments, each dedicated to a specific category of products—fruits and vegetables, dairy, meats, bakery, and so on. This categorization makes it easy for customers to find what they're looking for, aids the staff in managing inventory more effectively, and streamlines the process of restocking and organizing products.

Translating this analogy to data governance, we can think of an organization's data as the array of products offered in the grocery store. Just as the store is organized into departments, data within an organization can be categorized into domains and sub-domains. A domain represents a major category of data (e.g., customer data, product data, employee data). At the same time, sub-domains break down these categories further (e.g., customer contact information, product pricing details, employee performance records).

Incorporating Data Domains into NIDG Implementations

Incorporating data domains into Non-Invasive Data Governance implementations is similar to designing, setting up, and managing a grocery store's operations. It involves understanding the different types of data the organization deals with, identifying how this data is interconnected, and establishing clear guidelines for managing and governing this data. This structured approach not only improves data accessibility and quality but also ensures that data governance efforts are aligned with the organization's strategic objectives.

The following sections of this essay highlight considerations for managing and governing data domains while keeping with the grocery store analogy:

Identifying Data Domains and Sub-domains

The kickoff step in deploying NIDG closely resembles the methodical planning seen in grocery store layout designs, focusing on identifying various data domains and sub-domains within an organization. This step is reinforced by a deep understanding of the organizational data ecosystem, scrutinizing the relationships among distinct data sets and their contribution to the organization's operational objectives and overarching goals.

The process of identifying data domains and sub-domains under NIDG requires a detailed examination and cross-departmental collaboration, ensuring a thorough description of the data landscape. Similar to how a grocery store organizes its offerings into main departments like produce, dairy, and bakery, and further into sub-categories such as organic fruits, low-fat milk products, or artisan breads, an organization implementing NIDG will systematically map out primary data domains such as finance, customer relations, or operations. Following this, a deeper exploration into sub-domains—like accounts payable in finance, customer feedback in customer relations, and logistics in operations—is essential.

This granular approach to data domain identification, a core tenet of NIDG, ensures a focused and non-disruptive governance structure. By precisely defining policies, standards, and responsibilities within these domains, the organization fosters a more effective and efficient data management practice.

Such careful organization of data domains and sub-domains not only streamlines data governance but also enhances the overall data utility for the organization, drawing a parallel to the way well-structured grocery store aisles optimize the shopping experience.

Recognizing Roles and Responsibilities

Just as a grocery store meticulously recognizes department managers and staff to oversee specific sections, the NIDG model applies a similar principle to data management by acknowledging stewards or managers based on their data domain and sub-domain knowledge and authority. These stewards are tasked with the crucial responsibility of ensuring the data within their domain is of high quality, easily accessible, and secure, in accordance with the overarching data governance policies of the organization.

The NIDG approach enhances this process by recognizing and formalizing the roles already present within the organization. This strategy draws on the natural alignment between employees' existing functions and the needs of data governance. For example, paralleling the role of a grocery store's produce manager who guarantees the freshness and quality of fruits and vegetables, a data steward for customer information is charged with ensuring the accuracy, privacy, and readiness of customer data.

By recognizing clear responsibilities for each data domain and sub-domain, much like the differentiated care for various product categories in a store, NIDG fosters a system where data is managed efficiently and accountability is clear. This structured approach not only simplifies the complexities of data management but also bolsters data quality organization-wide, leading to improved decision-making and enhanced operational efficacy.

Establishing Governance Policies and Procedures

Formulating governance policies and procedures within the NIDG framework is akin to designing operational guidelines for a grocery store's various departments. This crucial step ensures that data within each domain and sub-domain is managed according to clear, predefined standards. These policies dictate the standards for data quality, set access controls, and outline procedures for the entire lifecycle management of data, ensuring its integrity and security.

Under NIDG, this process emphasizes enhancing and formalizing existing practices rather than introducing new, disruptive measures. It's about creating a governance structure that is as intuitive and natural to navigate as a well-organized grocery store, where the operational guidelines ensure that products are displayed effectively, inventory is meticulously tracked, and quality is consistently maintained. Just as specific protocols in a store ensure the freshness of produce or the efficient restocking of shelves, NIDG policies guide the collection, storage, processing, and sharing of data, ensuring its alignment with both regulatory standards and strategic business goals.

This framework not only empowers data stewards, like department managers, with clear mandates but also cultivates a culture of accountability and trust in the organization's data assets, enhancing decision-making and operational efficiency across the board.

Enhancing Data Accessibility and Quality

Incorporating NIDG principles enhances data accessibility and quality, much like how a well-organized grocery store optimizes the shopping experience. NIDG focuses on leveraging existing organizational structures and roles to improve the management of data domains, making data more accessible and of higher quality without disrupting current workflows. This approach involves the strategic use of systems and tools that facilitate the easy retrieval and sharing of data, coupled with ongoing efforts to clean, validate, and enrich data within each domain.

Implementing NIDG means applying practical, non-disruptive measures to ensure data is as navigable and reliable as grocery store aisles are to shoppers. Using data cataloging tools that provide clear metadata descriptions and lineage information, NIDG makes it straightforward for users to find and understand data, similar to how well-labeled aisles help shoppers locate items. Like regular product inspections for freshness, continuous quality improvement initiatives help maintain high data quality standards.

These initiatives, grounded in the NIDG framework, ensure that data across the organization is accessible and trusted for its integrity, thereby supporting informed decision-making in a manner that reflects the confidence shoppers have in their local grocery store's offerings.

Monitoring and Continuous Improvement

Incorporating NIDG into the process of monitoring and continuous improvement mirrors the way a grocery store fine-tunes its operations based on regular reviews. NIDG emphasizes a seamless integration of data governance practices into existing organizational processes, enabling continuous oversight without needing heavy-handed interventions. This approach involves the routine evaluation of data quality, adherence to governance policies, and the overall efficiency of data management practices across all data domains, ensuring that adjustments are made proactively to maintain high standards of data integrity and usability.

By adopting NIDG, organizations engage in a non-disruptive, continuous improvement cycle that assesses the health of data domains using established metrics and KPIs, much like a grocery store uses inventory checks and customer feedback to improve its offerings. Stakeholder engagement through surveys and forums acts as a feedback loop, providing direct insights into data usability issues and governance effectiveness. This feedback is instrumental in guiding refinements in governance policies and data management procedures, ensuring that the governance framework evolves in line with organizational needs and external developments.

The NIDG approach guarantees that data governance is not just a static policy but a dynamic, integral part of the organization's ongoing effort to enhance data quality and value, akin to the adaptive strategies of a successful grocery store.

Conclusion

Adopting a domain-oriented approach to data governance, as exemplified by the grocery store analogy, offers several benefits. It enhances the clarity and focus of data governance efforts, making it easier to identify and address specific data management challenges. It also facilitates better alignment between data governance initiatives and the organization's overall strategic goals, as data domains are often closely linked to key business functions and objectives.

This approach promotes a culture of data ownership and accountability, as individuals across the organization take on defined roles in managing and governing data within their areas of expertise. Organizations can achieve higher levels of data quality, security, and compliance by fostering a sense of responsibility and involvement in data governance.

Incorporating data domains and sub-domains into NIDG implementations, guided by the analogy of a grocery store's organization and management, is a critical strategy for improving the management and governance of organizational data. This approach simplifies the complex landscape of data governance and enhances operational efficiency, data quality, and strategic decision-making across the organization. By viewing data through the lens of domains and sub-domains, organizations can unlock the full potential of their data assets, driving growth and innovation in an increasingly data-driven world.

Stop Complaining About Your Data – And Do Something About It

Organizations are drowning in a sea of data, facing challenges that range from inconsistent quality to inefficient and ineffective management. It's easy to complain about the state of your data, but a more productive tactic involves taking actionable steps to address these issues. Enter Non-Invasive Data Governance (NIDG) — a methodology that empowers organizations to turn complaints into solutions, fostering a culture of proactive data management.

Understanding Non-Invasive Data Governance

Non-Invasive Data Governance is not about imposing strict controls or creating bureaucratic hurdles. Instead, it's a collaborative and incremental approach that integrates seamlessly into existing processes. The key principle is to involve stakeholders across the organization, turning them into advocates for better data practices.

In essence, NIDG operates on the principle that the best data governance strategies are those that work harmoniously with existing organizational structures. Rather than introducing rigid controls that disrupt daily operations, this approach acknowledges and respects the natural flow of work. It's not a top-down imposition of rules but a grassroots movement that empowers individuals at all levels to champion data quality. This collaborative philosophy is built on the understanding that stakeholders possess valuable insights into their respective domains, and their active involvement ensures that governance measures are effective and practical.

This collaborative and incremental approach doesn't view data governance as a one-size-fits-all solution. It recognizes the unique needs and challenges within different departments and business units. For instance, while finance teams might prioritize accuracy and compliance, marketing teams may value agility and flexibility. NIDG encourages tailoring governance practices to suit these diverse needs, fostering a culture where data management is seen as integral to achieving specific business objectives rather than a cumbersome compliance exercise. The result is a more responsive and adaptive governance framework that resonates with the varied priorities of stakeholders, ultimately leading to a more successful and sustainable data governance implementation.

Stop Complaining, Start Assessing

The first step is to stop complaining and start assessing the current state of your data. Non-Invasive Data Governance encourages organizations to conduct comprehensive data assessments. This involves identifying key data stakeholders, understanding their needs, and evaluating existing data management practices. By taking stock of the current situation, organizations gain insights into the specific pain points that need attention.

Embarking on the journey of NIDG requires a mindset shift from complaining to proactive assessment. This involves acknowledging that data quality or management challenges are not insurmountable obstacles, but opportunities for improvement. The assessment phase is not just a cursory glance at the data landscape; it's a deliberate and thorough examination that delves into the intricacies of data workflows, storage, and utilization. It encourages organizations to embrace a data-centric mindset, viewing data not merely as a byproduct, but as a strategic asset that can propel the organization forward.

Organizations can leverage various tools and methodologies during the assessment to conduct a nuanced analysis. This includes data profiling to understand the characteristics of different datasets, assessing data lineage to track its journey across systems, and evaluating data quality against predefined standards. The process is not just about identifying what is wrong but also recognizing what is working well. It's a holistic approach that considers both the challenges and successes, providing a comprehensive understanding of the data landscape. This nuanced assessment lays the foundation for targeted and effective interventions, ensuring that efforts are directed toward areas that yield the most significant impact on data quality and governance.

Define Purpose and Scope

Complaining often arises when there's a lack of clarity about why certain data practices are in place. Non-Invasive Data Governance emphasizes defining a clear purpose and scope for data management. This involves aligning data initiatives with organizational goals, compliance requirements, and strategic objectives. By clearly delineating the boundaries of data governance efforts, organizations can create a roadmap for targeted improvements.

Defining the purpose and scope within the NIDG framework is a crucial step that goes beyond mere paperwork; it's about instilling a sense of purpose in every data-related activity. This involves engaging stakeholders across different departments to gain a comprehensive understanding of their specific data needs and challenges. Organize workshops and collaborative sessions to foster open communication, ensuring that the purpose of data management resonates throughout the organization. This inclusivity not only unveils hidden insights, but also turns stakeholders into active participants, cultivating a shared responsibility for data governance.

Furthermore, the scope definition is not a one-size-fits-all approach; it's a tailored and dynamic process that adapts to the evolving needs of the organization. NIDG encourages a continuous feedback loop, allowing organizations to refine their scope based on emerging challenges or opportunities. It's not merely about setting boundaries but establishing a flexible framework that accommodates growth and innovation. As the purpose and scope become ingrained in the organizational culture, the transformation from complaint-driven to purpose-driven data management unfolds, fostering a proactive and collaborative environment.

Engage Stakeholders

One of the cornerstones of Non-Invasive Data Governance is active stakeholder engagement. Instead of imposing rigid rules, involve stakeholders in the decision-making process. Conduct workshops, interviews, and feedback sessions to understand their perspectives. By making stakeholders feel heard and valued, organizations create a collaborative environment where everyone is invested in the success of data governance initiatives.

Effective stakeholder engagement within the NIDG approach requires a strategic and ongoing effort to build relationships across the organization. Organizations can establish dedicated forums, such as data governance committees or working groups, where stakeholders from different departments come together regularly. These forums serve as platforms for open discussions, allowing stakeholders to share their insights, concerns, and expectations related to data governance. In addition, leveraging technology like collaborative platforms or communication tools can facilitate continuous engagement, ensuring that stakeholders stay informed and connected.

Moreover, engaging stakeholders is not a one-off activity; it's an iterative process that evolves with the organization. NIDG encourages organizations to regularly assess the effectiveness of their engagement strategies. This involves seeking feedback on the existing communication channels, understanding any emerging challenges, and adapting engagement approaches accordingly. By fostering a culture of continuous dialogue, organizations not only gain valuable input from stakeholders, but also cultivate a sense of ownership and commitment among them, transforming data governance from a top-down directive to a shared responsibility.

Establish Data Classification and Ownership

Data complaints often stem from ambiguity about data sensitivity and ownership. Non-Invasive Data Governance encourages the classification of data based on sensitivity levels — whether it's public, sensitive, or restricted. Simultaneously, collaborate with data owners to clearly define responsibilities and accountabilities. This ensures that data is not only classified appropriately but also managed by those who understand its intricacies.

Organizations can institute a structured and collaborative process to establish data classification and ownership within the NIDG framework. Workshops and sessions involving both data stakeholders and data owners can be organized to collectively define the criteria for classifying data into different categories. This participatory approach enhances the accuracy of data classification and builds consensus among stakeholders, fostering a shared understanding of the significance of different data types.

Additionally, defining data ownership involves more than assigning roles; it requires the development of clear communication channels between data owners and users. NIDG encourages the creation of accessible documentation outlining ownership responsibilities. Regular communication forums, such as quarterly meetings or newsletters, can further strengthen this collaboration. Organizations mitigate confusion and disputes by emphasizing transparency in the data governance process, leading to a more cohesive and effective approach to managing data across the entire ecosystem.

Implement Non-Invasive Controls

Rather than imposing restrictive controls, Non-Invasive Data Governance focuses on implementing controls that seamlessly integrate into existing workflows. This could include automated data quality checks, user-friendly metadata management, and collaborative data stewardship. By making these controls non-invasive, organizations minimize resistance and foster a more inclusive approach to data governance.

Implementing non-invasive controls within the NIDG framework involves a strategic blend of technology and cultural considerations. Automated data quality checks, for instance, can be introduced through user-friendly tools that operate in the background, requiring minimal manual intervention. This not only enhances the accuracy of data but also reduces the burden on end-users, promoting a positive perception of data governance initiatives. Additionally, incorporating collaborative data stewardship tools allows stakeholders to actively participate in the governance process, fostering a sense of ownership and responsibility for data quality.

Cultural aspects play a crucial role in ensuring the non-invasiveness of these controls. Organizations can conduct awareness campaigns and training sessions to familiarize teams with the benefits of these controls and dispel any apprehensions. Establishing a culture that values data quality and understands the non-invasive controls as enablers rather than restrictions contributes to a smoother integration of these measures into daily operations. The emphasis is on empowering users and creating an environment where data governance is seen as a facilitator rather than a hindrance to productivity.

Promote Data Literacy

Complaints about data often arise from a lack of understanding. Non-Invasive Data Governance advocates for promoting data literacy across the organization. Conduct training sessions, develop user-friendly documentation, and establish communication channels to educate stakeholders about the importance of data and the role they play in its governance. A more informed workforce is likely to become a more engaged and responsible one.

Promoting data literacy within the NIDG framework involves creating a comprehensive strategy that addresses the diverse needs and backgrounds of stakeholders. Organizations can conduct targeted training sessions tailored to different roles, ensuring that each group understands the specific aspects of data governance relevant to their responsibilities. These sessions should go beyond basic data concepts and delve into practical applications, showcasing how improved data practices contribute to better decision-making and overall organizational success. Additionally, developing user-friendly documentation, such as guidelines and FAQs, provides accessible resources for stakeholders to refer to as they navigate data governance processes.

Establishing effective communication channels is paramount in promoting data literacy. Regular newsletters, webinars, and interactive forums can serve as platforms for sharing insights, best practices, and success stories related to data governance. Encouraging an open dialogue where stakeholders can ask questions and seek clarification fosters a culture of continuous learning. By making data literacy an ongoing initiative, organizations can ensure that their workforce remains up to date with the evolving landscape of data governance, reinforcing the idea that everyone plays a vital role in maintaining data quality and integrity.

Continuous Improvement

Non-Invasive Data Governance is not a one-time fix; it's an ongoing continuous improvement process. Establish feedback loops, conduct regular reviews, and solicit input from stakeholders to identify areas for enhancement. By embracing a mindset of continuous improvement, organizations create a culture where addressing data challenges becomes a natural part of their operations.

Continuous improvement within the NIDG framework requires the establishment of robust feedback mechanisms that facilitate a constant flow of insights from stakeholders. Regular reviews of data governance practices, conducted at predefined intervals, allow organizations to assess the effectiveness of implemented strategies and identify areas for refinement. These reviews should involve key stakeholders from various departments, ensuring a comprehensive perspective on how data governance aligns with diverse organizational functions. Encouraging stakeholders to share their experiences, challenges, and suggestions provides valuable input for enhancing data governance practices.

Soliciting input from stakeholders can take various forms, including surveys, focus group sessions, or direct interviews. Organizations can leverage technology to create user-friendly feedback mechanisms, making it easy for stakeholders to contribute their observations. Analyzing this feedback systematically helps organizations prioritize improvement initiatives based on real-world challenges and user experiences. Moreover, creating a culture where continuous improvement is celebrated and acknowledged fosters a sense of ownership among stakeholders, reinforcing the notion that their input directly contributes to refining and optimizing data governance processes over time.

Conclusion

Complaining about data issues achieves little, but taking proactive steps through Non-Invasive Data Governance can lead to transformative change. By involving stakeholders, defining purpose, and implementing non-invasive controls, organizations can turn data complaints into success stories. It's time to stop complaining and start doing something about your data — the Non-Invasive Data Governance way.

Data Governance Doesn't Have to Be Scary

The mere mention of "data governance" can send shivers down the spines of executives and employees alike. The thought of implementing stringent rules and procedures for managing data often conjures images of bureaucratic nightmares and stifled innovation. However, it doesn't have to be this way. Contrary to popular belief, implementing an effective and sustainable data governance program doesn't have to threaten the organization and its culture. In fact, when done right, it can enhance productivity, foster innovation, and build trust among stakeholders. How? Let's explore the core principles of Non-Invasive Data Governance (NIDG) to understand why.

First and foremost, NIDG emphasizes Organic Integration. Rather than imposing governance measures from the top down, NIDG seeks to seamlessly integrate governance practices into existing organizational processes and structures. This means that data governance becomes a natural part of everyday workflows, enhancing efficiency without disrupting operations. By leveraging existing roles and processes, NIDG ensures that governance is seen as an enabler rather than a hindrance.

This approach offers significant benefits in terms of the acceptance and adoption of data governance programs within organizations. By integrating governance practices into existing workflows, employees are more likely to see the value of governance in their day-to-day activities. This not only reduces resistance to change but also fosters a culture where data governance is viewed as a necessary and beneficial aspect of organizational operations.

By aligning governance with existing processes, NIDG minimizes the need for extensive training and reorganization, further reducing the fear and uncertainty often associated with implementing new initiatives. Organic Integration not only enhances efficiency and productivity, but also promotes a positive attitude towards data governance, paving the way for its successful implementation and long-term sustainability.

Central to the NIDG approach is the concept of Recognition-Based Stewardship and Roles. Instead of creating new, specialized roles for data stewardship, NIDG identifies and empowers individuals who already handle data in various capacities. By recognizing their expertise and assigning stewardship responsibilities based on existing roles, NIDG fosters a sense of ownership and accountability among employees. This not only ensures that governance activities are carried out effectively but also avoids unnecessary hierarchy and bureaucracy.

Recognition-Based Stewardship and Roles play a crucial role in alleviating the fear of data governance within organizations. By leveraging existing talent and expertise, NIDG demonstrates a commitment to recognizing and valuing the contributions of employees. This approach not only encourages employees to take ownership of governance initiatives but also promotes a sense of trust and respect between management and staff.

By empowering individuals in their existing roles, NIDG eliminates the need for extensive training and restructuring, further reducing resistance to change. Overall, Recognition-Based Stewardship and Roles foster a collaborative and inclusive approach to governance, enhancing acceptance and buy-in from employees at all levels of the organization.

NIDG eliminates the need for extensive training and restructuring, further reducing resistance to change.

NIDG prioritizes Minimal Disruption. Rather than overhauling existing processes, NIDG aims to implement governance measures with minimal disruption to day-to-day operations. This approach reduces resistance to change and allows organizations to maintain productivity while enhancing data management practices. By aligning governance activities with operational needs and objectives, NIDG ensures that the focus remains on driving business value rather than merely complying with regulations.

The emphasis on Minimal Disruption in NIDG reduces the fear of data governance and facilitates the acceptance of the program within organizations. By minimizing disruptions to existing workflows, NIDG demonstrates a commitment to supporting employees in their roles while simultaneously improving data management practices. This approach fosters a culture of continuous improvement, where governance initiatives are seen as enhancements rather than disruptions.

By aligning governance activities with operational needs, NIDG ensures that employees understand the relevance and value of governance measures, further promoting acceptance and engagement across the organization.

NIDG promotes Continuous Improvement. Data governance is not a one-time project, but an ongoing process of refinement and adaptation. By embedding governance activities into daily operations, NIDG encourages a culture of continuous learning and optimization. This enables organizations to respond swiftly to evolving data management challenges and regulatory requirements, ensuring that governance practices remain effective and relevant over time.

This emphasis on Continuous Improvement in NIDG not only alleviates the fear of data governance but also enhances the acceptance of the program within organizations. By fostering a culture of continuous learning and optimization, NIDG demonstrates a commitment to staying abreast of industry best practices and adapting to changing needs.

This proactive approach reassures employees that governance measures are not static, but evolve in response to feedback and emerging challenges, fostering trust and engagement in the governance process. By integrating governance activities into daily operations, NIDG ensures that employees see the immediate benefits of governance initiatives, further reinforcing their acceptance and participation in the program.

Another key aspect of NIDG is Adaptability. Recognizing the dynamic nature of data and organizational requirements, NIDG allows for flexibility in governance approaches. This means that governance strategies can be adapted to suit changing circumstances, technologies, and business priorities. By remaining agile and responsive, organizations can stay ahead of the curve and effectively manage their data assets in an ever-changing landscape.

The emphasis on Adaptability in NIDG not only helps reduce the fear of data governance but also enhances the acceptance of the program within organizations. By allowing for flexibility in governance approaches, NIDG demonstrates a willingness to accommodate diverse needs and evolving priorities. This fosters a sense of ownership and empowerment among employees, as they can actively participate in shaping governance practices to align with their specific roles and responsibilities.

The ability to adapt governance strategies to changing circumstances ensures that organizations can proactively address emerging challenges and seize new opportunities, further reinforcing the value and relevance of the governance program.

NIDG emphasizes Clarity and Transparency. Clear communication and transparent decision-making are essential for building trust and buy-in among stakeholders. NIDG ensures that roles, responsibilities, and policies are clearly defined, enabling employees to understand the rationale behind governance measures and their impact on the organization. This transparency fosters a culture of trust and collaboration, laying the foundation for successful data governance initiatives.

The emphasis on Clarity and Transparency in NIDG not only reduces the fear of data governance but also enhances the acceptance of the program within organizations. By providing clear guidelines and transparent decision-making processes, NIDG builds confidence among employees, reassuring them that governance measures are fair, consistent, and aligned with organizational goals. This clarity helps dispel any misconceptions or concerns about the intentions behind governance initiatives, fostering a positive attitude towards data governance and encouraging active participation from all stakeholders.

Last but not least, NIDG adopts a Value-Oriented Approach. Rather than focusing solely on compliance and risk mitigation, NIDG aligns governance activities with strategic objectives and business outcomes. This means that resources are invested in areas that offer the greatest return on investment and contribute to the organization's overall success. By demonstrating the tangible value of data governance in driving innovation, efficiency, and competitiveness, NIDG ensures that governance initiatives are seen as integral to business success rather than as a necessary evil.

The Value-Oriented Approach of NIDG not only alleviates the fear of data governance but also fosters greater acceptance of the program within organizations. By highlighting the benefits of governance in terms of improved decision-making, enhanced data quality, and better business outcomes, NIDG shifts the perception of data governance from being a burdensome requirement to being a strategic asset. This approach encourages stakeholders to actively support and participate in governance initiatives, recognizing them as investments that yield long-term dividends for the organization's growth and success.

Conclusion

Non-Invasive Data Governance (NIDG) offers a refreshing approach to data management that doesn't have to induce fear or resistance. By embracing principles such as Organic Integration, Recognition-Based Stewardship, Minimal Disruption, Continuous Improvement, Adaptability, Clarity, Transparency, and a Value-Oriented Approach, organizations can transform data governance into a natural, beneficial aspect of their operations. Through these principles, NIDG not only reduces apprehension, but also fosters acceptance and active participation, paving the way for successful implementation and long-term sustainability of data governance initiatives.

Ask Not What Your Data Governance Program
Can Do for You ...

The famous statement "Ask not what your country can do for you, ask what you can do for your country," spoken by United States President John F. Kennedy in his inaugural address in 1961, captures a powerful message about civic duty and collective responsibility. In its essence lies the idea of individuals actively contributing to the betterment of society rather than solely expecting benefits or assistance from the government. Similarly, when applied to the world of data governance within organizations, this principle underscores the importance of personal involvement and proactive engagement in ensuring the success of formal data governance initiatives.

In the context of implementing an effective formal data governance program, it's not enough for individuals to simply expect the program to deliver benefits or solutions to their data-related challenges. Instead, they should take an active role in supporting and advancing the program's objectives. Just as citizens have a responsibility to contribute to the well-being of their country, employees within an organization have a responsibility to contribute to the success of its data governance efforts.

By embracing this mindset shift—asking what we can do for our data governance program—we recognize the importance of personal accountability, collaboration, and collective action in driving meaningful change and achieving sustainable results. It's about recognizing that each individual has a role to play in upholding data integrity, promoting data-driven decision-making, and safeguarding the organization's data assets.

NIDG is about recognizing that each individual has a role to play in upholding data integrity, promoting data-driven decision-making, and safeguarding the organization's data assets.

With this perspective in mind, let's explore the core principles of Non-Invasive Data Governance (NIDG) and discover how they can empower individuals to actively participate in and support implementing an effective and sustainable data governance program.

At the heart of NIDG lies the principle of Organic Integration. Unlike traditional governance models that impose rules and regulations from the top down, NIDG seeks to seamlessly integrate governance practices into existing organizational processes and structures. By leveraging existing roles and workflows, NIDG ensures that data governance becomes a natural part of everyday operations, enhancing efficiency without disrupting productivity. This approach minimizes resistance to change and fosters a culture where data governance is seen as an enabler rather than a hindrance.

NIDG emphasizes Recognition-Based Stewardship and Roles. Rather than creating new, specialized roles for data stewardship, NIDG identifies and empowers individuals who already handle data in various capacities. By recognizing their expertise and conveying stewardship responsibilities based on existing roles, NIDG fosters a sense of ownership and accountability among employees. This not only ensures that governance activities are carried out effectively but also avoids unnecessary hierarchy and bureaucracy, promoting a more inclusive and collaborative approach to data governance.

In addition to recognizing the importance of existing roles, NIDG prioritizes Minimal Disruption. Instead of overhauling existing processes, NIDG aims to implement governance measures with minimal disruption to day-to-day operations. By aligning governance activities with operational needs and objectives, NIDG ensures that the focus remains on driving business value rather than merely complying with regulations. This approach not only reduces resistance to change but also allows organizations to maintain productivity while enhancing data management practices.

NIDG promotes Continuous Improvement. Data governance is not a one-time project but an ongoing process of refinement and adaptation. By embedding governance activities into daily operations, NIDG encourages a culture of continuous learning and optimization. This enables organizations to respond swiftly to evolving data management challenges and regulatory requirements, ensuring that governance practices remain effective and relevant over time.

Another key aspect of NIDG is Adaptability. Recognizing the dynamic nature of data and organizational requirements, NIDG allows for flexibility in governance approaches. This means that governance strategies can be adapted to suit changing circumstances, technologies, and business priorities. By remaining agile and responsive, organizations can stay ahead of the curve and effectively manage their data assets in an ever-changing landscape.

NIDG also emphasizes Clarity and Transparency. Clear communication and transparent decision-making are essential for building trust and buy-in among stakeholders. NIDG ensures that roles, responsibilities, and policies are clearly defined, enabling employees to understand the rationale behind governance measures and their impact on the organization. This transparency fosters a culture of trust and collaboration, laying the foundation for successful data governance initiatives.

Last but not least, NIDG adopts a Value-Oriented Approach. Rather than focusing solely on compliance and risk mitigation, NIDG aligns governance activities with strategic objectives and business outcomes. By demonstrating the tangible value of data governance in driving innovation, efficiency, and competitiveness, NIDG ensures that governance initiatives are seen as integral to business success rather than as a necessary evil.

Conclusion

Embracing the principles of Non-Invasive Data Governance empowers organizations to rethink their approach to data governance. By integrating governance practices into existing workflows, recognizing the expertise of individuals, minimizing disruption, fostering continuous improvement, embracing adaptability, promoting clarity and transparency, and adopting a value-oriented mindset, organizations can transform data governance from a daunting obligation into a strategic asset. So, let us not ask what our data governance program can do for us, but rather what we can do for our data governance program.

Data Governance is a Team Sport

The concept of data governance often conjures images of strict policies, rigid frameworks, and top-down directives. However, the evolving landscape of data governance suggests a different analogy - one that is more inclusive, collaborative, and rooted in the day-to-day realities of organizational life. "Data Governance is a Team Sport" is more than just a catchy phrase. It summarizes the essence of a non-invasive approach to managing an organization's data assets. This perspective champions the idea that effective data governance is not the sole responsibility of a central team but a cooperative endeavor that involves every member of the organization. Teams that excel in sports at the professional level often demonstrate strength from the front office down to the people who take care of the players.

At the heart of the Non-Invasive Data Governance (NIDG) approach is the recognition that data governance is already happening across teams and departments. Whether it's the meticulous data entry by administrative staff, the careful data analysis by business analysts, or the strategic data oversight by management, these are all forms of data governance in action. Acknowledging these existing efforts is the first step in fostering a culture of shared responsibility and collaboration. It shifts the narrative from imposing new governance structures to enhancing and formalizing what is already working well. However, like any team sport, data governance faces its share of challenges. One of the most common hurdles is conflicting play calling among team members, which can arise from unclear roles, competing priorities, or simply resistance to change. Such conflicts not only disrupt the flow of data governance initiatives but can also lead to missed opportunities for improvement and innovation. Addressing these issues requires a leadership style (from the team's general manager, so to speak) that emphasizes open communication, mutual respect, and a clear articulation of roles and responsibilities. It's about creating an environment where every team member feels valued and understands how their contributions fit into the larger data governance (team) strategy.

Drawing on the team sport analogy further, the importance of practice and communication in achieving excellence cannot be overstated. In data governance, this translates to ongoing training, continuous learning, and regular dialogue across all levels of the organization. Just as athletes spend countless hours practicing their skills and strategies, data stewards and their colleagues must invest time in developing their data governance competencies and literacy. This includes not just technical skills, but also the ability to communicate effectively, negotiate priorities, and collaborate across departments. It is crucial to establish a culture where continuous improvement and open communication are valued above all. This means creating a safe environment for sharing knowledge, expressing ideas, and challenging the status quo without fear of retribution. Management must lead by example, actively participating in training sessions and encouraging their teams to do the same.

Management must lead by example, actively participating in training sessions and encouraging their teams to do the same. The organization should facilitate cross-departmental collaborations to break down silos, using structured forums and workshops where team members can share insights and learn from each other's experiences. Adopting this approach ensures that the principles of practice and communication are not just ideals but are actively lived by every member of the organization, driving the success of the data governance program.

Effective communication is the linchpin of successful data governance and team success. It involves more than just sharing information. It's about engaging in meaningful conversations that foster a common understanding and shared vision. Regular team meetings, newsletters, workshops, and forums are all valuable tools for keeping the lines of communication open. These platforms not only serve as opportunities for learning and sharing data best practices, but also as venues for airing concerns, celebrating successes, and navigating the complexities of data governance together.

To embed this process into the organizational fabric, it is imperative to establish structured communication channels that facilitate transparency and inclusivity. Leadership should prioritize the creation of a Data Governance Communication Plan that outlines how information is disseminated, and feedback is collected from every level of the organization. This strategy could include regular data governance updates in company-wide meetings, dedicated sections in internal newsletters, and establishing an online portal (home page) for data governance resources. Encouraging a culture where feedback is sought and valued from all organizational levels ensures that communication is a two-way street, enhancing the effectiveness of data governance initiatives and building a stronger, more united team.

In emphasizing that data governance is a team sport, it's crucial to recognize the diversity of the team members involved. From IT professionals and data scientists to business analysts and executive leaders, each member brings a unique set of skills and perspectives to the table. Leveraging this diversity is key to building a robust and resilient data governance program. It requires a leadership approach that is inclusive, adaptive, and committed to fostering a culture of collaboration and mutual support. Adopting this idea, organizations can create an environment where every team member feels valued and understood, regardless of their role or department. This involves establishing clear channels of communication, setting up cross-functional teams, and promoting joint problem-solving sessions where different perspectives are not only heard but actively integrated into decision-making processes. Such an approach encourages a sense of ownership and responsibility among all stakeholders, making the data governance journey a collective endeavor with shared goals and successes.

Just as every team sport has its rules and strategies, so too does data governance. However, in the spirit of NIDG, these rules should be guiding principles rather than rigid prescriptions. They should be flexible enough to accommodate the unique needs and contexts of different teams, yet consistent enough to ensure alignment with the organization's overall data strategy. Developing these guiding principles is a collaborative effort that benefits from the input and buy-in of all stakeholders involved. Embracing the idea that data governance is a team sport offers a refreshing and effective approach to managing an organization's data assets. It recognizes the value of existing governance activities, addresses the challenges of team dynamics, and emphasizes the importance of practice and communication in achieving success. By fostering a culture of collaboration, respect, and continuous improvement, organizations can unlock the full potential of their data governance initiatives.

Conclusion

Like any team sport, the journey to excellence in data governance requires dedication, teamwork, and a shared commitment to common goals. With the right mindset and approach, organizations can navigate the complexities of data governance and drive meaningful outcomes for all stakeholders involved.

Summary

In an era defined by artificial intelligence and data-driven decision-making, *Non-Invasive Data Governance Unleashed: Empowering People to Govern Data and AI* offers a transformative perspective on how organizations can address the pressing challenges of managing their data. This book emphasizes a practical, human-centric approach to governance that aligns with modern technological advancements while fostering a culture of accountability, innovation, and collaboration. With every chapter, readers gain actionable insights, strategic lessons, and practical tools to make data governance a cornerstone of their organizational success.

Chapter 1, Foundations of Data Governance established the essential building blocks of data governance, emphasizing the necessity of formalized frameworks to ensure data reliability and usability. Readers will understand the importance of data governance as a strategic enabler and how its effective implementation directly impacts an organization's success. Through discussions on ROI, various governance approaches, and the interplay between governance, IT, and information management, the chapter highlighted the importance of aligning governance with organizational goals while dispelling common misconceptions.

Chapter 2, The Human Element in Data Governance, underscored the critical role that individuals play in driving governance efforts. By exploring paradigm shifts in data stewardship, leadership engagement, and fostering a culture of accountability, the chapter equips organizations to embrace the human aspects of governance. The essays emphasizes the inclusive nature of stewardship and the need for awareness and participation across all levels of an organization, making governance a collective responsibility.

Chapter 3, AI and Data Governance, explored the intersection of AI and data governance, shedding light on how governance underpins the success of AI initiatives. By addressing risks associated with ungoverned data, the differences between AI models, and the foundational role of quality data, readers gain a roadmap for integrating governance into AI strategies. The chapter also provided a forward-looking perspective on how organizations can prepare for the evolving relationship between AI and data governance.

Chapter 4, Practical Strategies and Tools, provided a toolkit for implementing data governance in real-world scenarios. It provided guidance on selecting governance use cases, preparing data for AI, and redefining traditional roles to meet modern demands. Practical strategies for cost-effective governance, federated models, and decentralized environments empower organizations to adapt governance practices to their unique needs without compromising effectiveness or scalability.

Chapter 5, Data Stewardship, dove into how organizations can empower and formalize the roles of data stewards. By advocating for the recognition of existing roles and the democratization of stewardship, the chapter offered a vision for inclusive and future-ready governance. It emphasizes that the talent needed for governance success often already exists within organizations and highlights how stewardship roles can evolve alongside technological advancements.

Chapter 6, Data Governance in Action, focused on practical implementation strategies for data governance. It discusses prioritizing critical data elements, measuring the effectiveness of governance roles, and fostering engagement through innovative methods. The importance of communication and making governance memorable was highlighted as key to sustaining long-term success, offering readers creative ways to embed governance into organizational culture.

Chapter 7, Non-Invasive Data Governance, provided a comprehensive look at the Non-Invasive Data Governance (NIDG) methodology. By emphasizing practicality and integration, the chapter demonstrated how NIDG aligns governance practices with existing workflows and roles. It outlined the essential components of the NIDG framework, providing organizations with a roadmap to formalize and optimize governance efforts without disrupting operations.

Chapter 8, Future of Data Governance, explored how data governance can drive cultural and technological transformation. It emphasizes the role of stewards, the symbiotic relationship between governance and culture, and the importance of data literacy and modernization. Readers are encouraged to view governance not just as a compliance mechanism but as a strategic catalyst for innovation and organizational growth.

Chapter 9, Leadership and Governance, highlighted the importance of executive involvement and realistic goal setting. By addressing the challenges of internal dynamics and the need for structured governance councils, the chapter equips leaders with strategies to align governance efforts with organizational priorities. It underscored that strong leadership is essential for embedding governance into the organization's DNA.

Chapter 10, Metaphors, Analogies, and Stories in Data Governance, brought data governance to life through relatable metaphors and analogies. It inspired readers to take action by framing governance as an approachable and collaborative effort. By emphasizing the importance of teamwork, shared accountability, and proactive problem-solving, the chapter reinforced the idea that governance is a collective journey.

As the data landscape continues to evolve, *Non-Invasive Data Governance Unleashed: Empowering People to Govern Data and AI* provides a roadmap for organizations to navigate these changes with confidence. This book challenges traditional notions of governance, advocating for a practical, people-centered approach that integrates seamlessly with modern technologies and organizational goals. It reminds readers that data governance is not just a technical exercise or compliance requirement—it is a strategic enabler of innovation, trust, and growth.

The final takeaway from this book is clear: effective data governance is within reach for every organization. By empowering people, aligning processes, and leveraging tools strategically, organizations can transform governance from a burden into an opportunity. This journey is not about perfection but about progress—taking intentional steps to build a governance culture that supports both current needs and future aspirations. With the insights from this book, readers are equipped to lead their organizations into a new era of data-driven success.

Index

www.ingramcontent.com/pod-product-compliance
Lightning Source LLC
Chambersburg PA
CBHW062057050326
40690CB00016B/3127